TOP STOCKS

STOCKS

TWENTY-SEVENTH EDITION

2021

MARTIN ROTH'S

BEST-SELLING ANNUAL

TOP STOCKS

TWENTY-SEVENTH EDITION

2021

A SHAREBUYER'S GUIDE TO
LEADING AUSTRALIAN COMPANIES

WILEY

The author and publisher would like to thank Alan Hull (author of *Active Investing*, Revised Edition, *Trade My Way* and *Invest My Way*; www.alanhull.com) for generating the five-year share-price charts.

This twenty-seventh edition first published in 2021 by Wrightbooks an imprint of John Wiley & Sons Australia, Ltd

42 McDougall Street, Milton Qld 4064

Office also in Melbourne

Typeset in Adobe Garamond Pro Regular by 10/12 pt

First edition published as *Top Stocks* by Wrightbooks in 1995

New edition published annually

© Martin Roth 2021

The moral rights of the author have been asserted

ISBN: 9780730385059 (pbk.)
         9780730385035 (ebook)

Cover design: Wiley
Cover image: Stock market graph © Yaran / Shutterstock

Charts created using MetaStock

10 9 8 7 6 5 4 3 2 1

Disclaimer
The material in this publication is of the nature of general comment only, and does not represent professional advice. It is not intended to provide specific guidance for particular circumstances and it should not be relied on as the basis for any decision to take action or not take action on any matter which it covers. Readers should obtain professional advice where appropriate, before making any such decision. To the maximum extent permitted by law, the author and publisher disclaim all responsibility and liability to any person, arising directly or indirectly from any person taking or not taking action based on the information in this publication.

Contents

PART II: the tables

Preface

During 2020 Australia entered its first recession in 29 years as the COVID-19 pandemic crushed many businesses. Most will probably survive, but some will not. As the old stock market adage warns us, it is when the tide goes out that we learn who has been swimming naked.

But in fact, when the economic tide went out in 2020 it also revealed something else, something important — that Australia boasts many companies of very high quality. These are companies that make solid profits year after year, that have just moderate levels of debt and that pay regular dividends to their shareholders. Most importantly for readers of this book, they are exactly the kinds of companies that are found in *Top Stocks*.

Using the same stringent criteria as in all previous editions, fully 90 companies have qualified this year. Twenty-eight companies that were in *Top Stocks 2020* failed to meet the benchmarks and were excluded from this latest edition. At the same time, 13 new companies entered the book.

Guiding investors towards value stocks has been one of the paramount aims of the book from the very first edition. Indeed, one rationale for the book has always been to highlight the truth that Australia boasts many excellent companies that continue to make good profits year after year regardless of the direction of the financial markets. Despite the title, *Top Stocks* is actually a book about companies.

Right from the start it has been an attempt to help investors find the best public companies in Australia, using strict criteria. These criteria are explained fully later. But, in essence, all companies in the book must have been publicly listed for at least five years and must have been making a profit and paying a dividend for each of those five years. They must also meet tough benchmarks of profitability and debt levels. It is completely objective. My own personal views count for nothing. In addition, share prices have never been relevant.

Of course, such stocks could not withstand the tidal wave of a substantial market sell-off. They too would be affected, but they should be affected less. If they are good companies they will continue to thrive and to pay dividends. And they will bounce back faster than many others.

Of the 90 companies in *Top Stocks 2021* — 15 fewer than in last year's edition — fully 58 reported a higher after-tax profit in their latest full financial year (June 2020 for most of them). In addition, 54 recorded higher earnings per share and 42 paid a higher dividend.

And though, as I write above, share prices are not relevant for selection to *Top Stocks*, 55 of the companies in the book have provided investor returns — share price appreciation plus dividends — of an average of at least 10 per cent per year over a five-year period.

2020 financial results

The year 2020 was like no other in the history of *Top Stocks*. It makes it difficult to assess each company's latest financial results and make predictions about the future. Certainly few of the companies in the book were prepared to give guidance on revenues and profits for the coming year.

A large number of the corporations saw their operations affected by the COVID-19 pandemic. Some of them — several retailers, for example — actually benefited, but many suffered. Profits were down for some.

Consequently, many companies lowered their dividends. Even some companies whose businesses were going well decided to lower their dividend in order to bolster their finances, fearful of a worsening economy.

There were other twists. Many companies, with their businesses suffering, made one-off impairment charges against these businesses. It meant that statutory profits and underlying profits differed for many of the companies in this book.

In addition, quite a few companies had capital raisings during the year — often by selling more shares — fearing that economic conditions might worsen, and wishing to shore up their finances. This had the effect of boosting the number of shares on issue, which lowered earnings-per-share figures.

But there was more. During 2020 a new accounting standard regarding leases, named AASB 16, came into effect. This lowered some companies' profits. It also sometimes had the effect of raising their finance charges and their amortisation charges.

Consequently, some companies in this book presented both pre-AASB 16 and post-AASB 16 financial results.

As just one example, shoe retailer Accent Group announced that its June 2020 EBITDA (earnings before interest, taxation, depreciation and amortisation) figure was $121.7 million pre-AASB 16 and $203.4 million post-AASB 16, a big difference.

Its EBIT (earnings before interest and taxation) figure was $87.2 million pre-AASB 16 and $94.8 million post-AASB 16. Its after-tax profit was $58 million pre-AASB 16 and $55.7 million post-AASB 16.

Small companies

A particular attraction of *Top Stocks* is the manner in which the book each year places a spotlight on smaller, emerging companies that have just ascended into the rankings of the top 500 stocks, or that have only just been listed on the ASX for the required five years to make it into the book.

Here are three small companies — in *Top Stocks* for the first time — that show promise:

- Adairs. This home furnishings specialist retailer has high levels of customer recognition and loyalty in a big market with great potential as it continues to grow.
- Baby Bunting Group. Australia's only specialist baby goods retailer is opening new stores, exploring new markets and introducing new products as it expands its share of the $2.4 billion Australian baby goods retail market.
- PWR Holdings. This small high-tech company now supplies most Formula One racing teams with their cooling systems and is branching into other areas with great potential.

High-tech companies

It was back in *Top Stocks 2011* that I first alerted readers to the phenomenon of a growing number of high-tech companies making it into the book. Ten years earlier only one technology company — Computershare — had been in *Top Stocks*. But since 2011 a dozen or so have regularly qualified.

The Information Technology sector represents only around 4.5 per cent of market capitalisation in Australia (in the US it is more than 20 per cent), yet some of these companies have been outstanding performers.

They are generally small companies and it can sometimes be difficult for outsiders to understand just how they make their money. In addition, some are on high price/earnings ratios with low dividend yields. Thus, many investors avoid them.

But technology has infiltrated virtually every facet of our lives, and the best of these companies are set to grow. It is worth taking the time to learn more about them.

Information technology sector companies

	Year-on-year after-tax profit growth (%)	Dividend yield (%)
Altium	−39.1	1.1
Class	−23.8	2.7
Codan	39.7	1.8
Data#3	30.5	2.3
Dicker Data	67.3	3.8
DWS	0.8	6.7

	Year-on-year after-tax profit growth (%)	Dividend yield (%)
Hansen Technologies	21.9	2.1
Infomedia	15.1	2.6
Integrated Research	10.1	1.9
IRESS	1.6	4.5
Objective	21.8	0.6
Technology One	169.5	1.6

Gold

The gold price has continued to rise during 2020, putting a spotlight on gold stocks. Here are some from this edition of *Top Stocks*:

- Codan is a world leader in the production of gold detectors for small-scale miners.
- Evolution Mining produced 746 463 ounces of gold in the June 2020 year, with a forecast of 670 000 ounces to 730 000 ounces for the June 2021 year, rising to between 790 000 ounces and 850 000 ounces in June 2023.
- Northern Star Resources is one of Australia's largest gold producers. It sold 900 388 ounces of gold in the June 2020 year, with a forecast of 940 000 ounces to 1.06 million ounces for June 2021.
- Orica is a supplier of commercial explosives and sodium cyanide, with the gold sector representing around 20 per cent of sales.
- Regis Resources, a smaller gold production company, produced 352 042 ounces of gold in the June 2020 year, with a forecast of 355 000 ounces to 380 000 ounces in the June 2021 year.
- Sandfire Resources is predominantly a copper miner, but in the June 2020 year it also produced 42 263 ounces of gold, with a forecast of 36 000 ounces to 40 000 ounces in the June 2021 year.

Who is *Top Stocks* written for?

Top Stocks is written for all those investors wishing to exercise a degree of control over their portfolios. It is for those just starting out, as well as for those with plenty of experience but who still feel the need for some guidance through the thickets of more than 2000 listed stocks.

It is not a how-to book. It does not give step-by-step instructions to 'winning' in the stock market. Rather, it is an independent and objective evaluation of leading companies, based on rigid criteria, with the intention of yielding a large selection of stocks that can become the starting point for investors wishing to do their own research.

A large amount of information is presented on each company, and another key feature of the book is that the data is presented in a common format, to allow readers to make easy comparisons between companies.

It is necessarily a conservative book. All stocks must have been listed for five years even to be considered for inclusion. It is especially suited for those seeking out value stocks for longer-term investment.

Yet, perhaps ironically, the book is also being used by short-term traders seeking a good selection of financially sound and reliable companies whose shares they can trade.

In addition, many regular readers buy the book every year, and to them in particular I express my thanks.

What are the entry criteria?

The criteria for inclusion in *Top Stocks* are strict:

- All companies must be included in the All Ordinaries Index, which comprises Australia's 500 largest stocks (out of more than 2000). The reason for excluding smaller companies is that there is often little investor information available on many of them and some are so thinly traded as to be almost illiquid. In fact, the 500 All Ordinaries companies comprise, by market capitalisation, more than 95 per cent of the entire market.
- It is necessary that all companies be publicly listed since at least the end of 2015, and have a five-year record of profits and dividend payments each year.
- All companies are required to post a return-on-equity ratio of at least 10 per cent in their latest financial year.
- No company should have a debt-to-equity ratio of more than 70 per cent.
- It must be stressed that share price performance is NOT one of the criteria for inclusion in this book. The purpose is to select companies with good profits and a strong balance sheet. These may not offer the spectacular share-price returns of a high-tech start-up or a promising gold miner, but they should also present far less risk.
- There are several notable exclusions. Listed managed investments are out, as these mainly buy other shares or investments. Examples are Australian Foundation Investment Company and all the real estate investment trusts.
- A further exclusion are the foreign-registered stocks listed on the ASX. There is sometimes a lack of information available about such companies. In addition, their stock prices tend to move on events and trends in their home countries, making it difficult at times for local investors to follow them.

It is surely a tribute to the strength and resilience of Australian corporations that, once again, despite the volatility of recent years, so many companies have qualified for the book.

Changes to this edition

A total of 28 companies from *Top Stocks 2020* have been omitted from this new edition.

Three companies were acquired during the year:

- Pacific Energy
- Ruralco Holdings
- Wellcom Group

With interest rates continuing to fall, some corporations expanded their borrowings, and five companies from *Top Stocks 2020* saw their debt-to-equity ratio rise above the 70 per cent limit for this book:

- AMA Group
- Ampol (formerly Caltex Australia)
- Bell Financial Group
- CIMIC Group
- McMillan Shakespeare

The remaining 20 excluded companies had return-on-equity ratios that fell below the required 10 per cent:

- AGL Energy
- ALS
- APN Property Group
- Blackmores
- BlueScope Steel
- Cedar Woods Properties
- The Citadel Group
- Corporate Travel Management
- Flight Centre Travel Group
- GR Engineering Services
- Insurance Australia Group
- Monadelphous Group
- National Australia Bank
- Orora
- Sonic Healthcare
- Southern Cross Media Group
- TPG Telecom
- Treasury Wine Estates

- Virtus Health
- Webjet

There are 13 new companies in this book (although four of them have appeared in earlier editions of the book but were not in *Top Stocks 2020*).

The new companies in this book are:

- Adairs*
- Aristocrat Leisure
- Baby Bunting Group*
- Class*
- Dicker Data*
- Evolution Mining
- IDP Education*
- Integral Diagnostics*
- InvoCare*
- Pinnacle Investment Management Group*
- PWR Holdings*
- Ramsay Health Care
- Select Harvests

* Companies that have not appeared in any previous edition of *Top Stocks*.

Companies in every edition of *Top Stocks*

This is the 27th edition of *Top Stocks*. Just three companies have appeared in each one of those editions:

- ANZ Banking
- Commonwealth Bank of Australia
- Westpac Banking

Once again it is my hope that *Top Stocks* will serve you well.

Martin Roth
Melbourne
September 2020

Introduction

The 90 companies in this book have been placed as much as possible into a common format, for ease of comparison. Please study the following explanations in order to get as much as possible from the large amount of data.

The tables have been made as concise as possible, though they repay careful study, as they contain large amounts of information.

Note that the tables for the banks have been arranged a little differently from the others. Details of these are provided later in this Introduction.

Head
At the head of each entry is the company name, with its three-letter ASX code and the website address.

Share-price chart
Under the company name is a five-year share-price chart, to September 2020, provided by Alan Hull (www.alanhull.com), author of *Invest My Way*, *Trade My Way* and *Active Investing*.

Small table
Under the share-price chart is a small table with the following data.

Sector
This is the company's sector as designated by the ASX. These sectors are based on the Global Industry Classification Standard — developed by S&P Dow Jones Indices and MSCI — which was aimed at standardising global industry sectors. You can learn more about these at the ASX website.

Share price
This is the closing price on 4 September 2020. Also included are the 12-month high and low prices, as of the same date.

Market capitalisation

This is the size of the company, as determined by the stock market. It is the share price multiplied by the number of shares in issue. All companies in this book must be in the All Ordinaries Index, which comprises Australia's 500 largest stocks, as measured by market capitalisation.

Price-to-NTA-per-share ratio

The NTA-per-share figure expresses the worth of a company's net tangible assets — that is, its assets minus its liabilities and intangible assets — for each share of the company. The price-to-NTA-per-share ratio relates this figure to the share price.

A ratio of one means the company is valued exactly according to the value of its assets. A ratio below one suggests that the shares are a bargain, though usually there is a good reason for this. Profits are more important than assets.

Some companies in this book have a negative NTA-per-share figure — as a result of having intangible assets valued at more than their net assets — and a price-to-NTA-per-share ratio cannot be calculated.

See Table M, in the second part of this book, for a little more detail on this ratio.

Five-year share price return

This is the total return you could have received from the stock in the five years to September 2020. It is based on the share price appreciation (or depreciation) plus dividends, and is expressed as a compounded annual rate of return.

Dividend reinvestment plan

A dividend reinvestment plan (DRP) allows shareholders to receive additional shares in their company in place of the dividend. Usually — though not always — these shares are provided at a small discount to the prevailing price, which can make them quite attractive. And of course no broking fees apply.

Many large companies offer such plans. However, they come and go. When a company needs finance it may introduce a DRP. When its financing requirements become less pressing it may withdraw it. Some companies that have a DRP in place may decide to deactivate it for a time.

The information in this book is based on up-to-date information from the companies. But if you are investing in a particular company in expectations of a DRP, be sure to check that it is still on offer. The company's own website will often provide this information.

Price/earnings ratio

The price/earnings ratio (PER) is one of the most popular measures of whether a share is cheap or expensive. It is calculated by dividing the share price — in this case the closing price for 4 September 2020 — by the earnings per share figure. Obviously the share price is continually changing, so the PER figures in this book are for guidance only. Many newspapers publish each morning the latest PER for every stock.

Dividend yield

This is the latest full-year dividend expressed as a percentage of the share price. Like the price/earnings ratio, it changes as the share price moves. It is a useful figure, especially for investors who are buying shares for income, as it allows you to compare this income with alternative investments, such as a bank term deposit or a rental property.

Company commentary

Each commentary begins with a brief introduction to the company and its activities. Then follow the highlights of its latest business results. For the majority of the companies these are their June 2020 results, which were issued during July and August 2020. Finally there is a section on the outlook for the company.

Main table

Here is what you can find in the main table.

Revenues

These are the company's revenues from its business activities, generally the sale of products or services. However, it does not usually include additional income from such sources as investments, bank interest or the sale of assets. If the information is available, the revenues figure has been broken down into the major product areas.

As much as possible, the figures are for continuing businesses. When a company sells a part of its operations the financial results for the sold activities are now separated from the core results. This can mean that the previous year's results are restated — also excluding the sold business — to make year-on-year comparisons more valid.

Earnings before interest and taxation

Earnings before interest and taxation (EBIT) is the firm's profit from its operations before the payment of interest and tax. This figure is often used by analysts examining a company. The reason is that some companies have borrowed extensively to finance their activities, while others have opted for alternative means. By expressing profits before interest payments it is possible to compare more precisely the performance of these companies. The net interest figure — interest payments minus interest receipts — has been used for this calculation.

You will also find many companies using a measure called EBITDA, which is earnings before interest, taxation, depreciation and amortisation.

EBIT margin

This is the company's EBIT expressed as a percentage of its revenues. It is a gauge of a company's efficiency. A high EBIT margin suggests that a company is achieving success in keeping its costs low.

Gross margin

The gross margin is the company's gross profit as a percentage of its sales. The gross profit is the amount left over after deducting from a company's sales figure its cost of sales — that is, its manufacturing costs or, for a retailer, the cost of purchasing the goods it sells. The cost of goods sold figure does not usually include marketing or administration costs.

As there are different ways of calculating the cost of goods sold figure, this ratio is better used for year-to-year comparisons of a single company's efficiency, rather than in comparing one company with another.

Many companies do not present a cost of goods sold figure, so a gross margin ratio is not given for every stock in this book.

The revenues for some companies include a mix of sales and services. Where a breakdown is possible, the gross profit figure will relate to sales only.

Profit before tax/profit after tax

The profit before tax figure is simply the EBIT figure minus net interest payments. The profit after tax figure is, of course, the company's profit after the payment of tax, and also after the deduction of minority interests. Minority interests are that part of a company's profit that is claimed by outside interests, usually the other shareholders in a subsidiary that is not fully owned by the company. Many companies do not have any minority interests, and for those that do it is generally a tiny figure.

As much as possible, I have adjusted the profit figures to exclude non-recurring profits and losses, which are often referred to as significant items. It is for this reason that the profit figures in *Top Stocks* sometimes differ from those in the financial media or on financial websites, where profit figures normally include significant items.

Significant items are those that have an abnormal impact on profits, even though they happen in the normal course of the company's operations. Examples are the profit from the sale of a business, the expenses of a business restructuring, the write-down of property, an inventory write-down, a bad-debt loss or a write-off for research and development expenditure.

Significant items are controversial. It is often a matter of subjective judgement as to what is included and what excluded. After analysing the accounts of hundreds of companies while writing the various editions of this book, it is clear that different companies use varying interpretations of what is significant.

Further, when they do report a significant item there is no consistency as to whether they use pre-tax figures or after-tax figures. Some report both, making it easy to adjust the profit figures in the tables in this book. But difficulties arise when only one figure is given for significant items.

In normal circumstances most companies do not report significant items. But investors should be aware of this issue. My publisher occasionally receives emails from readers enquiring why a profit figure in this book is so different from that reported elsewhere. In virtually all cases the reason is that I have stripped out a significant item.

It is also worth noting my observation that a growing number of companies present what they call an underlying profit (called a cash profit for the banks), in addition to their reported (statutory) profit. This underlying profit will exclude not only significant items but also discontinued businesses and sometimes other related items. Where all the relevant figures are available, I have used these underlying figures for the tables in this book.

It should also be noted that when a company sells or terminates a significant business it will now usually report the profit or loss of that business as a separate item. It will also usually backdate its previous year's accounts to exclude that business, so worthwhile comparisons can be made of continuing businesses.

The tables in this book usually refer to continuing businesses only.

Earnings per share
Earnings per share is the after-tax profit divided by the number of shares. Because the profit figure is for a 12-month period, the number of shares used is a weighted average of those on issue during the year. This number is provided by the company in its annual report and its results announcements.

Cashflow per share
The cashflow per share ratio tells — in theory — how much actual cash the company has generated from its operations.

In fact, the ratio in this book is not exactly a true measure of cashflow. It is simply the company's depreciation and amortisation figures for the year added to the after-tax profit, and then divided by a weighted average of the number of shares. Depreciation and amortisation are expenses that do not actually utilise cash, so can be added back to after-tax profit to give a kind of indication of the company's cashflow.

By contrast, a true cashflow — including such items as newly raised capital and money received from the sale of assets — would require quite complex calculations based on the company's statement of cashflows.

However, many investors use the ratio as I present it, because it is easy to calculate, and it is certainly a useful guide to approximately how much funding the company has available from its operations.

Dividend
The dividend figure is the total for the year, interim and final. It does not include special dividends. The level of franking is also provided.

Net tangible assets per share
The NTA per share figure tells the theoretical value of the company — per share — if all assets were sold and all liabilities paid. It is very much a theoretical figure, as there is no guarantee that corporate assets are really worth the price put on them in the balance sheet. Intangible assets such as goodwill, newspaper mastheads and patent

rights are excluded because of the difficulty in putting a sales price on them, and also because they may in fact not have much value if separated from the company.

As already noted, some companies in this book have a negative NTA, due to the fact that their intangible assets are so great, and no figure can be listed for them.

Where a company's most recent financial results are the half-year figures, these are used to calculate this ratio.

Interest cover

The interest cover ratio indicates how many times a company could make its interest payments from its pre-tax profit. A rough rule of thumb says a ratio of at least three times is desirable. Below that and fast-rising interest rates could imperil profits. The ratio is derived by dividing the EBIT figure by net interest payments. Some companies have interest receipts that are higher than their interest payments, which turns the interest cover into a negative figure, so it is not listed.

Return on equity

Return on equity is the after-tax profit expressed as a percentage of the shareholders' equity. In theory, it is the amount that the company's managers have made for you — the shareholder — on your money. The shareholders' equity figure used is an average for the year.

Debt-to-equity ratio

This ratio is one of the best-known measures of a company's debt levels. It is total borrowings minus the company's cash holdings, expressed as a percentage of the shareholders' equity. Some companies have no debt at all, or their cash position is greater than their level of debt, which results in a negative ratio, so no figure is listed for them.

Where a company's most recent financial results are the half-year figures, these are used to calculate this ratio.

Current ratio

The current ratio is simply the company's current assets divided by its current liabilities. Current assets are cash or assets that can, in theory, be converted quickly into cash. Current liabilities are normally those payable within a year. Thus, the current ratio measures the ability of a company to repay its short-term debt in a hurry, should the need arise. The surplus of current assets over current liabilities is referred to as the company's working capital.

Where a company's most recent financial results are the half-year figures, these are used to calculate this ratio.

Banks

The tables for the banks are somewhat different from those for most other companies. EBIT and debt-to-equity ratios have little relevance for them, as they have such high interest payments (to their customers). Other differences are examined below.

Operating income

Operating income is used instead of sales revenues. Operating income is the bank's net interest income — that is, its total interest income minus its interest expense — plus other income, such as bank fees, fund management fees and income from businesses such as corporate finance and insurance.

Net interest income

Banks borrow money — that is, they accept deposits from savers — and they lend it to businesses, homebuyers and other borrowers. They charge the borrowers more than they pay those who deposit money with them, and the difference is known as net interest income.

Operating expenses

These are all the costs of running the bank. Banks have high operating expenses, and one of the keys to profit growth is cutting these expenses. Add the provision for doubtful debts to operating expenses, then deduct the total from operating income, and you get the pre-tax profit.

Non-interest income to total income

Banks have traditionally made most of their income from savers and from lending out money. But they are also working to diversify into new fields, and this ratio is an indication of their success.

Cost-to-income ratio

As noted, the banks have high costs — numerous branches, expensive computer systems, many staff, and so on — and they are all striving to reduce these. The cost-to-income ratio expresses their expenses as a percentage of their operating income, and is one of the ratios most often used as a gauge of efficiency. The lower the ratio drops the better.

Return on assets

Banks have enormous assets, in sharp contrast to, say, a high-tech start-up whose main physical assets may be little more than a set of computers and other technological equipment. So the return on assets — the after-tax profit expressed as a percentage of the year's average total assets — is another measure of efficiency.

PART I
THE COMPANIES

1300SMILES Limited

ASX code: ONT

www.1300smiles.com.au

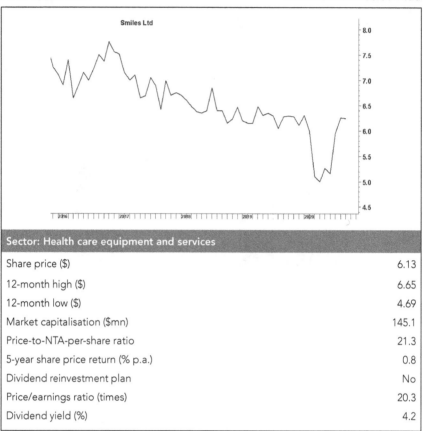

Smiles Ltd

Sector: Health care equipment and services	
Share price ($)	6.13
12-month high ($)	6.65
12-month low ($)	4.69
Market capitalisation ($mn)	145.1
Price-to-NTA-per-share ratio	21.3
5-year share price return (% p.a.)	0.8
Dividend reinvestment plan	No
Price/earnings ratio (times)	20.3
Dividend yield (%)	4.2

Townsville-based 1300SMILES, founded in 2000, runs a chain of some 35 dental practices in 10 major population centres of Queensland and in South Australia and New South Wales. Its main role is the provision of dental surgeries and practice management services to self-employed dentists, allowing them to focus on dental services. It also manages its own small dental business. The founder and managing director, Dr Daryl Holmes, owns around 60 per cent of the company equity.

Latest business results (June 2020, full year)

1300SMILES was hit by the COVID-19 pandemic, with many of its clinics forced to close temporarily for some weeks between March and May 2020, while activities at other clinics were severely limited. This led to a decline in revenues and profits for the year, despite a rebound in June 2020, which generated the company's highest-ever monthly revenues figure. The company also reports what it calls over-the-counter revenues, which represent the amount actually received by its dentistry businesses before the deduction of patient fees by self-employed dentists. On this basis — which the company believes gives a fairer measure of the scale of its operations than its reported statutory sales figure — total company revenues fell 3 per cent to $57.1 million. During the year the company acquired new multi-dentist practices in Gatton and in Laidley, both in Queensland. It sold two smaller operations.

Outlook

The dental business in Australia is fragmented, with around 70 per cent of dentists working in their own private practices or in small partnerships. However, as stricter regulatory and compliance requirements drive up costs, a gradual consolidation is taking place, and 1300SMILES is one of the leaders in this trend. The company buys dental practices, then retains the dentists, who pay a fee to 1300SMILES for services received, including marketing, administration, billing and collection, facilities certification and licensing. The company continues to seek out new practices to buy, though it was unsuccessful late in 2019 in its attempt to acquire a much larger rival, Albano, which manages the Maven chain of practices. It has taken a small stake in the ASX-listed Smiles Inclusive. 1300SMILES believes that, after being forced to close during the period of the pandemic, some older dentists will choose not to return to dentistry and will keep their practices closed. It has reported that from June 2020 it has not only been seeing many new patients, but has also been experiencing an unprecedented stream of applications from dentists wishing to join the 1300SMILES business.

Year to 30 June	2019	2020
Revenues ($mn)	40.3	39.8
EBIT ($mn)	10.7	10.2
EBIT margin (%)	26.4	25.7
Profit before tax ($mn)	10.8	9.8
Profit after tax ($mn)	7.8	7.1
Earnings per share (c)	32.82	30.18
Cash flow per share (c)	42.40	53.43
Dividend (c)	25	25.75
Percentage franked	100	100
Net tangible assets per share ($)	0.28	0.29
Interest cover (times)	~	23.8
Return on equity (%)	19.9	17.6
Debt-to-equity ratio (%)	21.4	20.2
Current ratio	1.0	1.1

Accent Group Limited

ASX code: AX1   www.accentgr.com.au

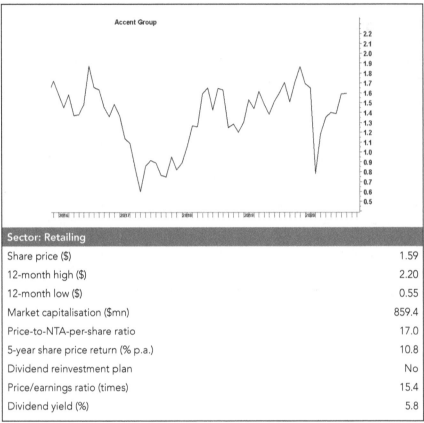

Sector: Retailing	
Share price ($)	1.59
12-month high ($)	2.20
12-month low ($)	0.55
Market capitalisation ($mn)	859.4
Price-to-NTA-per-share ratio	17.0
5-year share price return (% p.a.)	10.8
Dividend reinvestment plan	No
Price/earnings ratio (times)	15.4
Dividend yield (%)	5.8

Sydney company Accent Group is a nationwide footwear wholesaler and retailer that has grown rapidly through a series of mergers and acquisitions. Its brands now include The Athlete's Foot — established in 1976 — Hype DC, Platypus, Podium Sports, Skechers, Merrell, CAT, Vans, Dr. Martens, Saucony, Timberland, Sperry Top-Sider, Palladium and Stance. The company's wholesale division distributes footwear and apparel. Accent also operates in New Zealand.

Latest business results (June 2020, full year)

Sales and profits rose, despite the company closing all stores from late-March until May, resulting in a loss of more than $55 million in sales. Total sales of $948.9 million — including franchise stores — were up 1.5 per cent, with company-owned stores achieving 4.5 per cent growth to $807.1 million. On a like-for-like basis, sales rose 1.9 per cent. Digital sales were up 69 per cent, to represent 17 per cent of total turnover. In just the fourth quarter digital sales grew 142 per cent, with half of these sales to new customers. Wholesale sales were down, as demand fell during April and May 2020. The company qualified for $23.9 million in government wage subsidies in

Australia and New Zealand, and also received $7.6 million in rental concessions. During the year the company opened 57 new stores, including its first store under its new sports and lifestyle brand PIVOT, and closed 12. At June 2020 it operated a network of 524 stores.

Outlook

Accent maintains its ambitious growth strategy and expects profits to continue rising, with a mid- to long-term objective of annual earnings-per-share growth of at least 10 per cent. It expects to open 30 to 40 new stores during the June 2021 year. It sees particular potential in its new PIVOT brand, aimed at the $4 billion value sports and lifestyle market, and expects to open up to 12 PIVOT stores during the June 2021 year, with an eventual target of 100. It also has ambitious plans for Stylerunner, the online activewear retailer that it acquired in November 2019 after it fell into receivership. It plans to open up to six Stylerunner stores during the June 2021 year, while also boosting its online presence. Accent believes it has seen a structural shift towards online shopping, and it plans to invest in boosting this business. Its contactable customer database grew by more than two million customers to 6.8 million customers during the June 2020 year. Its goal is that digital sales will eventually represent 30 per cent of total turnover.

Year to 28 June*	2019	2020
Revenues ($mn)	796.3	829.8
EBIT ($mn)	80.6	94.8
EBIT margin (%)	10.1	11.4
Profit before tax ($mn)	77.0	80.3
Profit after tax ($mn)	53.9	55.7
Earnings per share (c)	10.02	10.31
Cash flow per share (c)	15.28	29.92
Dividend (c)	8.25	9.25
Percentage franked	100	100
Net tangible assets per share ($)	0.09	0.09
Interest cover (times)	22.6	6.6
Return on equity (%)	13.6	13.7
Debt-to-equity ratio (%)	12.3	7.6
Current ratio	1.2	1.0

* 30 June 2019

Adairs Limited

ASX code: ADH   www.adairs.com.au

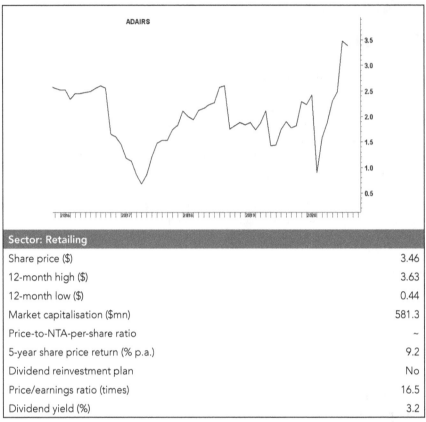

Sector: Retailing	
Share price ($)	3.46
12-month high ($)	3.63
12-month low ($)	0.44
Market capitalisation ($mn)	581.3
Price-to-NTA-per-share ratio	~
5-year share price return (% p.a.)	9.2
Dividend reinvestment plan	No
Price/earnings ratio (times)	16.5
Dividend yield (%)	3.2

Melbourne-based home furnishings specialist Adairs dates back to 1918 and the opening of a store in Chapel Street in Prahran, Melbourne. It has since grown into a nationwide chain of stores specialising in bed linen, bedding, towels, homewares, soft furnishings, children's furnishings and some bedroom furniture. It has also expanded to New Zealand, and it operates a flourishing online business. In December 2019 it acquired the New Zealand–based online furniture retailer Mocka.

Latest business results (June 2020, full year)

A combination of soaring online sales, the Mocka acquisition and government subsidies helped generate an excellent result, despite temporary store closures in Australia and New Zealand during early 2020. Total store sales fell 7 per cent to $265 million, although on a like-for-like basis — excluding the impact of the store closures — they rose by nearly 4 per cent. By contrast, online sales soared 61 per cent for Adairs, and by 110 per cent when Mocka revenues are included. Total online sales of $124 million were nearly a third of company turnover. Mocka made a 30-week contribution, with revenues of $30 million and EBIT of $6.7 million, significantly higher than expectations. The company benefited from more than $11 million in JobKeeper wage subsidies.

Outlook

Adairs manages popular brands with high levels of customer recognition and loyalty. With an addressable Australian home furnishings market of some $12 billion it sees enormous scope for growth. It has become a significant beneficiary of what could be a structural trend towards online shopping — induced by the COVID-19 pandemic — and also of rising demand for homewares, as people are forced to spend more time in their homes. It believes its online operations could see significant further growth, and it plans to invest heavily in this business. It is fast-tracking an expansion of its warehouse facilities to support this. It also continues to open new retail outlets, with an emphasis on larger stores, which generally are more profitable than smaller ones. At June 2020 it operated a total of 167 stores nationwide and in New Zealand, two more than a year earlier. During the June 2021 year it expects to open three to five new stores and enlarge a similar number. It is also building a new national distribution centre in Melbourne, and expects this to generate annual cost savings of around $3.5 million from the June 2022 year. Adairs imports much of its product range and it will benefit from any appreciation in the value of the dollar.

Year to 28 June*	2019	2020
Revenues ($mn)	344.4	388.9
EBIT ($mn)	43.4	59.0
EBIT margin (%)	12.6	15.2
Gross margin (%)	57.2	57.1
Profit before tax ($mn)	42.3	52.8
Profit after tax ($mn)	29.6	35.3
Earnings per share (c)	17.87	21.00
Cash flow per share (c)	22.51	44.40
Dividend (c)	14.5	11
Percentage franked	100	100
Net tangible assets per share ($)	0.03	~
Interest cover (times)	37.5	9.6
Return on equity (%)	25.3	27.3
Debt-to-equity ratio (%)	7.0	0.7
Current ratio	1.5	0.8

* 30 June 2019

Adbri Limited

ASX code: ABC
www.adbri.com.au

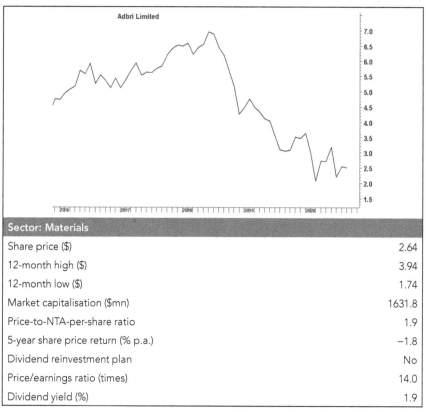

Sector: Materials	
Share price ($)	2.64
12-month high ($)	3.94
12-month low ($)	1.74
Market capitalisation ($mn)	1631.8
Price-to-NTA-per-share ratio	1.9
5-year share price return (% p.a.)	−1.8
Dividend reinvestment plan	No
Price/earnings ratio (times)	14.0
Dividend yield (%)	1.9

Adelaide-based Adbri, the new name for Adelaide Brighton, was established in 1882 and is one of Australia's leaders in the production and supply of construction materials, notably cement and lime. In addition, its Hy-Tec business and its Mawson Group joint venture are suppliers of pre-mixed concrete, and it has a business as a supplier of aggregates, through Mawson Group and Hurd Haulage. The Adbri Masonry operation is a leading producer of concrete masonry products. Adbri's major customers include the residential, non-residential and engineering construction sectors, as well as the infrastructure, alumina, steel and mining industries.

Latest business results (June 2020, half year)

Continuing weakness in the residential sector sent revenues and profits down from the June 2019 half. Cement sales volumes fell by 6 per cent, due especially to weak demand from New South Wales. By contrast, mining projects helped boost sales in Western Australia. Lime sales volumes rose by 4 per cent, thanks especially to increased demand from Western Australian gold and nickel miners. Concrete volumes were down by 13 per cent, with strength in Victoria more than offset by falling sales in

New South Wales and Queensland. Concrete product volume sales were down, although revenues and profit rose, thanks to a higher mix of sales to the retail sector.

Outlook

Adbri is a key supplier to the construction and resources industries, and its fortunes are heavily dependent on trends in these sectors. It expects to benefit as governments at all levels seek to boost the economy through such means as infrastructure spending, home-building grants and stamp duty relief. In addition, it sees the low-interest environment as providing support. It expects the resources sector to remain firm, with growing demand for cement and lime. The company is a prominent supplier to the gold mining industry and is a beneficiary of booming conditions for that sector. It has embarked on a productivity program aimed at stripping $30 million from its annual cost base. In 2013 Adelaide Brighton initiated the process of selling surplus land, and it believes that over 10 years it could realise up to $130 million in sales. With the current weakness in its businesses, it plans to bring forward some land sales. However, in July 2020 the company announced that Alcoa of Australia would not be renewing a major lime supply contract that expires in June 2021, depriving Adbri of around $70 million in annual revenues. The company has said it is working to devise strategies to mitigate the consequent loss of earnings.

Year to 31 December	2018	2019
Revenues ($mn)	1630.6	1517.0
EBIT ($mn)	273.5	186.4
EBIT margin (%)	16.8	12.3
Gross margin (%)	35.5	35.2
Profit before tax ($mn)	259.1	167.9
Profit after tax ($mn)	191.0	122.9
Earnings per share (c)	29.36	18.86
Cash flow per share (c)	42.80	33.23
Dividend (c)	20	5
Percentage franked	100	100
Interest cover (times)	19.0	10.1
Return on equity (%)	15.4	10.1
Half year to 30 June	2019	2020
Revenues ($mn)	755.7	700.7
Profit before tax ($mn)	76.0	65.3
Profit after tax ($mn)	55.3	47.6
Earnings per share (c)	8.50	7.30
Dividend (c)	0	4.75
Percentage franked	~	100
Net tangible assets per share ($)	1.30	1.40
Debt-to-equity ratio (%)	45.9	34.6
Current ratio	2.6	4.3

Altium Limited

ASX code: ALU

www.altium.com

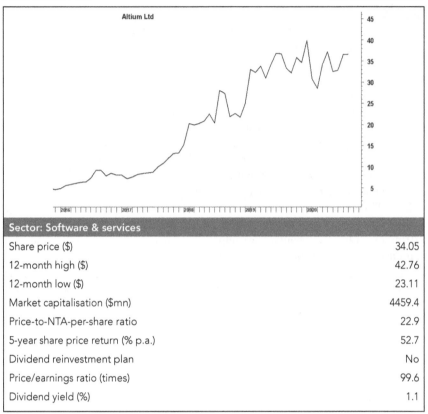

Sector: Software & services	
Share price ($)	34.05
12-month high ($)	42.76
12-month low ($)	23.11
Market capitalisation ($mn)	4459.4
Price-to-NTA-per-share ratio	22.9
5-year share price return (% p.a.)	52.7
Dividend reinvestment plan	No
Price/earnings ratio (times)	99.6
Dividend yield (%)	1.1

Sydney-based software company Altium was founded in Tasmania in 1985. It was originally named Protel. Its specialty is the provision of software that allows engineers to design printed circuit boards (PCBs). Its core product is Altium Designer. A much smaller division, Microcontrollers and Embedded Systems, is responsible for the Tasking-brand set of embedded tools for code development. Another smaller division, Electronic Parts, Search and Discovery, provides an electronic parts search tool. Altium now has most of its operations abroad, but retains its Sydney headquarters and its ASX listing.

Latest business results (June 2020, full year)

Altium delivered a ninth straight year of double-digit revenue and pre-tax profit growth. However, the recalculation of tax assets and liabilities led to a substantially higher tax bill for the year, and the after-tax profit fell sharply. The company reported that the COVID-19 pandemic led to a marked slowdown in demand in the second half. The core Boards and Systems division experienced steady growth from all regions, with surging demand for the Altium NEXUS product, which provides Altium Designer customers with a variety of enhanced design capabilities. Sales of this product soared 133 per cent to US$15.5 million. The Electronic Parts, Search and Discovery division recorded a modest 6 per cent rise in sales. The Microcontrollers and Embedded Systems division, which is focused on the automotive industry, saw no growth for the year. Note that Altium reports its finances in American dollars. All figures in this book are converted to Australian dollars using prevailing exchange rates.

Outlook

Printed circuit boards are incorporated in most electronic devices, and demand for them continues to grow. The strong rise in smart electronic connected devices is partly behind this trend. It is expensive for a customer to switch once it makes a decision to employ Altium software, and the company has a high level of recurring subscription fee income. It has a strong reputation for its PCB design software, with high profit margins and a growth rate significantly higher than the industry average. It has set itself a June 2025 target of US$500 million in total revenues, but now concedes that it may miss this goal by six months to a year. Another target is for 100 000 subscribers to its Altium Designer services by 2025, compared with 51 000 at June 2020. It has launched its new Altium 365 cloud-based platform and expects this to become a significant driver of future growth. At June 2020 Altium had no debt and more than US$90 million in cash holdings.

Year to 30 June	2019	2020
Revenues ($mn)	239.9	274.1
Boards & systems (%)	77	79
Microcontrollers & embedded systems (%)	13	11
Electronic parts, search & discovery (%)	10	10
EBIT ($mn)	79.0	93.5
EBIT margin (%)	32.9	34.1
Profit before tax ($mn)	80.0	93.7
Profit after tax ($mn)	73.5	44.8
Earnings per share (c)	56.35	34.20
Cash flow per share (c)	62.57	46.50
Dividend (c)	34	39
Percentage franked	0	0
Net tangible assets per share ($)	1.46	1.49
Interest cover (times)	~	~
Return on equity (%)	31.3	16.9
Debt-to-equity ratio (%)	~	~
Current ratio	1.8	2.0

Alumina Limited

ASX code: AWC   www.aluminalimited.com

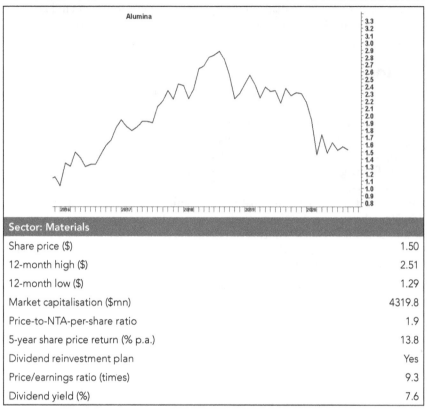

Sector: Materials	
Share price ($)	1.50
12-month high ($)	2.51
12-month low ($)	1.29
Market capitalisation ($mn)	4319.8
Price-to-NTA-per-share ratio	1.9
5-year share price return (% p.a.)	13.8
Dividend reinvestment plan	Yes
Price/earnings ratio (times)	9.3
Dividend yield (%)	7.6

Melbourne-based Alumina traces its origins back to the late 1950s and the mining of bauxite by WMC Limited. This led in 1961 to the establishment of a joint venture company between WMC and the Aluminium Company of America (Alcoa). In 2002 WMC spun off its interest in this business into a separate company, Alumina. Today Alumina's sole business activity is ownership of 40 per cent of the equity of Alcoa World Alumina and Chemicals (AWAC), in partnership with Alcoa, which holds the other 60 per cent. AWAC is an international business, responsible for about 10 per cent of global alumina production. It manages bauxite mines in Western Australia, Brazil, Saudi Arabia and Guinea. It also operates alumina refineries in Western Australia, Texas, Brazil, Saudi Arabia and Spain. Other businesses include the Alcoa Steamship operation and the Portland aluminium smelter in Victoria, in which it holds a 55 per cent equity share.

Latest business results (June 2020, half year)

Falling alumina prices sent revenues and profits tumbling. The company divides its operations into three segments, bauxite mining, alumina refining and Portland aluminium smelting. The mining business produced 20.3 million tonnes of bauxite, up from 19.9 million tonnes in the June 2019 half, at an average cash cost of US$9.60 per tonne, down from US$10.50. Most production is for the company's own use, although there are also some third-party sales. It refined 6.4 million tonnes of alumina at its own refineries, up from 6.2 million tonnes in June 2019, at an average cash cost of US$193 per tonne, down from US$218. However, the average price received of US$266 per tonne was a big drop from US$375 in the June 2019 half and US$424 in the June 2018 half. The Portland smelter produced 78 000 tonnes of aluminium, down from 80 000 tonnes in June 2019. Note that Alumina reports its results in US dollars. The Australian dollar figures in this book — converted at prevailing exchange rates — are for guidance only.

Outlook

Alumina benefits from high-quality bauxite reserves and low-cost alumina refining operations. Its shares have attracted attention for a high dividend yield. However, its financial results are directly linked to global alumina and aluminium prices. These have recently been recovering from some substantial weakness, partly due to production problems at the giant Alunorte refinery in Brazil. A Chinese economic revival could also boost prices. Alumina and Alcoa may choose to sell or even close the loss-making Portland smelter if they are unable to reach agreement on reducing power prices.

Year to 31 December	2018	2019
Revenues ($mn)	925.6	604.9
EBIT ($mn)	848.5	472.4
EBIT margin (%)	91.7	78.1
Profit before tax ($mn)	847.2	466.7
Profit after tax ($mn)	847.2	466.6
Earnings per share (c)	29.43	16.21
Cash flow per share (c)	29.44	16.21
Dividend (c)	32.43	11.43
Percentage franked	100	100
Interest cover (times)	636.4	82.7
Return on equity (%)	28.6	16.7
Half year to 30 June	2019	2020
Revenues ($mn)	311.5	149.4
Profit before tax ($mn)	297.0	137.1
Profit after tax ($mn)	297.0	137.1
Earnings per share (c)	9.86	4.70
Dividend (c)	6.29	4.06
Percentage franked	100	100
Net tangible assets per share ($)	0.96	0.80
Debt-to-equity ratio (%)	2.8	4.8
Current ratio	0.3	34.2

Ansell Limited

ASX code: ANN   www.ansell.com

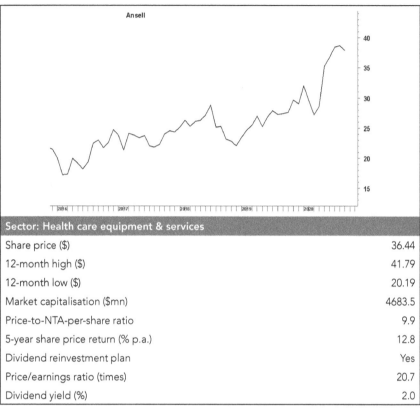

Sector: Health care equipment & services	
Share price ($)	36.44
12-month high ($)	41.79
12-month low ($)	20.19
Market capitalisation ($mn)	4683.5
Price-to-NTA-per-share ratio	9.9
5-year share price return (% p.a.)	12.8
Dividend reinvestment plan	Yes
Price/earnings ratio (times)	20.7
Dividend yield (%)	2.0

Melbourne-based Ansell has roots that stretch back to the manufacture of pneumatic bicycle tyres in the 19th century. It is today a global leader in a variety of safety and healthcare products. It makes a wide range of examination and surgical gloves for the medical profession. It also makes gloves and other hand and arm protective products for industrial applications, including for single use, along with household gloves. It has offices and production facilities in 55 countries, and more than 90 per cent of company revenues derive from abroad. Though still based in Australia, the company has its operational headquarters in the US.

Latest business results (June 2020, full year)

Ansell became a beneficiary of the COVID-19 pandemic, as demand soared for its single-use gloves and personal protective equipment, and revenues and profits rose. However, the company's traditional medical supplies business was hit by the postponement of much elective surgery in 2020, and demand for industrial gloves also suffered in a weak economic environment. The Healthcare division saw EBIT surge 35 per cent on a constant currency basis, on a sales gain of 14 per cent, thanks to higher volumes, pricing initiatives and favourable raw material costs, partially offset by COVID-19-related expenses. The Industrial division reported single-digit increases in sales and profits, with particularly strong growth in demand for chemical protection clothing. Note that Ansell reports its results in US dollars. The Australian dollar figures in this book — converted at prevailing exchange rates — are for guidance only.

Outlook

Ansell has a strong portfolio of products, which gives it a degree of pricing power. It has achieved success in its research and development efforts, with a continuing stream of innovative and high-margin products. Thanks to a major company transformation program, which still continues, it has been able to lower its manufacturing costs. It also continues to seek appropriate acquisition opportunities. It expects COVID-19 to remain a challenge during the June 2021 financial year, and possibly into the next financial year also, with continuing strong demand for the company's protective wear. However, it is seeing raw material shortfalls, which will place pressure on pricing and could lead to some product shortages. It is also forecasting some further weakness in industrial demand. It is stepping up investments aimed at boosting production capacity and continues to focus on automation as a means to drive efficiencies. Its early forecast is for June 2021 earnings per share of US$1.26 to US$1.38, up from US$1.22 in June 2020.

Year to 30 June	2019	2020
Revenues ($mn)	2081.9	2338.7
Healthcare (%)	53	55
Industrial (%)	47	45
EBIT ($mn)	278.2	314.2
EBIT margin (%)	13.4	13.4
Gross margin (%)	39.0	39.2
Profit before tax ($mn)	262.8	293.2
Profit after tax ($mn)	209.6	229.0
Earnings per share (c)	154.90	175.74
Cash flow per share (c)	194.12	238.58
Dividend (c)	64.93	72.46
Percentage franked	0	0
Net tangible assets per share ($)	3.41	3.67
Interest cover (times)	18.0	15.0
Return on equity (%)	10.3	11.4
Debt-to-equity ratio (%)	10.5	7.9
Current ratio	3.1	2.4

ARB Corporation Limited

ASX code: ARB

www.arb.com.au

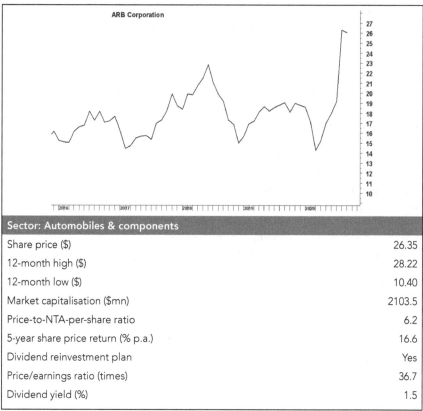

ARB Corporation

Sector: Automobiles & components	
Share price ($)	26.35
12-month high ($)	28.22
12-month low ($)	10.40
Market capitalisation ($mn)	2103.5
Price-to-NTA-per-share ratio	6.2
5-year share price return (% p.a.)	16.6
Dividend reinvestment plan	Yes
Price/earnings ratio (times)	36.7
Dividend yield (%)	1.5

Melbourne-based ARB, founded in 1975, is a prominent manufacturer of specialty automotive accessories, and an international leader in the design and production of specialised equipment for four-wheel-drive vehicles. These include its Air Locker air-operated locking differential system. It also makes and distributes a wide range of other products, including bull bars, roof racks, tow bars, canopies and the Old Man Emu range of suspension products. It operates a network of 67 ARB-brand stores throughout Australia, including 27 that are company-owned. It has established manufacturing facilities in Thailand, with distribution centres in the United States, the Czech Republic, Thailand and Dubai. It exports to more than 100 countries, and overseas business represents nearly one-third of total company turnover.

Latest business results (June 2020, full year)

Sales rose and profits edged up in a challenging year. The company reported that monthly sales grew at a relatively consistent pace of 7.6 per cent during the year until March 2020, when they began to fall significantly, followed by a substantial rebound beginning in May 2020. Some 61 per cent of total income is from the Australian after-market, comprising ARB stores and other retailers, as well as vehicle dealers and fleet operators. For the second straight year demand just edged up, hurt by a slowdown in domestic sales of SUVs and four-wheel-drive utilities. By contrast, exports were up by 17 per cent, following 10 per cent growth in the previous year. Original equipment manufacturer sales to Australian vehicle makers fell by 13 per cent, hurt by the decline in new vehicle sales in Australia.

Outlook

The COVID-19 pandemic disrupted ARB's manufacturing operations in both Australia and Thailand, and with order inflow surging again from May 2020 the company found itself unable to meet demand in an orderly manner. Nevertheless, it is optimistic about the longer-term outlook, believing that international travel restrictions in many of its markets will lead to increases in domestic travel by private vehicle. It regards product development as a key element in helping it maintain a competitive edge, with research and development spending of $12 million in June 2020, down from $13 million in the previous year. A new 20 000-square-metre warehouse in Thailand has lowered global distribution costs and boosted efficiency. ARB-brand stores are an important generator of sales and the company is steadily rolling out new outlets, with three new ones planned to open during the June 2021 year. At June 2020 ARB had no debt and more than $41 million in cash holdings.

Year to 30 June	2019	2020
Revenues ($mn)	443.9	465.4
EBIT ($mn)	77.9	79.8
EBIT margin (%)	17.6	17.1
Gross margin (%)	42.8	41.4
Profit before tax ($mn)	77.7	78.1
Profit after tax ($mn)	57.1	57.3
Earnings per share (c)	71.86	71.80
Cash flow per share (c)	89.31	99.03
Dividend (c)	39.5	39.5
Percentage franked	100	100
Net tangible assets per share ($)	3.98	4.22
Interest cover (times)	360.7	47.6
Return on equity (%)	17.6	15.9
Debt-to-equity ratio (%)	~	~
Current ratio	3.8	3.1

Aristocrat Leisure Limited

ASX code: ALL

www.aristocrat.com

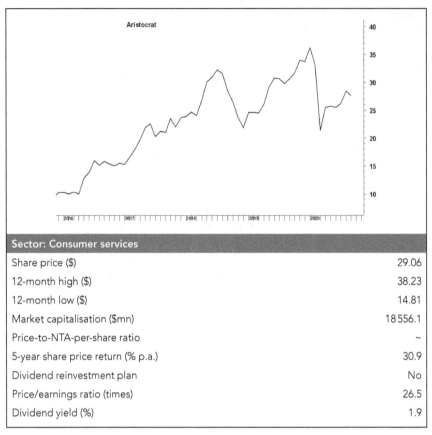

Sector: Consumer services	
Share price ($)	29.06
12-month high ($)	38.23
12-month low ($)	14.81
Market capitalisation ($mn)	18 556.1
Price-to-NTA-per-share ratio	~
5-year share price return (% p.a.)	30.9
Dividend reinvestment plan	No
Price/earnings ratio (times)	26.5
Dividend yield (%)	1.9

Sydney-based Aristocrat, founded in 1953, is Australia's leading developer and manufacturer of electronic machines for the gaming industry, and it is also among the world's largest. It is licensed by some 300 gaming jurisdictions worldwide and it operates in more than 90 countries. Its products and services include gaming machines, interactive video terminal systems, electronic tables, gaming machine support services and casino management systems. It is actively bringing a large selection of its games to online and mobile devices.

Latest business results (March 2020, half year)

Sales rose but profits fell as Aristocrat was hit by the early impact of the COVID-19 pandemic. This led to a significant fall in gaming machine sales, as many customers were forced to close their venues, sparking a sharp decline in capital spending. The company's major market is the Americas, and though sales declined by just 5 per cent, profits were down 14 per cent. There were steeper declines in the Australia/New Zealand market. By contrast, digital sales and profits surged by double-digit amounts. Digital sales now represent 46 per cent of total company turnover, up from 39 per cent a year earlier.

Outlook

Aristocrat enjoys a strong position in the global gaming industry, with high market shares in many regions. Nevertheless, this remains a competitive business, and the company is highly dependent on a continuing stream of attractive new products. To develop these, it must recruit and retain large numbers of highly skilled creative specialists and technology experts, and this has been one of its key challenges. In any case, until gaming venues reopen and patrons return it can expect subdued demand for its products. Personnel costs represent about 70 per cent of company operating expenses, and Aristocrat is working to reduce its short-term cost base through staffing reductions — some on a temporary basis — as well as salary cuts and the transition of some full-time roles to part-time. It has also suspended its shareholder dividend. Meanwhile, its digital business continues to grow strongly, thanks to popular games that include 'RAID: Shadow Legends', 'Lightning Link' and 'Cashman Casino'. Revenues from digital products have now overtaken hardware and licensing revenues from the Americas, previously the main driver of company expansion, although profit margins are substantially less. The company has formed a new Digital Leadership Team, and expects further strong growth for this business, especially while social distancing rules remain in force. With much of its income coming from outside Australia, its earnings are heavily influenced by currency rate trends.

Year to 30 September	2018	2019
Revenues ($mn)	3509.5	4397.4
EBIT ($mn)	868.5	1099.0
EBIT margin (%)	24.7	25.0
Profit before tax ($mn)	763.1	973.5
Profit after tax ($mn)	542.6	698.8
Earnings per share (c)	85.03	109.64
Cash flow per share (c)	113.58	145.58
Dividend (c)	46	56
Percentage franked	100	100
Interest cover (times)	8.2	8.8
Return on equity (%)	35.3	36.1
Half year to 31 March	2019	2020
Revenues ($mn)	2105.3	2251.8
Profit before tax ($mn)	491.7	403.7
Profit after tax ($mn)	356.5	305.9
Earnings per share (c)	55.90	47.90
Dividend (c)	22	0
Percentage franked	100	~
Net tangible assets per share ($)	~	~
Debt-to-equity ratio (%)	102.9	64.1
Current ratio	1.7	1.9

ASX Limited

ASX code: ASX www.asx.com.au

Sector: Diversified financials	
Share price ($)	85.90
12-month high ($)	91.32
12-month low ($)	63.02
Market capitalisation ($mn)	16 629.8
Price-to-NTA-per-share ratio	13.6
5-year share price return (% p.a.)	21.7
Dividend reinvestment plan	No
Price/earnings ratio (times)	33.4
Dividend yield (%)	2.8

ASX (Australian Securities Exchange) was formed in 1987 through the amalgamation of six independent stock exchanges that formerly operated in the state capital cities. Each of those exchanges had a history of share trading dating back to the 19th century. Though originally a mutual organisation of stockbrokers, in 1998 ASX became a listed company, with its shares traded on its own market. It expanded in 2006 when it merged with the Sydney Futures Exchange. Today it provides primary, secondary and derivative market services, along with clearing, settlement and compliance services. It is also a provider of a range of comprehensive market data and technical services.

Latest business results (June 2020, full year)

ASX posted another solid result, with revenues and profits higher and all divisions showing growth. It was the company's tenth consecutive profit increase. The best result came from the smallest division, Equity Post-Trade Services, with revenues up 17 per cent, reflecting a 29 per cent jump in the value of trades centrally cleared in the market during the year. The Trading Services division saw an 11.5 per cent rise, which was also a result of higher levels of market trading, along with a 10.7 per cent increase in information services revenues. The Listings and Issuer Services division recorded a 7.3 per cent increase, with a rise in secondary capital raisings — as companies sought to strengthen their finances when the COVID-19 pandemic hit — more than offsetting a decline in new listing revenues. There were 83 new listings during the year, down from 111 in the previous year. The largest division, Derivatives and OTC Markets, saw the smallest rise, up 4.5 per cent, with an increase in futures and OTC revenues offsetting a decline in equity options revenues.

Outlook

ASX's profits are highly geared to levels of market activity. Nevertheless, such is the diverse variety of instruments available to investors nowadays that even market weakness does not necessarily lead to a decline in trading volumes. The company also enjoys a high degree of protection in its operations, with little effective competition for many of its businesses. In line with its vision of becoming one of the world's most technologically advanced financial marketplaces, it boosted its capital spending to $80.4 million, from $75.1 million in the previous year. In particular, it plans to replace its CHESS equities clearing and settlement system with a major new platform using distributed ledger technology — also sometimes referred to as blockchain — to become operational by April 2022.

Year to 30 June	2019	2020
Revenues ($mn)	873.2	949.0
Derivatives and OTC markets (%)	36	34
Trading services (%)	26	27
Listings and issuer services (%)	26	25
Equity post-trade services (%)	12	14
EBIT ($mn)	606.3	637.0
EBIT margin (%)	69.4	67.1
Profit before tax ($mn)	705.1	720.8
Profit after tax ($mn)	492.0	498.6
Earnings per share (c)	254.16	257.56
Cash flow per share (c)	278.86	284.42
Dividend (c)	228.7	238.9
Percentage franked	100	100
Net tangible assets per share ($)	7.53	6.32
Interest cover (times)	~	~
Return on equity (%)	12.5	13.1
Debt-to-equity ratio (%)	~	~
Current ratio	1.1	1.1

AUB Group Limited

ASX code: AUB   www.aubgroup.com.au

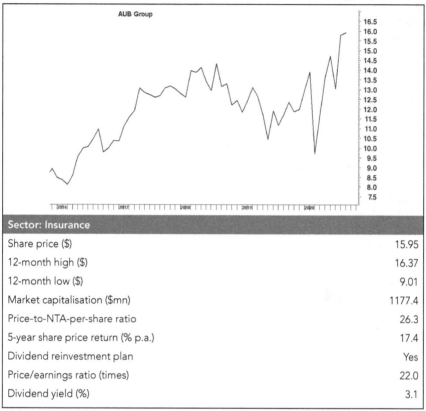

Sector: Insurance	
Share price ($)	15.95
12-month high ($)	16.37
12-month low ($)	9.01
Market capitalisation ($mn)	1177.4
Price-to-NTA-per-share ratio	26.3
5-year share price return (% p.a.)	17.4
Dividend reinvestment plan	Yes
Price/earnings ratio (times)	22.0
Dividend yield (%)	3.1

Sydney-based AUB Group, formerly known as Austbrokers Holdings, was established in 1985. It manages a network of insurance businesses throughout Australia and New Zealand. Its principal business is insurance broking, and it typically holds an equity stake of at least 50 per cent in each business, usually in partnership with the original owners. It also manages the SURA underwriting agency business, which operates agencies in many specialised areas of the insurance business. A third division provides risk services to insurers, brokers and corporate clients.

Latest business results (June 2020, full year)

AUB enjoyed another good year, with a solid rise in revenues and profits. The core Australian broking operation contributes more than half the company's turnover. It reported a double-digit rise in profits, thanks to new business and an increase in premiums for commercial insurance. There was also a contribution from the company's 40 per cent holding in online insurance distribution platform BizCover, acquired in February 2020. New Zealand broking, representing about 15 per cent of turnover, delivered a fourth straight year of double-digit profit growth as the company continued to build this business. However, the SURA underwriting business saw revenues and profits down, due to competitive challenges and the impact of the COVID-19 pandemic on some clients.

Outlook

AUB has achieved success with its model of buying a stake in an insurance broking house but, in most cases, continuing to operate it with the original owners. This has allowed the businesses to preserve their local identity and management, while benefiting from the support of a large group. The company is able to help its members develop their businesses through growth initiatives, including the addition of new products, and sometimes through appropriate bolt-on acquisitions. Since entering the New Zealand market in 2014 it has become that country's largest broking management group. It is a beneficiary of rising premiums, and expects further 5 per cent to 6 per cent growth in the June 2021 year. It sees great potential in its new ExpressCover online platform — developed together with BizCover — for simplifying the insurance process for small and medium-sized businesses. It has abandoned its attempt to take over a major rival, Coverforce Holdings, but continues to seek other acquisitions. In August 2020 it acquired a 73 per cent stake in Experien Insurance Services, a specialty brokerage focused on the medical and dental professions. AUB's early forecast is for underlying after-tax profit in the June 2021 year of $58.5 million to $61 million.

Year to 30 June	2019	2020
Revenues ($mn)	276.4	303.5
EBIT ($mn)	70.1	82.8
EBIT margin (%)	25.3	27.3
Profit before tax ($mn)	66.8	76.6
Profit after tax ($mn)	46.4	53.4
Earnings per share (c)	66.64	72.45
Cash flow per share (c)	82.89	101.74
Dividend (c)	46	50
Percentage franked	100	100
Net tangible assets per share ($)	0.19	0.61
Interest cover (times)	21.8	13.4
Return on equity (%)	13.1	12.6
Debt-to-equity ratio (%)	7.1	30.0
Current ratio	1.1	1.2

Australia and New Zealand Banking Group Limited

ASX code: ANZ
www.anz.com.au

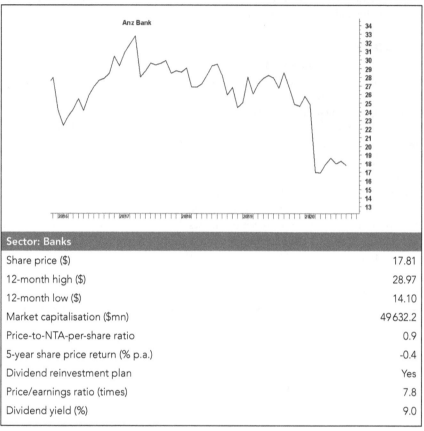

Anz Bank

Sector: Banks	
Share price ($)	17.81
12-month high ($)	28.97
12-month low ($)	14.10
Market capitalisation ($mn)	49 632.2
Price-to-NTA-per-share ratio	0.9
5-year share price return (% p.a.)	-0.4
Dividend reinvestment plan	Yes
Price/earnings ratio (times)	7.8
Dividend yield (%)	9.0

Melbourne-based ANZ has its roots in the establishment of the Bank of Australasia in London in 1835. It is today one of the country's four banking giants and one of the largest companies. It is a market leader in New Zealand banking, and it is also active throughout Asia and the Pacific region. Altogether, it has a presence in some 15 Asian markets, including a major technology and back office operation in Bangalore, India.

Latest business results (March 2020, half year)

Profits fell sharply on both a statutory and a cash basis, due especially to a $1.67 billion credit impairment charge as the bank warned of a material deterioration in the economic outlook and expected large credit losses. During the half some 105 000 Australians requested home loan repayment deferrals on $36 billion worth of borrowings, representing 14 per cent of the home loans portfolio. Repayment deferrals were also provided on $7.5 billion worth of loans to commercial customers. The bank wrote down the value of its Asian investments by $815 million. ANZ's institutional banking operation, one of its traditional strengths, actually saw some excellent business, with cash profits up 20 per cent from the September 2019 half before the impact of credit impairment provisioning. However, the core Australian banking business and New Zealand banking both experienced weakness, even before the impact of provisioning.

Outlook

ANZ believes the Australian economy will take three to five years to recover from the impact of the lockdown measures and it is investigating a range of measures to help struggling customers, including partial repayments, deferred repayments and special interest rates. A slowing economy and continuing low interest rates could put pressure on the interest-rate margin, which would further hurt profits, and it is working to cut costs, notably employee expenses. It may also reduce dividend payment. It continues to restructure its operations. Having significantly streamlined its extensive Asian activities, it is now working to boost business in selected Asian markets. In particular, it is optimistic about the potential for increased institutional banking operations in China, where it is already a banker to e-commerce giants Alibaba, Tencent, Baidu and JD.com. In January 2020 it completed the sale of its OnePath pensions and investments business to IOOF Holdings. In September 2020 it completed the NZ$762 million sale of its asset finance business in New Zealand, UDC Finance, to Japan's Shinsei Bank.

Year to 30 September	2018	2019
Operating income ($mn)	19 367.0	19 029.0
Net interest income ($mn)	14 514.0	14 339.0
Operating expenses ($mn)	9 401.0	9 071.0
Profit before tax ($mn)	9 278.0	9 163.0
Profit after tax ($mn)	6 487.0	6 470.0
Earnings per share (c)	224.60	228.23
Dividend (c)	160	160
Percentage franked	100	85
Non-interest income to total income (%)	24.5	24.6
Cost-to-income ratio (%)	48.1	48.3
Return on equity (%)	11.0	10.8
Return on assets (%)	0.7	0.7
Half year to 31 March	2019	2020
Operating income ($mn)	9 746.0	8 579.0
Profit before tax ($mn)	4 988.0	2 300.0
Profit after tax ($mn)	3 564.0	1 413.0
Earnings per share (c)	123.00	46.70
Dividend (c)	80	25
Percentage franked	100	100
Net tangible assets per share ($)	18.94	19.89

Australian Ethical Investment Limited

ASX code: AEF   www.australianethical.com.au

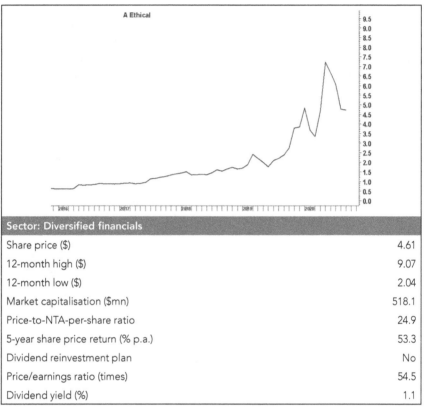

Sector: Diversified financials	
Share price ($)	4.61
12-month high ($)	9.07
12-month low ($)	2.04
Market capitalisation ($mn)	518.1
Price-to-NTA-per-share ratio	24.9
5-year share price return (% p.a.)	53.3
Dividend reinvestment plan	No
Price/earnings ratio (times)	54.5
Dividend yield (%)	1.1

Australian Ethical, based in Sydney, was founded in 1986. It is a wealth management company that specialises in investments in corporations that meet a set of ethical criteria. It operates a range of wholesale and retail funds, incorporating Australian and international shares, emerging companies and fixed interest. It also manages the Australian Ethical Advocacy Fund, which seeks to engage directly with companies to pursue improved corporate behaviours. The company donates up to 10 per cent of its profits to charities and activist groups through its Australian Ethical Foundation.

Latest business results (June 2020, full year)

Continuing growth in new customer numbers and in net money inflows, along with an increased performance fee, delivered another year of double-digit gains in revenues and profits. Net inflows of $660 million were double the figure of the previous year, with more than 70 per cent of this coming from superannuation funds. Unlike in the previous year, there were also increased inflows from managed funds and institutional investors. Altogether, the customer base grew by 20 per cent. The company received a performance fee of $3.6 million — up from $0.8 million in the previous year — relating to the outperformance of the Emerging Companies Fund. Two separate fee reductions were implemented during the year as the benefits of scale were passed on to customers. Funds under management of $4.05 billion at June 2020 were up 19 per cent from a year earlier.

Outlook

Australian Ethical is a small company but is one of the leaders in a growing trend towards ethical investment. One reason it has attracted attention for its funds is because of its perceived independence. Some rival ethical or green funds are actually managed by large institutional investors. The company's pledge is that it seeks out positive investments that support its three pillars of people, planet and animals. Its Ethical Charter gives details of the criteria it uses for its investments, and it provides a public list of the companies in which it is prepared to invest. It also publishes position papers on many topical issues. The company has been engaged in a marketing campaign aimed at boosting its image, and believes this has been a factor in its recent growth. Nevertheless, despite its strong position, Australian Ethical remains heavily exposed to financial markets at a time of uncertainty and volatility, and its businesses could be hurt in any sustained market downturn. At June 2020 the company had no debt and more than $21 million in cash holdings.

Year to 30 June	2019	2020
Revenues ($mn)	41.0	49.9
EBIT ($mn)	8.8	13.0
EBIT margin (%)	21.5	26.0
Profit before tax ($mn)	9.1	13.1
Profit after tax ($mn)	6.5	9.3
Earnings per share (c)	5.99	8.46
Cash flow per share (c)	6.32	9.27
Dividend (c)	5	5
Percentage franked	100	100
Net tangible assets per share ($)	0.15	0.19
Interest cover (times)	~	~
Return on equity (%)	40.5	49.1
Debt-to-equity ratio (%)	~	~
Current ratio	2.4	2.5

Australian Pharmaceutical Industries Limited

ASX code: API　　　　　　　　　　　　　　　　　www.api.net.au

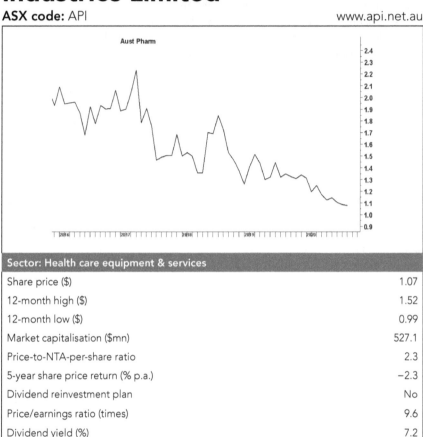

Aust Pharm

Sector: Health care equipment & services	
Share price ($)	1.07
12-month high ($)	1.52
12-month low ($)	0.99
Market capitalisation ($mn)	527.1
Price-to-NTA-per-share ratio	2.3
5-year share price return (% p.a.)	−2.3
Dividend reinvestment plan	No
Price/earnings ratio (times)	9.6
Dividend yield (%)	7.2

Melbourne-based Australian Pharmaceutical Industries (API) dates back to the 1910 establishment of the Chemists' Cooperative Company in New South Wales. It has steadily grown and is today one of Australia's largest pharmaceuticals wholesalers and retailers. Its brands include Priceline Pharmacy, Soul Pattinson Chemist, Pharmacist Advice, Club Premium, Pharmacy Best Buys and Clear Skincare. It also maintains a small Consumer Brands division, manufacturing a range of pharmaceutical, health and beauty products. Washington H. Soul Pattinson owns 19 per cent of the company's equity.

Latest business results (February 2020, half year)

Revenues were up but profits were down, as the company's Priceline business was hit by competitive pressures, with some stores also affected by bushfires in the Eastern States. The Consumer Brands division was hurt by supplier delays for some critical raw materials. Pharmacy distribution revenues rose 5 per cent to $1.5 billion as the company attracted new pharmacy groups as customers. Total sales for the Priceline retail network — most of the 488 stores are owned on a franchise basis — edged a little higher, though fell when low-margin dispensary sales are excluded. The Consumer

Brands division — just 1.4 per cent of total company turnover — recorded a decline in revenues and profits. The Clear Skincare division — still only 1.2 per cent of company turnover — achieved double-digit increases in sales and profits from 59 clinics. A big reduction in company debt, following the sale of the company's shareholding in rival Sigma Healthcare, led to a $2 million decline in interest payments.

Outlook

API is one of the three companies that dominate the wholesale pharmaceutical market in Australia. The other two are Sigma Healthcare and EBOS. An ageing population supports a slow increase in drugs demand. However, this business is heavily regulated by the government's Pharmaceutical Benefits Scheme (PBS), and it is difficult to achieve much growth in profits. Consequently, the company is working to grow by other means, and to diversify into non-PBS product areas. The COVID-19 pandemic has led to strong increases in demand for personal care and health care products such as hand sanitisers and cold and flu products, but has also led to higher costs, including the temporary closure of Clear Skincare clinics. The company is working to lower its cost base, and has closed two of its distribution centres. Its $127 million acquisition in 2018 of the Clear Skincare business has provided it with an entry to the highly promising market for non-invasive aesthetic services, and it plans a steady rollout of new clinics.

Year to 31 August	2018	2019
Revenues ($mn)	4026.3	4010.7
EBIT ($mn)	88.9	94.0
EBIT margin (%)	2.2	2.3
Gross margin (%)	12.3	12.9
Profit before tax ($mn)	76.5	73.7
Profit after tax ($mn)	54.7	55.1
Earnings per share (c)	11.11	11.19
Cash flow per share (c)	16.84	17.09
Dividend (c)	7.5	7.75
Percentage franked	100	100
Interest cover (times)	7.2	4.6
Return on equity (%)	10.3	10.7
Half year to 29 February*	2019	2020
Revenues ($mn)	1977.1	2033.1
Profit before tax ($mn)	36.3	29.1
Profit after tax ($mn)	26.8	26.3
Earnings per share (c)	5.44	4.40
Dividend (c)	3.75	0
Percentage franked	100	~
Net tangible assets per share ($)	0.46	0.46
Debt-to-equity ratio (%)	51.4	14.9
Current ratio	1.4	1.3

* 28 February 2019

Baby Bunting Group Limited

ASX code: BBN   www.babybunting.com.au

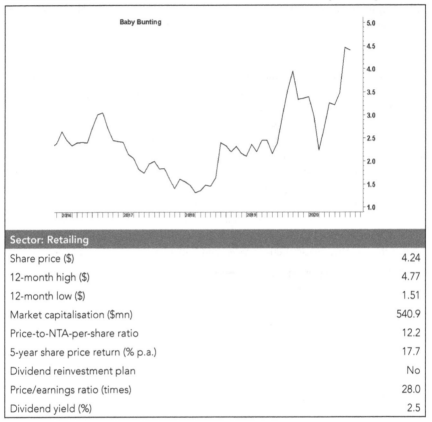

Sector: Retailing	
Share price ($)	4.24
12-month high ($)	4.77
12-month low ($)	1.51
Market capitalisation ($mn)	540.9
Price-to-NTA-per-share ratio	12.2
5-year share price return (% p.a.)	17.7
Dividend reinvestment plan	No
Price/earnings ratio (times)	28.0
Dividend yield (%)	2.5

Melbourne retailer Baby Bunting started in 1979 with the opening of a store in the suburb of Balwyn. It has since grown into a nationwide chain of stores specialising in some 6000 lines of baby and nursery products, including prams, car seats, carriers, furniture, nursery items, safety goods, babywear, manchester, toys, feeding products and maternity wear.

Latest business results (June 2020, full year)

In a volatile period, Baby Bunting achieved solid growth in revenues and underlying profits. On a same-store basis, sales rose 4.9 per cent, and the company also opened three new stores. The second half saw some disruption from the COVID-19 pandemic, with panic buying of nappies, baby wipes and some other products leading to temporary shortages. However, the company was able to keep all its stores open, and with customers forced to remain at home, it enjoyed increased demand for furniture, toys and bedding, more than offsetting weaker sales of prams and car seats. There was a significant jump in sales of private label and exclusive products, up 47.9 per cent from the previous year. Online sales grew by 39.1 per cent to comprise 14.5 per cent of total turnover. This growth might have been stronger but for a new company website platform, launched in July 2019, that caused numerous problems. In its accounts Baby Bunting recognised a non-cash impairment of $3.2 million in its investment in digital technology, and on a statutory basis its profits fell for the year.

Outlook

Baby Bunting occupies a strong position in the $2.4 billion Australian baby goods retail market. With the demise of some competitors, it is now the only specialist baby goods retailer with a national presence, and its major rivals are stores such as Kmart, Target and Big W. It has numerous strategies for growth. It plans to open some four to eight new stores each year, with an eventual target of more than 100 throughout Australia, up from 56 at June 2020. It has begun shipping online orders to New Zealand, and is investigating an entry to the New Zealand market. It is experiencing strong growth and high margins for its private-label and exclusive product ranges, which have grown from 27.6 per cent of total sales in June 2019 to 36.5 per cent in June 2020, with a long-term target of 50 per cent. The company is also moving into new product areas and it is streamlining its supply chain, with a new distribution centre set to open in 2021.

Year to 28 June*	2019	2020
Revenues ($mn)	368.0	405.2
EBIT ($mn)	26.1	33.2
EBIT margin (%)	7.1	8.2
Gross margin (%)	34.9	36.2
Profit before tax ($mn)	20.4	27.5
Profit after tax ($mn)	14.4	19.3
Earnings per share (c)	11.42	15.17
Cash flow per share (c)	29.49	35.05
Dividend (c)	8.4	10.5
Percentage franked	100	100
Net tangible assets per share ($)	0.38	0.35
Interest cover (times)	4.6	5.8
Return on equity (%)	15.2	20.8
Debt-to-equity ratio (%)	~	~
Current ratio	1.0	1.0

* 30 June 2019

Bapcor Limited

ASX code: BAP www.bapcor.com.au

Sector: Retailing	
Share price ($)	7.01
12-month high ($)	7.53
12-month low ($)	2.85
Market capitalisation ($mn)	2 379.3
Price-to-NTA-per-share ratio	10.7
5-year share price return (% p.a.)	16.9
Dividend reinvestment plan	No
Price/earnings ratio (times)	23.1
Dividend yield (%)	2.5

Melbourne company Bapcor started in 1971 as Burson Auto Parts, supplying a range of automotive products to workshops and service stations. It grew steadily, organically and by acquisition, opening stores throughout Australia, and taking its present name in 2016. It now services the automotive aftermarket under numerous brands, including Autobarn, Midas and ABS. It has extensive operations in Australia and New Zealand, and in 2018 it opened its first stores in Thailand, in partnership with a local auto specialist company. It operates from more than 1000 locations in Australia, New Zealand and Thailand.

Latest business results (June 2020, full year)

Revenues grew as the company continued to expand its network of stores, but the COVID-19 pandemic hit operations, and profits edged down. The Trade division, comprising the Burson Auto Parts and the Precision Automotive Equipment business units, is the largest of Bapcor's operating segments. It saw revenues up 7.1 per cent, including same-store growth of 6 per cent, with profits rising by 3.7 per cent. The Specialist Wholesale division comprises a range of small outlets that focus on sourcing replacement parts for the automotive aftermarket. The acquisition of truck parts specialist Truckline and Diesel Drive in December 2019 helped this division to a substantial increase in revenues and profits. The Retail division comprises company-owned and franchised stores and workshops under the Autobarn, Autopro, Sprint Auto Parts, Midas and ABS names. This division recorded a double-digit boost to sales and profits, with a 240 per cent surge in online sales. However, New Zealand business was hurt by the lockdowns in that country, and sales and profits fell. During the year the company added a total of 45 new businesses to its network.

Outlook

Bapcor is a leader in the supply of a huge range of auto parts to more than 30 000 auto workshop customers, and this business is expected to continue to grow as the population increases, even in the event of an economic slowdown. A worsening economy can actually help the company, as car owners tend to put off the purchase of a new car and instead spend money on maintaining their existing car, boosting the demand for more parts. It is also possible that restrictions on international travel, along with moves away from public transport, will lead to greater car usage. The move to Thailand takes Bapcor to a car market the size of Australia's but with a very fragmented auto parts sector. The company's long-term target is for more than 1500 stores.

Year to 30 June	2019	2020
Revenues ($mn)	1296.6	1462.7
Trade (%)	39	37
Specialist wholesale (%)	30	34
Retail (%)	19	19
Bapcor New Zealand (%)	12	10
EBIT ($mn)	145.9	144.1
EBIT margin (%)	11.3	9.8
Gross margin (%)	46.9	46.5
Profit before tax ($mn)	130.6	125.3
Profit after tax ($mn)	94.3	89.1
Earnings per share (c)	33.45	30.35
Cash flow per share (c)	39.52	57.61
Dividend (c)	17	17.5
Percentage franked	100	100
Net tangible assets per share ($)	~	0.66
Interest cover (times)	9.6	7.7
Return on equity (%)	13.9	10.5
Debt-to-equity ratio (%)	46.1	10.5
Current ratio	2.3	2.0

Beach Energy Limited

ASX code: BPT www.beachenergy.com.au

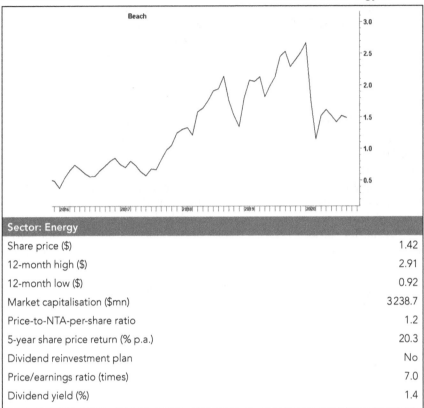

Sector: Energy	
Share price ($)	1.42
12-month high ($)	2.91
12-month low ($)	0.92
Market capitalisation ($mn)	3238.7
Price-to-NTA-per-share ratio	1.2
5-year share price return (% p.a.)	20.3
Dividend reinvestment plan	No
Price/earnings ratio (times)	7.0
Dividend yield (%)	1.4

Adelaide-based Beach Energy, with a history dating back to 1961, is a major oil and gas producer, and a key supplier of gas to eastern states. Its operations are concentrated on five production hubs — the Cooper/Eromanga Basin region of South Australia and Queensland, the Bass Basin in the Bass Strait, the Otway Basin of Victoria and South Australia, the Perth Basin and the Taranaki Basin in New Zealand. It also maintains an active exploration and development program in other areas of Australia and New Zealand.

Latest business results (June 2020, full year)

Lower oil prices sent revenues and profits down. Total production of 26.7 million barrels of oil equivalent (boe) was down from 29.4 million barrels in the previous year. The average realised oil price of $80.90 per barrel was sharply down from $101.80 in the previous year. However, the average realised gas/ethane price rose 7 per cent. During the year the company drilled 178 wells, up from 134 in the June 2019 year, with a success rate of 81 per cent, including new gas discoveries in the Perth and Otway basins. It also commissioned a new gas plant in South Australia.

Outlook

Confronted by lower oil prices, Beach has modified its ambitious growth program in order to prioritise cash flow. It expects to reduce its planned June 2021 capital spending budget by around 30 per cent, to between $650 million and $750 million, with a postponement of the start of production at its new offshore Victorian Otway wells. In the five years to June 2024 it expects total capital spending of some $4.2 billion, and it believes that by the June 2025 year it will be producing 37 million boe annually. It expects to engage in extensive drilling and development activity in the Perth Basin, following the discovery of gas at its Beharra Springs site. It also plans further development of its Western Flank oil and gas operation in the Cooper/Eromanga Basin. For the June 2021 year the company forecasts production of between 26 million boe and 28.5 million boe, and EBITDA of $900 million to $1 billion, compared with $1.1 billion in June 2020. At June 2020 Beach had net cash holdings of more than $50 million and it is in a strong position to take advantage of weak oil prices by acquiring assets that are being sold by other energy producers. This could include ExxonMobil's stake in the Gippsland Basin oil and gas fields in the Bass Strait.

Year to 30 June	2019	2020
Revenues ($mn)	2077.7	1728.2
EBIT ($mn)	848.1	653.0
EBIT margin (%)	40.8	37.8
Gross margin (%)	41.9	38.9
Profit before tax ($mn)	790.0	639.0
Profit after tax ($mn)	560.2	461.0
Earnings per share (c)	24.59	20.22
Cash flow per share (c)	47.54	39.73
Dividend (c)	2	2
Percentage franked	100	100
Net tangible assets per share ($)	1.02	1.21
Interest cover (times)	14.6	46.6
Return on equity (%)	26.6	17.8
Debt-to-equity ratio (%)	~	~
Current ratio	1.0	1.1

Beacon Lighting Group Limited

ASX code: BLX   www.beaconlighting.com.au

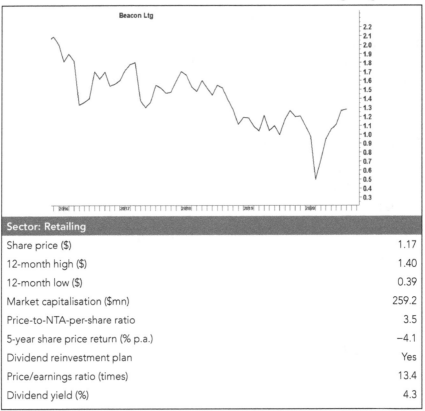

Sector: Retailing	
Share price ($)	1.17
12-month high ($)	1.40
12-month low ($)	0.39
Market capitalisation ($mn)	259.2
Price-to-NTA-per-share ratio	3.5
5-year share price return (% p.a.)	−4.1
Dividend reinvestment plan	Yes
Price/earnings ratio (times)	13.4
Dividend yield (%)	4.3

Melbourne-based lighting specialist Beacon dates back to the launch of the first Beacon Lighting store in 1967. It steadily expanded throughout Australia, and today has more than 110 stores, supplying a wide range of lighting fixtures and light globes, as well as ceiling fans. Its Beacon Lighting Commercial division supplies many commercial projects, including volume residential developments, apartment complexes, aged care facilities, hotels and retail fit-outs. It also operates an international wholesale business, based in Hong Kong and with a showroom in China.

Latest business results (June 2020, full year)

Sales and underlying profits rose in a strong result that benefited from the COVID-19 pandemic, as customers spent more time engaged in home renovation projects. Sales actually fell by 3.7 per cent in the first half, but rebounded with 9.5 per cent growth in the second half. Rising demand enabled the company to reduce the levels of discounting it had been using to drive sales, boosting margins. On a same-store basis, sales were up 7.2 per cent for the year, with a positive contribution from all states and territories. Online sales jumped 50.6 per cent to $16.2 million. International sales were up 22.9 per cent to $8.5 million. During the year the company closed two stores. At the statutory level, profits were higher, thanks to the sale and leaseback of the company's Parkinson distribution centre in Queensland, partially offset by losses from the closure of its low-margin solar lighting business.

Outlook

Beacon's business is closely linked to trends in the housing market, which recently has been weak. However, the company has developed a variety of strategies for growth. It expects to open at least five new stores during the June 2021 year, with an eventual target of 170 stores throughout Australia. With online sales growing strongly, it is investing in upgrading its digital presence. It is working to boost exports, with sales offices in Hong Kong, Germany and the United States. Its Light Source Solutions Roadway division supplies LED street lighting. Masson for Light works with architects to supply designer lights for prestige construction projects. The company has introduced its Beacon Design Studio service, which now operates in selected stores, and it is opening a concept designer showroom for custom lighting in Melbourne. The sale of its Parkinson distribution centre enabled Beacon to pay down debt, and at June 2020 it had net cash holdings of $14.5 million. With much of its product range imported, Beacon is vulnerable to currency fluctuations.

Year to 28 June*	2019	2020
Revenues ($mn)	233.6	251.6
EBIT ($mn)	25.1	33.5
EBIT margin (%)	10.7	13.3
Gross margin (%)	65.4	65.5
Profit before tax ($mn)	23.1	27.4
Profit after tax ($mn)	16.4	19.1
Earnings per share (c)	7.52	8.70
Cash flow per share (c)	9.60	19.83
Dividend (c)	4.55	5
Percentage franked	100	100
Net tangible assets per share ($)	0.33	0.33
Interest cover (times)	13.0	5.5
Return on equity (%)	20.5	22.5
Debt-to-equity ratio (%)	38.6	~
Current ratio	1.7	1.6

* 30 June 2019

BHP Group Limited

ASX code: BHP www.bhp.com

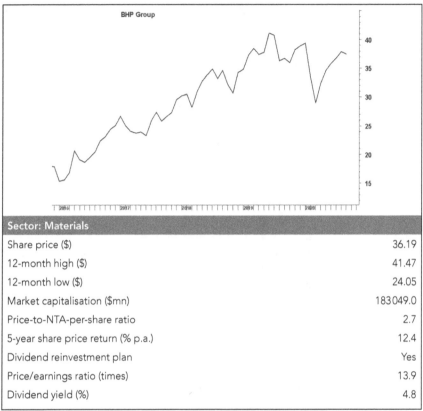

Sector: Materials	
Share price ($)	36.19
12-month high ($)	41.47
12-month low ($)	24.05
Market capitalisation ($mn)	183049.0
Price-to-NTA-per-share ratio	2.7
5-year share price return (% p.a.)	12.4
Dividend reinvestment plan	Yes
Price/earnings ratio (times)	13.9
Dividend yield (%)	4.8

BHP Group was formed in 2001 from the merger of BHP, which was founded as Broken Hill Proprietary in 1885, and Billiton, which dates back to 1851. With its headquarters in Melbourne, it is today one of the world's largest diversified resources companies, with a powerful portfolio of assets incorporating iron ore, copper, coal, nickel, potash, and oil and gas. It has operations in many countries.

Latest business results (June 2020, full year)

Profits edged down as lower prices hit the company's coal and petroleum businesses. By contrast, the core iron ore operation was a beneficiary of a 16 per cent rise in the average price for the year, along with record sales volumes from the Jimblebar and Yandi mines. The iron ore division rose to represent nearly half the company's total revenues and about three-quarters of underlying profit. Copper revenues and profits were little changed from the previous year, with lower average prices largely offset by higher production and cost-cutting gains. Petroleum revenues and profits slumped as the company's production volumes fell and the average realised crude oil price dropped by 26 per cent. Similarly, the company's coal business saw revenues and profits down on the back of falling prices and lower production levels. Note that BHP reports its results in US dollars. The Australian dollar figures in this book — converted at prevailing exchange rates — are for guidance only.

Outlook

BHP has been working over some years to lower its cost base, and this is helping to protect it at a time of global slowdown. In particular, it claims that its West Australian iron ore business now has the cheapest operating costs among all its rivals. It expects capital spending of around US$7 billion in the June 2021 year, down from US$7.6 billion in June 2020 as it defers some of its major petroleum projects in the face of lower oil prices. For June 2022 it expects spending of about US$8.5 billion. Multi-billion-dollar projects under way include the Spence copper mine expansion project in Chile, the Mad Dog petroleum venture in the Gulf of Mexico, the South Flank iron ore project in Western Australia and the Jansen potash infrastructure project in Canada. It is also launching a major scheme to introduce autonomous — driverless — trucks to some of its Australian coal and iron ore sites. It has announced plans to divest itself of its thermal coal assets in New South Wales and Colombia and its coking coal mines in Queensland.

Year to 30 June	2019	2020
Revenues ($mn)	61 511.1	62 218.8
Iron ore (%)	39	48
Copper (%)	24	25
Coal (%)	21	15
Petroleum (%)	13	9
EBIT ($mn)	23 694.4	23 140.6
EBIT margin (%)	38.5	37.2
Profit before tax ($mn)	22 216.7	21 820.3
Profit after tax ($mn)	13 147.2	13 130.4
Earnings per share (c)	253.81	259.65
Cash flow per share (c)	417.36	434.81
Dividend (c)	215.11	174.86
Percentage franked	100	100
Net tangible assets per share ($)	13.15	13.56
Interest cover (times)	16.0	17.5
Return on equity (%)	18.4	19.2
Debt-to-equity ratio (%)	17.8	26.1
Current ratio	1.9	1.4

Brambles Limited

ASX code: BXB   www.brambles.com

Sector: Commercial & professional services	
Share price ($)	10.87
12-month high ($)	13.42
12-month low ($)	8.97
Market capitalisation ($mn)	16359.7
Price-to-NTA-per-share ratio	4.5
5-year share price return (% p.a.)	5.3
Dividend reinvestment plan	No
Price/earnings ratio (times)	24.3
Dividend yield (%)	2.7

Sydney-based Brambles has a history that dates back to 1875, when Walter Bramble opened a butcher's business, later expanding into transportation and logistics. Today, following a long series of acquisitions, it is the global leader in pallets, crates and container pooling services under the brand name CHEP (Commonwealth Handling Equipment Pool, a term used by the Australian government to designate pallets and other assets left in Australia by the United States Army after World War II). It owns approximately 330 million pallets, crates and containers through a network of more than 750 service centres in 60 countries.

Latest business results (June 2020, full year)

Around 80 per cent of Brambles's business is related to consumer goods, particularly grocery items. Consequently, when the COVID-19 pandemic erupted, and consumers began stockpiling goods, the company saw a surge in business, as global grocery supply chains struggled to meet significantly higher levels of demand. Sales revenues for the year rose 6 per cent on a constant currency basis and profits were also up. Nevertheless, the company also suffered from the pandemic, with a sharp decline in the automotive supplies business and in the company's Kegstar brewery keg pooling subsidiary. By division, the best result came from CHEP Americas, thanks to strong volume growth and supply chain efficiencies. CHEP EMEA, covering Europe, Africa and the Middle East, was hurt by higher transportation costs and some pandemic issues, and profits edged down. CHEP Asia-Pacific achieved a modest increase in constant-currency sales and underlying profit. Note that Brambles reports its results in US dollars. The Australian dollar figures in this book — converted at prevailing exchange rates — are for guidance only.

Outlook

Brambles is heavily influenced by trends in global trade and, more generally, the global economy. Consequently, it could suffer as economies weaken around the world in the wake of the pandemic. With half its revenues coming from the Americas, it was a beneficiary of a firm US economy. Nevertheless, American operations have been suffering from high costs, with profit margins that are substantially below those prevailing elsewhere. The company is working to drive down costs and in the June 2020 year it achieved a 1 per cent improvement in American margins. Its target is for a 2 per cent to 3 per cent improvement by June 2022. It also plans an expansion into new markets. Its early forecast is for revenues growth of up to 4 per cent and profit growth up to 5 per cent in the June 2021 year.

Year to 30 June	2019	2020
Revenues ($mn)	6382.4	6860.3
CHEP Americas (%)	50	52
CHEP EMEA (%)	40	39
CHEP Asia-Pacific (%)	10	9
EBIT ($mn)	1029.0	1111.6
EBIT margin (%)	16.1	16.2
Profit before tax ($mn)	906.1	994.5
Profit after tax ($mn)	630.7	691.6
Earnings per share (c)	39.58	44.66
Cash flow per share (c)	81.80	101.95
Dividend (c)	29	29
Percentage franked	48	30
Net tangible assets per share ($)	3.17	2.40
Interest cover (times)	8.4	9.5
Return on equity (%)	13.7	14.7
Debt-to-equity ratio (%)	13.4	39.0
Current ratio	1.6	1.1

Breville Group Limited

ASX code: BRG   www.brevillegroup.com.au

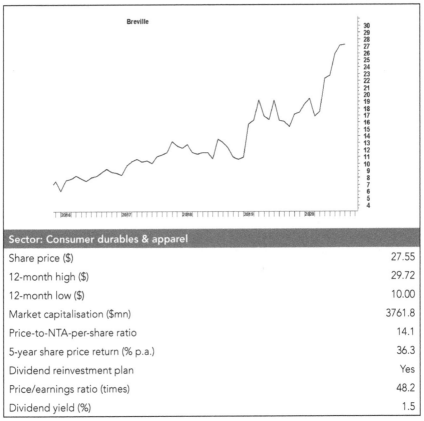

Sector: Consumer durables & apparel	
Share price ($)	27.55
12-month high ($)	29.72
12-month low ($)	10.00
Market capitalisation ($mn)	3761.8
Price-to-NTA-per-share ratio	14.1
5-year share price return (% p.a.)	36.3
Dividend reinvestment plan	Yes
Price/earnings ratio (times)	48.2
Dividend yield (%)	1.5

Sydney-based Breville Group traces its origins to the production of the first Breville radio in 1932. It later moved into the home appliance business and was subsequently acquired by Housewares International. In 2008 Housewares changed its name to Breville Group, and today the company is a leading designer and distributor of kitchen home appliances under the Breville and Kambrook brands. Its subsidiary in the UK distributes Breville products under the Sage brand. Breville sells its products in some 80 countries, and international business is responsible for around 80 per cent of company turnover.

Latest business results (June 2020, full year)

In a turbulent year for the company, revenues and underlying profits showed healthy gains. All regions of activity were strong, but with particularly impressive growth, for a second consecutive year, in demand from European consumers. Breville segments its operations into two broad divisions, Global Product and Distribution. The former, responsible for the sale of products designed and developed by Breville, again generated around 80 per cent of company turnover, with revenues up 25 per cent and EBIT rising by 14.5 per cent. This good result came despite some supply delays from manufacturers in China as well as retail trading restrictions in many countries. The company's entry to the Spanish and French markets helped boost European sales by 60 per cent. The Distribution division achieved a 24 per cent jump in EBIT on 27 per cent sales growth, thanks especially to some strong demand in Australia and New Zealand.

Outlook

Breville has been achieving great success with its strategy of developing its own lines of premium home appliances for the North American, European and Australia/New Zealand markets. North America alone now represents more than half of company revenues, thanks to a continuing series of attractive, high-margin products, and Europe is on track to overtake Australia/New Zealand as the second-largest region. Despite supply issues, the company has been a beneficiary of the COVID-19 pandemic as households, unable to eat out, are increasingly acquiring a broad range of home appliances that allow them to replicate outdoor dining experiences in their own homes. Breville continues to expand, including planned market launches in Italy, Portugal and Mexico. It is also working on product innovation, and sees particularly high potential for its new lines of air fryers and sous vide cookers. At June 2020 the company had no debt and cash holdings of more than $128 million, which it can employ for its expansion initiatives.

Year to 30 June	2019	2020
Revenues ($mn)	760.0	952.2
EBIT ($mn)	97.3	113.1
EBIT margin (%)	12.8	11.9
Gross margin (%)	35.7	33.7
Profit before tax ($mn)	94.3	104.9
Profit after tax ($mn)	67.4	75.0
Earnings per share (c)	51.80	57.21
Cash flow per share (c)	64.57	76.73
Dividend (c)	37	41
Percentage franked	60	60
Net tangible assets per share ($)	1.44	1.95
Interest cover (times)	32.1	13.8
Return on equity (%)	22.7	20.4
Debt-to-equity ratio (%)	~	~
Current ratio	2.6	2.4

Brickworks Limited

ASX code: BKW　　　　　　　　　www.brickworks.com.au

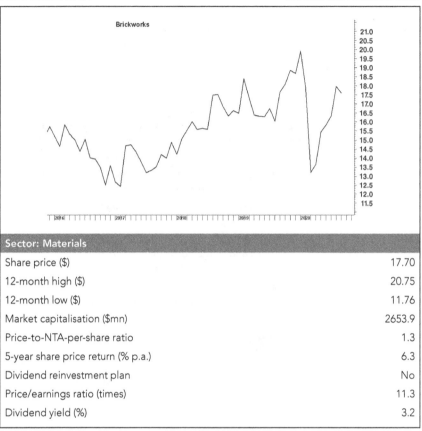

Sector: Materials	
Share price ($)	17.70
12-month high ($)	20.75
12-month low ($)	11.76
Market capitalisation ($mn)	2653.9
Price-to-NTA-per-share ratio	1.3
5-year share price return (% p.a.)	6.3
Dividend reinvestment plan	No
Price/earnings ratio (times)	11.3
Dividend yield (%)	3.2

Sydney-based Brickworks, founded in 1934, is one of Australia's largest manufacturers of building products used especially in the home construction sector. Its brands include Austral Bricks, Austral Masonry, Austral Precast, Bristile Roofing, Bowral Bricks, Nubrik, GB Masonry and UrbanStone. It also manages an extensive land portfolio based on surplus and redundant building products sites, and it operates an industrial property trust in a joint venture with Goodman. In November 2018 it acquired America's fourth-largest brick manufacturer, Glen-Gery, followed by the acquisition of Sioux City Brick in August 2019 and four manufacturing sites and other assets from Redland Brick in February 2020. In a cross-shareholding arrangement, it owns 39 per cent of the equity of Washington H. Soul Pattinson, while Soul Pattinson owns 44 per cent of the equity in Brickworks.

Latest business results (January 2020, half year)

In a bad period for the company, revenues edged higher but profits fell sharply. A big slowdown in building activity across the country, particularly multi-residential construction in New South Wales and Queensland, had a significant negative impact on Austral Precast and Austral Masonry. Maintenance shutdowns for many of its brick plants and a $4 million increase in gas costs also hurt the company. Consequently, domestic building products EBIT crashed 62 per cent to just $10 million. US building products contributed $110 million in revenues, with EBIT of $6 million. The company's property portfolio contributed $89 million in EBIT, down 33 per cent due to a lack of land sales during the period. Its shareholding in Soul Pattinson resulted in EBIT of $39 million, down 36 per cent, due mainly to a weaker contribution from New Hope Corporation, in which Soul Pattinson is the major shareholder.

Outlook

Brickworks was hit by the COVID-19 pandemic, which forced it to suspend operations at some plants in both Australia and the US. Its domestic businesses have also seen some shortages of imported products. The company has expressed concerns about the longer-term outlook for Australian manufacturing businesses, with rising energy costs a particular worry. It is now looking to North America for growth. Following the Redland acquisition it is operating 12 brick plants and one manufactured stone plant in the US, along with an extensive network of company-owned retail outlets. Its target is for annual North American sales of around 400 million bricks worth some A$290 million. Domestically, it sees bright prospects for its joint venture industrial property trust, as online shopping boosts demand for well-located warehouse facilities.

Year to 31 July	2018	2019
Revenues ($mn)	785.2	918.7
EBIT ($mn)	281.4	308.9
EBIT margin (%)	35.8	33.6
Gross margin (%)	32.0	32.1
Profit before tax ($mn)	267.2	286.0
Profit after tax ($mn)	225.6	234.2
Earnings per share (c)	151.08	156.50
Cash flow per share (c)	170.76	181.48
Dividend (c)	54	57
Percentage franked	100	100
Interest cover (times)	19.9	13.5
Return on equity (%)	11.2	11.1
Half year to 31 January	2019	2020
Revenues ($mn)	442.5	448.6
Profit before tax ($mn)	200.9	122.0
Profit after tax ($mn)	159.7	100.3
Earnings per share (c)	106.75	67.00
Dividend (c)	19	20
Percentage franked	100	100
Net tangible assets per share ($)	13.04	13.37
Debt-to-equity ratio (%)	11.3	21.0
Current ratio	1.2	2.5

Class Limited

ASX code: CL1

www.class.com.au

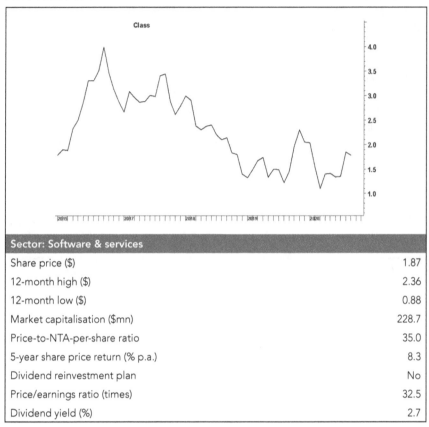

Sector: Software & services	
Share price ($)	1.87
12-month high ($)	2.36
12-month low ($)	0.88
Market capitalisation ($mn)	228.7
Price-to-NTA-per-share ratio	35.0
5-year share price return (% p.a.)	8.3
Dividend reinvestment plan	No
Price/earnings ratio (times)	32.5
Dividend yield (%)	2.7

Sydney technology company Class was established in 2005 to provide software to the wealth accounting sector. In 2009 it launched its flagship Class Super product for the administration of self-managed superannuation funds and in 2015 it launched Class Portfolio, which provides investment portfolio accounting, administration and reporting functions. It is now a leading supplier of cloud-based software products for accountants, administrators and advisers in the wealth accounting sector. In January 2020 it acquired corporate compliance and documentation technology company NowInfinity 3505 and in August 2020 it acquired corporate compliance specialist Smartcorp.

Latest business results (June 2020, full year)

Revenues rose as demand continued to grow for the company's products. But profits fell, due in particular to higher depreciation and amortisation charges, acquisition costs incurred during the year and a big jump in employee expenses. However, at the

EBITDA level profits actually edged up. The number of accounts for Class Super grew 2.8 per cent to 176 318. Class claims a 28.9 per cent market share for this business. The number of accounts for Class Portfolio grew 21.2 per cent to 9253. The company's capital spending for the year rose from $7.6 million in June 2019 to $9.9 million.

Outlook

Class has a strong reputation, solid market share and extremely high retention rates for its core Class Super product, which enables customers to automate key processes, reduce operating costs, improve data accuracy and reduce compliance risk. However, this is largely a mature product with just limited scope for growth. Consequently, the company is investigating new product areas. In October 2020 it launches a new product, Class Trust, which helps users to set up and administer a trust. Through simplifying and automating the trust administration process the company believes this product has the potential to open up a large new market worth some $117 million per year. The acquisition of NowInfinity 3505, for a price of up to $25 million, gives Class a leadership position in the document and corporate compliance market, and allows the company to broaden its relationship with accounting and legal services clients. The $4.2 million acquisition of Smartcorp, another leader in corporate compliance, further enhances this position. Thanks to the launch of Class Trust and the two acquisitions, Class believes it now has an addressable market worth some $365 million, and it sees great scope for growth. Its June 2021 forecast is for revenues of $53 million, with an EBITDA of at least $21.2 million, up from $18.2 million in June 2020.

Year to 30 June	2019	2020
Revenues ($mn)	38.3	43.9
EBIT ($mn)	12.2	10.1
EBIT margin (%)	31.9	23.0
Profit before tax ($mn)	12.5	10.1
Profit after tax ($mn)	9.0	6.8
Earnings per share (c)	7.66	5.75
Cash flow per share (c)	12.56	12.53
Dividend (c)	5	5
Percentage franked	100	100
Net tangible assets per share ($)	0.18	0.05
Interest cover (times)	~	480.9
Return on equity (%)	31.8	19.4
Debt-to-equity ratio (%)	~	~
Current ratio	4.9	2.2

Clover Corporation Limited

ASX code: CLV   www.clovercorp.com.au

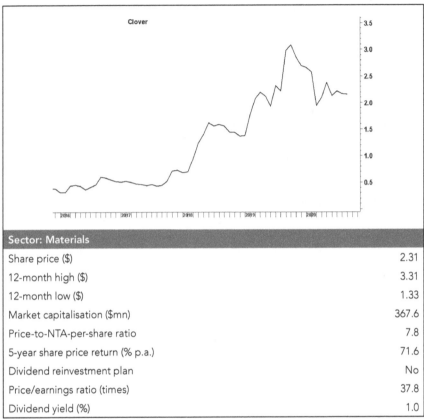

Sector: Materials	
Share price ($)	2.31
12-month high ($)	3.31
12-month low ($)	1.33
Market capitalisation ($mn)	367.6
Price-to-NTA-per-share ratio	7.8
5-year share price return (% p.a.)	71.6
Dividend reinvestment plan	No
Price/earnings ratio (times)	37.8
Dividend yield (%)	1.0

Melbourne-based Clover, founded in 1988 as a family-owned company, develops value-added nutrients for use in foods or as nutritional supplements. Its key product is docosahexaenoic acid (DHA), a form of omega 3. It sells this under the Nu-Mega and Ocean Gold range of tuna oils. It also markets nutritional oil powders, based on technology developed by the Commonwealth Scientific and Industrial Research Organisation (CSIRO). In addition, the company has developed technology that allows nutritional oils to be added to infant formula, foods and beverages. Overseas customers account for about half of company sales.

Latest business results (January 2020, half year)

Revenues and profit rose again, though at a more subdued pace than previously. The Australia/New Zealand segment comprises about 56 per cent of company turnover and sales jumped by 21 per cent. However, Clover said this was partially a reflection of customers moving production from Asian facilities to facilities in Australia and New Zealand. In addition, Chinese customers have been cautious about building inventory levels in the midst of uncertainty over proposed infant formula legislation changes. Consequently, sales to Asia, representing 27 per cent of company business, dropped by 17 per cent. However, Europe and North America, comprising the remaining 17 per cent of company sales, continued to race ahead. European sales were up 31 per cent, following a 53 per cent jump in the January 2019 half, and American revenues soared by 57 per cent, compared to a 42 per cent rise a year earlier.

Outlook

Thanks to its excellent technology, Clover is experiencing strong demand for its DHA products, especially from the infant formula market. It is now placing a particular emphasis on European markets, thanks to new European Union (EU) legislation requiring a minimum DHA content in infant formula, and has established a warehouse in the Netherlands, with a full-time sales agent. It also expects strong Chinese demand to resume, though this will in part depend on the progress of proposed legislation similar to that in the EU. It is developing new products, aimed especially at the American health and sports nutrition markets. Developments include a new vegan encapsulated product, pressed tablets, organic products, powdered drinks and health bars. In particular, it is working to deliver omega 3 in food, rather than in tablets. Clover enjoyed a spike in sales in the early months of the COVID-19 pandemic, particularly to infant formula manufacturers, as consumers — apparently fearful of possible shortages — rushed to stockpile supplies.

Year to 31 July	2018	2019
Revenues ($mn)	63.0	76.7
EBIT ($mn)	10.8	14.3
EBIT margin (%)	17.2	18.6
Profit before tax ($mn)	10.6	14.0
Profit after tax ($mn)	7.6	10.1
Earnings per share (c)	4.59	6.12
Cash flow per share (c)	5.02	6.36
Dividend (c)	1.75	2.375
Percentage franked	100	100
Interest cover (times)	57.2	44.9
Return on equity (%)	21.5	24.3
Half year to 31 January	2019	2020
Revenues ($mn)	34.3	37.6
Profit before tax ($mn)	6.2	6.4
Profit after tax ($mn)	4.5	4.6
Earnings per share (c)	2.71	2.79
Dividend (c)	0.625	0
Percentage franked	100	~
Net tangible assets per share ($)	0.23	0.30
Debt-to-equity ratio (%)	3.1	32.0
Current ratio	4.2	4.9

Cochlear Limited

ASX code: COH   www.cochlear.com

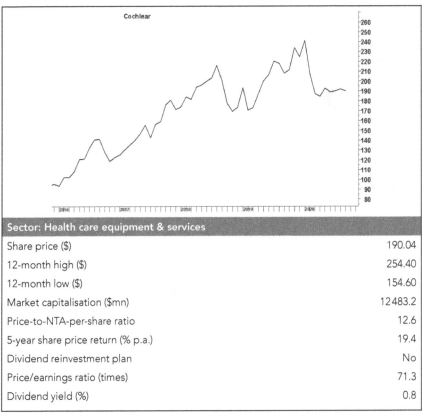

Sector: Health care equipment & services	
Share price ($)	190.04
12-month high ($)	254.40
12-month low ($)	154.60
Market capitalisation ($mn)	12 483.2
Price-to-NTA-per-share ratio	12.6
5-year share price return (% p.a.)	19.4
Dividend reinvestment plan	No
Price/earnings ratio (times)	71.3
Dividend yield (%)	0.8

Sydney-based Cochlear, founded in 1981, has around 60 per cent of the world market for cochlear bionic-ear implants, which are intended to assist the communication ability of people suffering from severe hearing impediments. It also sells the Baha bone-anchored hearing implant, as well as a range of acoustic products. With manufacturing facilities and technology centres in Australia, Sweden, Belgium and the US, it has sales in over 100 countries, and overseas business accounts for more than 90 per cent of revenues and profits.

Latest business results (June 2020, full year)

In a dreadful year, underlying profits crashed as the COVID-19 pandemic halted elective surgery in many countries, leading to a decline in implant demand. In addition, the company was hit by heavy legal costs in a patent infringement lawsuit in the United States. It recorded this as a $416 million exceptional expense, and at the statutory level it reported a large loss for the year. Cochlear implant sales fell 7 per cent to 31 662 units, with revenues down 3 per cent. Services revenues fell 7 per cent.

Acoustics revenues dropped by 20 per cent, with a loss of market share from competitor product launches in the first half, compounded by the delays in elective surgery in the second half.

Outlook

Cochlear continues to launch new products at an impressive rate, with research and development spending of $185 million in the June 2020 year, roughly in line with June 2019, and this is helping it maintain its market leadership. It is experiencing strong demand for its new Nucleus Profile Plus Series implants. These are the world's thinnest implants with the benefit that they enable the implant recipient to undergo a magnetic resonance imaging scan without the need to remove the internal magnet. It sees great potential for its new Osia 2 acoustic system, which delivers a significant improvement in performance and quality of life for bone conduction patients. It was approved in the US in November 2019, with approval in Europe expected by mid 2021. The company is also working to expand its markets. It views hearing-impaired adults in developed countries as offering great potential, and in recent years this has become a fast-growing market segment. Cochlear is building a $50 million implant production facility in China, aimed especially at servicing fast-growing emerging markets. This will be its first implant manufacturing facility outside Australia, and will boost total company production capacity by 50 per cent when it is completed by the end of 2020.

Year to 30 June	2019	2020
Revenues ($mn)	1426.7	1352.3
Cochlear implants (%)	58	61
Services (%)	30	29
Acoustics (%)	12	10
EBIT ($mn)	370.1	206.9
EBIT margin (%)	25.9	15.3
Gross margin (%)	75.4	74.5
Profit before tax ($mn)	365.6	198.0
Profit after tax ($mn)	276.7	153.8
Earnings per share (c)	480.82	266.48
Cash flow per share (c)	547.72	400.76
Dividend (c)	330	160
Percentage franked	100	100
Net tangible assets per share ($)	5.22	15.09
Interest cover (times)	82.2	23.2
Return on equity (%)	41.4	14.5
Debt-to-equity ratio (%)	14.2	~
Current ratio	1.8	1.8

Codan Limited

ASX code: CDA   www.codan.com.au

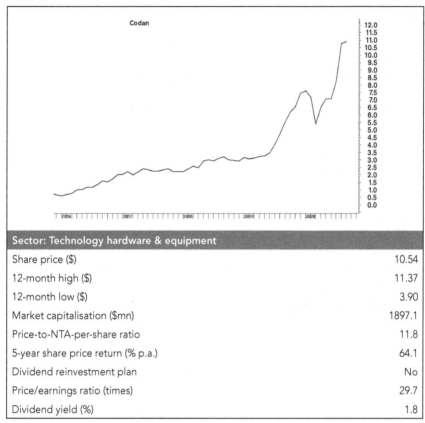

Sector: Technology hardware & equipment	
Share price ($)	10.54
12-month high ($)	11.37
12-month low ($)	3.90
Market capitalisation ($mn)	1897.1
Price-to-NTA-per-share ratio	11.8
5-year share price return (% p.a.)	64.1
Dividend reinvestment plan	No
Price/earnings ratio (times)	29.7
Dividend yield (%)	1.8

Adelaide electronics company Codan was founded in 1959. It is a leading world manufacturer of metal-detecting products, including metal detectors for hobbyists, gold detectors for small-scale miners and landmine detectors for humanitarian applications. A second division produces high-frequency communication radios for military and humanitarian use. A smaller business, the company's Perth-based Minetec subsidiary, provides electronic productivity and safety devices and services for the mining industry. Codan sells to more than 150 countries, and overseas sales represent around 90 per cent of company revenues.

Latest business results (June 2020, full year)

Codan enjoyed an excellent year, with strong growth in sales and profits, thanks to surging demand for its metal-detecting equipment and several major contracts for its communications products. The core Metal Detection division saw sales up by 30 per cent and profits up 45 per cent. The successful release of the new Vanquish detector helped the company gain market share in the recreational sector, while its three models for artisanal gold mining continued to dominate their market. The

Communications division enjoyed a 34 per cent rise in sales and a 43 per cent jump in profits. There was strong demand for the company's tactical communications systems, and several large land mobile radio contracts. The small Tracking Solutions division, incorporating the Minetec business, saw sales down, and its loss widened, as Codan restructures this business.

Outlook

Codan is a significant force in three niche high-tech product areas. When demand is high, and the company can get the product mix right, there is the potential for strong profit growth. Its high-margin metal detectors dominate the African artisanal gold mining market, with a new model to be released during the June 2021 year. In the recreational market it has achieved success with its new Vanquish detector, along with continuing strong demand for the Equinox model. Sales seem set to expand as the company moves into new markets. The Communications division is seeing continuing interest in tactical communications systems, which are aimed especially at militaries in Africa, Latin America, the Middle East and Asia. However, travel restrictions from the COVID-19 pandemic have limited marketing endeavours, and the company says the tactical communications order book has fallen. However, it reports growing sales of its land mobile radios. The company expects the Minetec unit to return to profitability in the June 2021 year as Codan transitions this business into a software systems operation that delivers supporting technology to the US giant Caterpillar, with which Codan has a global licensing agreement.

Year to 30 June	2019	2020
Revenues ($mn)	270.8	348.0
Metal detection (%)	67	68
Communications (%)	28	30
EBIT ($mn)	63.4	88.9
EBIT margin (%)	23.4	25.5
Gross margin (%)	56.6	56.5
Profit before tax ($mn)	63.3	89.0
Profit after tax ($mn)	45.7	63.8
Earnings per share (c)	25.51	35.47
Cash flow per share (c)	34.03	46.95
Dividend (c)	9	18.5
Percentage franked	100	100
Net tangible assets per share ($)	0.69	0.89
Interest cover (times)	918.4	~
Return on equity (%)	22.9	27.8
Debt-to-equity ratio (%)	~	~
Current ratio	1.9	2.2

Collins Foods Limited

ASX code: CKF   www.collinsfoods.com

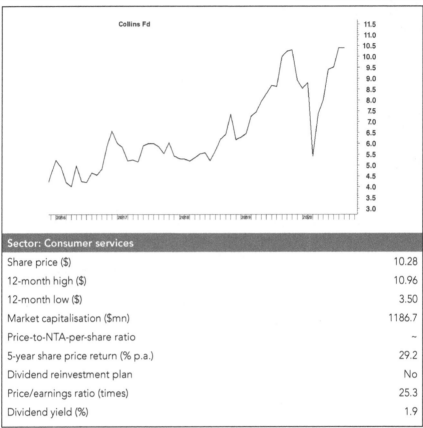

Sector: Consumer services	
Share price ($)	10.28
12-month high ($)	10.96
12-month low ($)	3.50
Market capitalisation ($mn)	1186.7
Price-to-NTA-per-share ratio	~
5-year share price return (% p.a.)	29.2
Dividend reinvestment plan	No
Price/earnings ratio (times)	25.3
Dividend yield (%)	1.9

Collins Foods, based in Brisbane, dates back to 1968 when it obtained the KFC fried chicken franchise for Queensland. Today it owns and operates KFC outlets across Australia, and is the country's largest KFC franchisee. It also owns KFC stores in Germany and the Netherlands. It operates the Sizzler restaurant business, with company-owned restaurants in Australia and a large number of franchise outlets in Thailand, China and Japan. It has launched the Taco Bell Mexican restaurant brand in Australia.

Latest business results (May 2020, full year)

Sales and profits rose again, thanks to organic growth and new-store business. In addition, the May 2020 figures represent 53 weeks, compared to 52 weeks for April 2019. KFC Australia saw revenues and profits rise by around 10 per cent, thanks to impressive same-store sales growth of 3.5 per cent, along with the opening of nine new restaurants. European revenues rose 8 per cent, despite a 5.8 per cent drop in overall same-store sales, thanks to the opening of four new restaurants. European profits were largely flat on the previous year. The opening of eight new Taco Bell outlets offset the closure of three Sizzler restaurants, and Taco Bell/Sizzler revenues were up, though this business unit remained in the red. At the end of the period the company operated 240 franchised KFC restaurants in Australia, 23 in the Netherlands and 17 in Germany. It operated 12 franchised Taco Bell outlets in Australia. It owned and operated nine Sizzler restaurants in Australia, with 73 franchised stores in Asia, mainly in Thailand. Note that this book uses underlying profit figures supplied by the company. On a statutory basis, the company's after-tax profit actually fell, from $39.1 million to $31.3 million.

Outlook

Collins has experienced significant disruptions from the COVID-19 pandemic. Stores in shopping malls have seen substantially reduced sales, and dine-in restrictions at many stores have also had a negative impact. At the same time, business has benefited from growing demand for takeaway food by people confined to their homes, and the company has been working to boost delivery services. It continues to expand, and expects to open nine to 12 new KFC restaurants in Australia during the April 2021 year. However, in Europe, due to COVID-19 uncertainty, it has revised down its new restaurant opening plans to three or four, down from five or six. It will also slow its rollout of new Taco Bell restaurants, with between four and six expected to open in the April 2021 year.

Year to 3 May*	2019	2020
Revenues ($mn)	901.2	981.7
KFC restaurants Australia (%)	80	80
KFC restaurants Europe (%)	14	14
Taco Bell & Sizzler (%)	6	6
EBIT ($mn)	76.0	101.7
EBIT margin (%)	8.4	10.4
Gross margin (%)	52.4	52.4
Profit before tax ($mn)	65.2	69.7
Profit after tax ($mn)	45.0	47.3
Earnings per share (c)	38.63	40.57
Cash flow per share (c)	75.00	79.97
Dividend (c)	19.5	20
Percentage franked	100	100
Net tangible assets per share ($)	~	~
Interest cover (times)	7.1	3.2
Return on equity (%)	13.2	13.4
Debt-to-equity ratio (%)	60.3	56.2
Current ratio	0.9	1.0

* 28 April 2019

Commonwealth Bank of Australia

ASX code: CBA   www.commbank.com.au

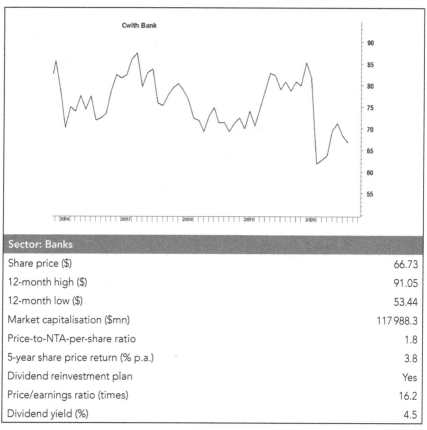

Sector: Banks	
Share price ($)	66.73
12-month high ($)	91.05
12-month low ($)	53.44
Market capitalisation ($mn)	117 988.3
Price-to-NTA-per-share ratio	1.8
5-year share price return (% p.a.)	3.8
Dividend reinvestment plan	Yes
Price/earnings ratio (times)	16.2
Dividend yield (%)	4.5

The Commonwealth Bank, based in Sydney, was founded in 1911. It is today one of Australia's largest banks, and one of the country's top providers of home loans, personal loans and credit cards, as well as the largest holder of deposits. Commonwealth Securities is Australia's largest online stockbroker. It has significant interests in New Zealand, through ASB Bank. It owns Bankwest in Western Australia.

Latest business results (June 2020, full year)

Operating income rose but the cash profit fell for the third consecutive year as the bank took a hit from the COVID-19 pandemic. As of June 2020 it was deferring repayments for 145 000 home loan customers and for 67 000 business lending clients, and it increased its loan impairment expense by $1.3 billion over the year to $2.5 billion. Pressure from falling interest rates sent the bank's net interest margin down by two basis points to 2.07 per cent. Volume growth in home lending and household deposits boosted operating income. Operating expenses edged up, due to rising staff and IT expenses. On a divisional basis, the core Retail Banking Services division — which includes the home loans and retail deposit businesses – actually enjoyed a small rise in profits. But the Business and Private Banking division and the Institutional Banking and Markets division both saw earnings well down. New Zealand too was weak. On a statutory, non-cash basis the bank's profits rose, thanks to significant gains achieved from the divestment of some businesses.

Outlook

Commonwealth Bank occupies a powerful position in the domestic economy as well as in the local banking industry. Thanks to a large branch network, offering many cross-selling opportunities, it has pricing power that has generally enabled it to maintain a cost advantage over some of its rivals. It expects the Australian economy to fall by around 4 per cent in calendar 2020, but then to rebound by about 2 per cent in 2021, thanks to a pipeline of new infrastructure projects and a strong outlook for mining and agricultural exports. It continues to strive to reduce costs, with a target of a cost-to-income ratio that eventually falls below 40 per cent. It is also working to streamline its operations, in order to concentrate on its basic banking businesses. In May 2020 it announced the $1.7 billion sale of 55 per cent of its stake in its Colonial First State funds management operation. It is also investigating the divestment of its interests in non-core mortgage, financial planning and insurance businesses.

Year to 30 June	2019	2020
Operating income ($mn)	23 579.0	23 761.0
Net interest income ($mn)	18 224.0	18 610.0
Operating expenses ($mn)	10 824.0	10 895.0
Profit before tax ($mn)	11 554.0	10 348.0
Profit after tax ($mn)	8 221.0	7 296.0
Earnings per share (c)	465.78	412.50
Dividend (c)	431	298
Percentage franked	100	100
Non-interest income to total income (%)	22.7	21.7
Net tangible assets per share ($)	34.88	36.80
Cost-to-income ratio (%)	45.9	45.9
Return on equity (%)	12.0	10.3
Return on assets (%)	0.8	0.7

Credit Corp Group Limited

ASX code: CCP www.creditcorpgroup.com.au

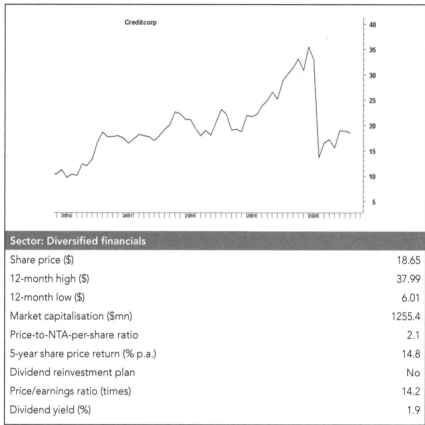

Sector: Diversified financials	
Share price ($)	18.65
12-month high ($)	37.99
12-month low ($)	6.01
Market capitalisation ($mn)	1255.4
Price-to-NTA-per-share ratio	2.1
5-year share price return (% p.a.)	14.8
Dividend reinvestment plan	No
Price/earnings ratio (times)	14.2
Dividend yield (%)	1.9

Sydney-based Credit Corp was formed in 1992, although it has its origins in companies that started in the early 1970s. It provides debt collection services to companies in numerous industries, including the finance, insurance, legal and government sectors, though with a specialty in consumer credit card debt. It has operations in the United States and in New Zealand. It also runs a consumer lending business in Australia and New Zealand.

Latest business results (June 2020, full year)

Another jump in the company's US debt collection business, combined with continuing firm growth domestically and in New Zealand, helped Credit Corp to a solid result. However, the economic slowdown led it to make a substantial impairment charge against parts of its portfolio of debt assets, and on a statutory basis its profits were well down. The company's core business — representing nearly 60 per cent of turnover — is its Australia/New Zealand debt collection operations, and revenues and the after-tax profit both rebounded, after falling in the previous year. US revenues and profits both rose by more than 40 per cent, and this business now represents some 15 per cent of total company turnover and 10 per cent of after-tax profit. The Australia/ New Zealand consumer lending operation saw revenues and profits higher, though the loan book of $181 million at June 2020 was down from $212 million a year earlier. Having repaid much of its own debt, Credit Corp at June 2020 held net cash assets of more than $26 million.

Outlook

Credit Corp's main business effectively involves buying consumer debt at a discount to its face value, and then seeking to recover an amount in excess of the purchase price. Often this recovery takes the form of phased payments over an extended period, and Credit Corp thus has substantial recurring income. Setting an appropriate price for the acquisition of parcels of debt is one of the keys to success, and Credit Corp has acquired considerable expertise in this. It believes that economic slowdown and rising levels of unemployment will lead to an increasing number of debtors being unable to pay the company what they owe, and consequently it has taken an impairment charge against its holdings. But it also now expects to experience significantly increased opportunities to purchase consumer debt from banks and other creditors, contributing to its own long-term growth. The company's early forecast is for a June 2021 after-tax profit of $60 million to $75 million.

Year to 30 June	2019	2020
Revenues ($mn)	313.8	354.8
EBIT ($mn)	112.5	124.6
EBIT margin (%)	35.8	35.1
Profit before tax ($mn)	100.5	113.9
Profit after tax ($mn)	70.3	79.6
Earnings per share (c)	141.92	131.21
Cash flow per share (c)	146.67	149.18
Dividend (c)	72	36
Percentage franked	100	100
Net tangible assets per share ($)	8.43	8.82
Interest cover (times)	9.4	11.6
Return on equity (%)	18.7	15.0
Debt-to-equity ratio (%)	25.9	~
Current ratio	7.5	5.0

CSR Limited

ASX code: CSR

www.csr.com.au

Sector: Materials	
Share price ($)	3.74
12-month high ($)	5.16
12-month low ($)	2.75
Market capitalisation ($mn)	1815.3
Price-to-NTA-per-share ratio	1.8
5-year share price return (% p.a.)	10.2
Dividend reinvestment plan	No
Price/earnings ratio (times)	13.7
Dividend yield (%)	2.7

Sydney-based CSR, founded in 1855 as a sugar refiner, is now a leading manufacturer of building products for residential and commercial construction, with distribution throughout Australia and New Zealand. Its brands include Gyprock plasterboard, Bradford insulation, Monier roof tiles, Hebel concrete products and PGH Bricks and Pavers. It is also a joint venture partner in Australia's second-largest aluminium smelter at Tomago. In addition, it operates a residential and industrial property development business, based on former industrial sites.

Latest business results (March 2020, full year)

Profits fell for the second straight year — following five consecutive annual rises — as the company was hit by a slowdown in residential construction. The core Building Products division saw revenues and profits down. There were solid performances from the Gyprock plasterboard and the Bradford insulation businesses. However, this was more than offset by lower earnings from PGH Bricks and Pavers, Hebel concrete products and the AFS formwork business. The company's earnings also suffered from a lack of property sales during the year. In the March 2019 year property sales had contributed EBIT of nearly $39 million. By contrast, the aluminium business recorded a good result, with EBIT surging 63 per cent despite a slight dip in revenues. This was largely due to favourable currency movements and hedging gains.

Outlook

CSR was a major beneficiary of the strength of the Australian house construction and renovation market, but is now being hurt by weakness in this industry. Nevertheless, with the Australian population continuing to grow, it is optimistic about the long-term outlook for its building products operations, and it is working to boost capacity. It has completed a $75 million expansion of its Hebel facility in New South Wales, doubling its production capacity, and is also boosting its construction systems production capacity at both New South Wales and Victoria. An extensive hedging program will help stabilise profits for the aluminium business, but the company remains concerned about rising energy costs, which it says are some of the highest in the world. Its property division remains active, with new residential and industrial projects in western Sydney and continuing work at Chirnside Park in Melbourne. The sale of an industrial site at Horsley Park in western Sydney will generate a profit of $53 million for the March 2021 year, and a further series of major projects is expected to underpin property earnings for the coming 10 years. The COVID-19 pandemic has led to a slowing of some operations.

Year to 31 March	2019	2020
Revenues ($mn)	2322.8	2212.5
Building products (%)	73	72
Aluminium (%)	27	28
EBIT ($mn)	264.3	209.8
EBIT margin (%)	11.4	9.5
Gross margin (%)	29.9	30.3
Profit before tax ($mn)	256.4	192.8
Profit after tax ($mn)	181.7	134.8
Earnings per share (c)	36.11	27.32
Cash flow per share (c)	49.03	47.52
Dividend (c)	26	10
Percentage franked	75	50
Net tangible assets per share ($)	2.19	2.04
Interest cover (times)	33.5	12.3
Return on equity (%)	15.1	12.0
Debt-to-equity ratio (%)	~	~
Current ratio	2.1	2.3

Data#3 Limited

ASX code: DTL   www.data3.com

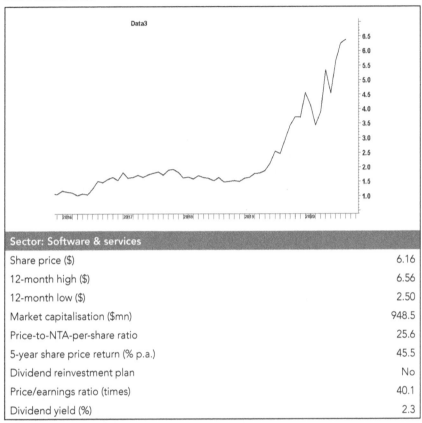

Sector: Software & services	
Share price ($)	6.16
12-month high ($)	6.56
12-month low ($)	2.50
Market capitalisation ($mn)	948.5
Price-to-NTA-per-share ratio	25.6
5-year share price return (% p.a.)	45.5
Dividend reinvestment plan	No
Price/earnings ratio (times)	40.1
Dividend yield (%)	2.3

Brisbane-based IT consultant Data#3 was formed in 1984 from the merger of computer software consultancy Powell, Clark and Associates with IBM typewriter dealer Albrand Typewriters and Office Machines. Today it operates from offices around Australia and in Fiji, providing information and communication technology services — notably software licensing and software asset management — to a wide range of businesses that include banking and finance, mining, tourism and leisure, legal, health care, manufacturing, distribution, government and utilities.

Latest business results (June 2020, full year)

Data#3 delivered a second consecutive excellent result, thanks in particular to continuing demand among clients for cloud-based services. Altogether, public cloud-based revenues grew 60 per cent to $581 million. The company now divides its activities broadly into three segments. The first of these, software solutions, involves managing clients' software investments. It enjoyed strong growth during the year, including new business wins and a shift to cloud offerings, with revenues up 25 per cent to $985 million. A second segment, infrastructure solutions, helps clients maximise returns from infrastructure investments in servers, storage, networks and devices, and this business saw revenues up 9 per cent to $413 million. A third, much smaller, business segment is services. This had a mixed year, with growth in new project activity offset by a decline in maintenance work. The 77-per-cent-owned subsidiary Discovery Technology, which provides wi-fi-based IT location and analytical services, saw a substantial recovery, moving from loss to profit.

Outlook

Data#3 has adopted a three-year strategic plan with three key long-term objectives — to deliver sustained profit growth, to boost its services revenues, with enhanced margins, and to expand its cloud services revenues. It expects that technology will play a major role in Australia's economic recovery from the COVID-19 pandemic. In the longer term it believes companies are set for a digital transformation based on such technologies as artificial intelligence, the internet of things, blockchain and 3D printing, presenting many opportunities for new business. The company is a major reseller for Microsoft products, and stands to benefit as Microsoft becomes a global leader in public cloud services. In 2018 Data#3 was selected by the federal government's Digital Transformation Agency as its sole provider of Microsoft licensing services, extending the existing nine-year relationship for a further three years. It believes its Discovery Technology subsidiary will become a significant participant in the fast-moving data and analytics market. At June 2020 Data#3 had no debt and cash holdings of more than $255 million, and it continues to seek out expansion opportunities.

Year to 30 June	2019	2020
Revenues ($mn)	1414.4	1623.8
EBIT ($mn)	25.8	34.1
EBIT margin (%)	1.8	2.1
Profit before tax ($mn)	26.6	34.1
Profit after tax ($mn)	18.1	23.6
Earnings per share (c)	11.76	15.35
Cash flow per share (c)	13.40	18.54
Dividend (c)	10.7	13.9
Percentage franked	100	100
Net tangible assets per share ($)	0.20	0.24
Interest cover (times)	~	2621.5
Return on equity (%)	39.6	47.6
Debt-to-equity ratio (%)	~	~
Current ratio	1.1	1.1

Dicker Data Limited

ASX code: DDR

www.dickerdata.com.au

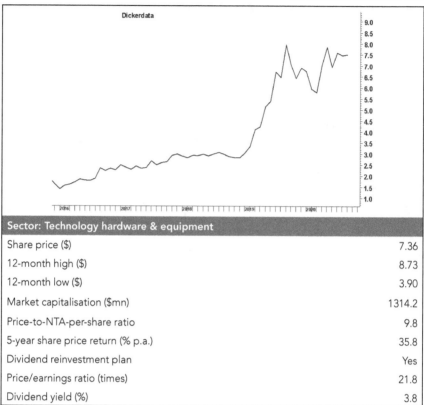

Sector: Technology hardware & equipment	
Share price ($)	7.36
12-month high ($)	8.73
12-month low ($)	3.90
Market capitalisation ($mn)	1314.2
Price-to-NTA-per-share ratio	9.8
5-year share price return (% p.a.)	35.8
Dividend reinvestment plan	Yes
Price/earnings ratio (times)	21.8
Dividend yield (%)	3.8

Sydney-based technology distributor Dicker Data dates back to its establishment by David Dicker in 1978. Today it is a leader in Australia and New Zealand in the wholesale distribution of computer hardware, software and related products, with more than 5000 customers, and a particular focus on small and medium-sized companies. Chief executive officer David Dicker and co-founder and director Fiona Brown between them own more than 70 per cent of the company's equity.

Latest business results (June 2020, half year)

Dicker Data became a beneficiary of the COVID-19 pandemic, as a big increase in remote working led to a surge in demand for computer equipment and software. Hardware sales generate about three-quarters of company turnover, and sales grew 11.4 per cent. Software sales surged 43.6 per cent, with particular growth in renewable and subscription products. Ten new vendors contributed sales of $26 million. New Zealand represents about 7 per cent of total income, and sales surged by nearly 32 per cent, though with little contribution to profit.

Outlook

Dicker Data has a strong position in Australia's IT distribution sector, with an approximate 27 per cent market share in the corporate and commercial segment. Though this is a low-margin business, it has grown to such a scale that it has become very profitable. The company is unusual in that CEO David Dicker takes no salary. In addition, its policy is to pay out its entire profits in dividends, and these are generally distributed quarterly. It has become a major beneficiary of the digital transformation of businesses in Australia, and believes the remote-working trend will continue, with people's homes becoming sub-branches of their offices. It expects the roll-out of 5G digital connectivity to have a revolutionary impact in accelerating the development of artificial intelligence and machine learning technologies, leading to increased demand for both hardware and software. It is seeing strong growth in recurring subscription revenues for its software. It has started a new financial services business to provide credit to customers, and sees this as a fresh source of income. To support future growth and to help streamline its operations it is building a major new $55 million distribution centre in Sydney with 80 per cent more capacity than its current facility. Dicker Data has expressed a desire to expand through a move offshore. As the distribution business depends heavily on strong relationships with IT vendors, the company expects to move overseas by acquiring an existing corporation that has already built these relationships.

Year to 31 December	2018	2019
Revenues ($mn)	1490.7	1758.5
EBIT ($mn)	51.8	81.4
EBIT margin (%)	3.5	4.6
Profit before tax ($mn)	46.2	75.9
Profit after tax ($mn)	32.5	54.3
Earnings per share (c)	20.22	33.69
Cash flow per share (c)	21.84	36.53
Dividend (c)	20.2	28
Percentage franked	100	100
Interest cover (times)	9.3	14.7
Return on equity (%)	41.9	62.1
Half year to 30 June	2019	2020
Revenues ($mn)	850.8	1005.8
Profit before tax ($mn)	32.3	42.0
Profit after tax ($mn)	23.8	29.4
Earnings per share (c)	14.73	17.08
Dividend (c)	10	15
Percentage franked	100	100
Net tangible assets per share ($)	0.38	0.75
Debt-to-equity ratio (%)	120.8	45.8
Current ratio	1.0	1.2

DWS Limited

ASX code: DWS   www.dws.com.au

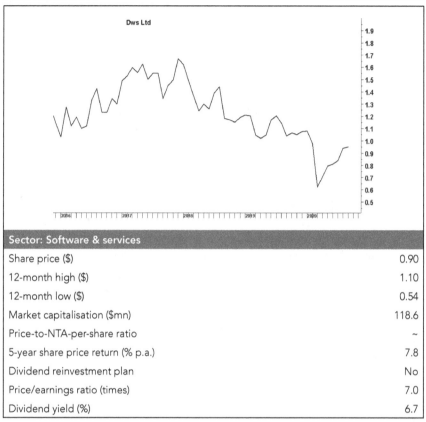

Sector: Software & services	
Share price ($)	0.90
12-month high ($)	1.10
12-month low ($)	0.54
Market capitalisation ($mn)	118.6
Price-to-NTA-per-share ratio	~
5-year share price return (% p.a.)	7.8
Dividend reinvestment plan	No
Price/earnings ratio (times)	7.0
Dividend yield (%)	6.7

Melbourne-based DWS is an IT services company established in 1991. It specialises in the design, development and maintenance of software for a range of clients across many industries. It also manages the IT services and consultancy businesses Phoenix, Symplicit and Projects Assured. It operates from offices in Melbourne, Sydney, Adelaide, Canberra and Brisbane. The DWS founder and chief executive officer, Danny Wallis, owns 42 per cent of the company equity. In October 2019 the company acquired the software services and products specialist Object Consulting.

Latest business results (June 2020, full year)

Revenues and normalised profits generally marked time as the COVID-19 pandemic hurt business, with some projects delayed or cancelled. In addition, the company suffered from lower-than-expected demand from several sectors. The acquisition of the Projects Assured consultancy in mid 2018 and of Object Consulting led to a 28 per cent jump in work for federal and state governments. This has now risen to represent 43 per cent of total company turnover, up from just 14 per cent in June 2018 and 35 per cent in June 2019. By contrast, sales to the banking and finance sector fell below company expectations, dropping 11 per cent, and this work has now fallen from 34 per cent of company turnover to 29 per cent. The other main sector, information technology and communications, was also weaker than expected, with sales down 25 per cent. The number of billable consultants fell from 751 at June 2019 to 720 a year later, reflecting the second-half decline in business and the underperformance of the Symplicit business. DWS also reported some heavy one-off expenses related to the Projects Assured and Object Consulting acquisitions, and at the statutory level profits fell.

Outlook

The acquisitions of Projects Assured for approximately $43 million and of Object Consulting for $4.3 million have greatly diversified DWS's operations, and it has now become a major supplier of IT-related products and services to the public sector. Object Consulting in particular offers a high exposure to state government contracts. The company is now working to leverage these businesses, with the aim of further diversifying its operations. Nevertheless, despite the acquisitions, the company is still dependent on its home state of Victoria for more than 40 per cent of its work, and the state's weakened economy could hurt business. DWS is working to boost its work in the information technology and communications sector, which has slumped from $24.8 million in June 2018 to $11.6 million in June 2020.

Year to 30 June	2019	2020
Revenues ($mn)	163.5	167.9
EBIT ($mn)	25.9	24.7
EBIT margin (%)	15.8	14.7
Profit before tax ($mn)	22.9	22.4
Profit after tax ($mn)	16.8	16.9
Earnings per share (c)	12.74	12.84
Cash flow per share (c)	14.22	15.72
Dividend (c)	8	6
Percentage franked	100	100
Net tangible assets per share ($)	~	~
Interest cover (times)	8.6	11.0
Return on equity (%)	23.5	24.3
Debt-to-equity ratio (%)	46.9	35.8
Current ratio	1.3	1.1

Evolution Mining Limited

ASX code: EVN   www.evolutionmining.com.au

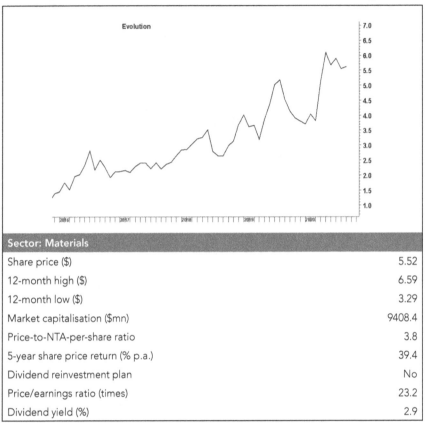

Sector: Materials	
Share price ($)	5.52
12-month high ($)	6.59
12-month low ($)	3.29
Market capitalisation ($mn)	9408.4
Price-to-NTA-per-share ratio	3.8
5-year share price return (% p.a.)	39.4
Dividend reinvestment plan	No
Price/earnings ratio (times)	23.2
Dividend yield (%)	2.9

Gold mining company Evolution Mining, based in Sydney, was formed in 2011 from the merger of Catalpa Resources and Conquest Mining and the acquisition of two mines from Newcrest Mining. It now operates five fully-owned mines — Cowal in New South Wales, Mt Carlton and Mt Rawdon in Queensland, Mungari in Western Australia and Red Lake in Ontario, Canada. It also holds an interest in the Ernest Henry copper-gold project in Queensland. It has sold its Cracow mine.

Latest business results (June 2020, full year)

A rising gold price sent revenues and profits soaring. The average gold price received by the company was $2274 per ounce, compared to $1760 in the previous year. Total gold production for the year of 746 463 ounces was a touch down from 753 001 ounces in the June 2019 year. Production costs for the year averaged $1043 per ounce, up from $924. Total exploration expenditure of $82.8 million was up from $52.1 million, due especially to the company's efforts to boost production at the Cowal mine. The result also included copper and silver revenues of $203.7 million, roughly in line with the previous year.

Outlook

Evolution's strategy is to build its gold reserves through developing or acquiring new assets, while also improving the quality of its portfolio and driving down expenses in order to remain a low-cost producer. In particular, it has aimed at delivering operational stability and predictability through the ownership of a number of similar-sized mines, rather than holding just a single mine or a dominant mine. Its target is to own six to eight mines, and it has said it is continually looking for additional long-life, low-cost assets to add to its portfolio. It has high hopes for its Red Lake asset in Canada, which it acquired in April 2020 for US$375 million plus contingency payments based on future production. It plans a major investment in this mine, aimed at boosting production and lowering operating costs, and believes that it could eventually be producing well in excess of 200 000 ounces of gold annually. It is also investing in new underground facilities at its Cowal mine, and believes production there could rise to more than 300 000 ounces per year. In June 2020 it sold its Cracow mine to Aeris Resources for a sum of up to $125 million. Evolution has set a gold production target of 670 000 ounces to 730 000 ounces for the June 2021 year, rising to between 790 000 ounces and 850 000 ounces in June 2023.

Year to 30 June	2019	2020
Revenues ($mn)	1509.8	1941.9
Cowal (%)	29	32
Ernest Henry (%)	23	20
Mungari (%)	14	15
Mr Rawdon (%)	11	10
Cracow (%)	10	10
EBIT ($mn)	330.3	594.2
EBIT margin (%)	21.9	30.6
Gross margin (%)	25.0	33.8
Profit before tax ($mn)	314.8	576.5
Profit after tax ($mn)	218.2	405.4
Earnings per share (c)	12.86	23.81
Cash flow per share (c)	34.96	48.33
Dividend (c)	9.5	16
Percentage franked	100	100
Net tangible assets per share ($)	1.42	1.45
Interest cover (times)	21.3	33.5
Return on equity (%)	9.3	16.6
Debt-to-equity ratio (%)	~	7.7
Current ratio	2.3	2.0

Fiducian Group Limited

ASX code: FID   www.fiducian.com.au

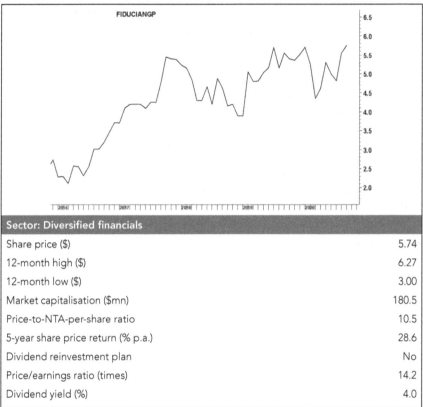

Sector: Diversified financials	
Share price ($)	5.74
12-month high ($)	6.27
12-month low ($)	3.00
Market capitalisation ($mn)	180.5
Price-to-NTA-per-share ratio	10.5
5-year share price return (% p.a.)	28.6
Dividend reinvestment plan	No
Price/earnings ratio (times)	14.2
Dividend yield (%)	4.0

Sydney financial services company Fiducian Group was founded in 1996 by executive chairman Indy Singh. Initially it specialised in the provision of masterfund, client administration and financial planning services to financial advisory groups. It has since expanded and is now a holding company with five divisions — Fiducian Portfolio Services is in charge of trustee and superannuation services; Fiducian Investment Management Services operates the company's managed funds; Fiducian Service is the administration service provider for all the company's products; Fiducian Financial Services manages the company's financial planning businesses; and Fiducian Business Services provides accounting and business services. In 2019 the company acquired the financial planning business of Tasmanian financial services group MyState.

Latest business results (June 2020, full year)

Revenues and underlying profits rose once more in a solid result. For reporting purposes the company divides its operations into three broad segments. The largest of these now is financial planning, which enjoyed a 21 per cent jump in revenues and with funds under advice growing from $2.7 billion in June 2019 to $3 billion.

However, this operation remained in the red as the company continued to invest in buying up new businesses to add to its network of advisers. The funds management business saw revenues and profits rise. The corporate and platform administration segment incorporates all the company's other businesses, and revenues and profits were also higher. At June 2020 the total funds under management, advice and administration of $8 billion was up by 8 per cent from a year earlier.

Outlook

Fiducian managed nine company-owned financial planning offices at June 2020, as well as 32 franchised offices, with a total of 74 authorised representatives across Australia. It is continually boosting these numbers as new offices join the group and it has also been achieving solid organic growth. During the June 2020 year it acquired new business that added $412 million to its funds under advice, and it has reported that it has a strong pipeline of acquisition opportunities and new franchisees wishing to join the group. The funds management business offers 15 funds, and the company believes that its method of choosing fund managers with differing investment styles offers the ability to deliver above-average returns with greater diversification and reduced risks. Fiducian management have stated that they expect profits to continue to grow in the June 2021 year. However, the company is vulnerable to any major downturn in financial markets. At June 2020 it had no debt and cash holdings of nearly $14 million.

Year to 30 June	2019	2020
Revenues ($mn)	48.9	54.7
Financial planning (%)	35	37
Funds management (%)	36	36
Corporate and platform administration (%)	29	27
EBIT ($mn)	15.5	17.0
EBIT margin (%)	31.7	31.1
Profit before tax ($mn)	16.0	17.3
Profit after tax ($mn)	12.0	12.7
Earnings per share (c)	38.45	40.47
Cash flow per share (c)	44.15	51.31
Dividend (c)	22.3	23
Percentage franked	100	100
Net tangible assets per share ($)	0.47	0.54
Interest cover (times)	~	~
Return on equity (%)	36.5	34.9
Debt-to-equity ratio (%)	~	~
Current ratio	2.4	2.4

Fortescue Metals Group Limited

ASX code: FMG   www.fmgl.com.au

Sector: Materials	
Share price ($)	17.52
12-month high ($)	19.56
12-month low ($)	8.13
Market capitalisation ($mn)	53 943.5
Price-to-NTA-per-share ratio	2.8
5-year share price return (% p.a.)	62.9
Dividend reinvestment plan	Yes
Price/earnings ratio (times)	7.9
Dividend yield (%)	10.0

Perth-based Fortescue was founded in 2003. It has been responsible for discovering and developing some of the largest iron ore mines in the world. It is today one of the world's largest iron ore producers, with operations that are centred on several mine sites in the Pilbara region. It also operates its own heavy-haul railway between its mines and its Herb Elliott Port at Port Hedland. More than 90 per cent of its sales are to China.

Latest business results (June 2020, full year)

Fortescue posted another excellent result, thanks to higher production and continuing rises in the iron ore price. Sales of 178.2 million tonnes were up 6 per cent from the previous year, and the average price of US$79 per tonne was 21 per cent higher. Average production costs of US$12.94 per tonne were down 1 per cent, thanks to a continuing focus on productivity and innovation initiatives. Net debt — borrowings minus cash holdings — continued to fall, down from US$2.1 billion in June 2019 to US$258 million in June 2020. Note that Fortescue reports its results in US dollars. The Australian dollar figures in this book — converted at prevailing exchange rates — are for guidance only.

Outlook

Its heavy debt burden brought Fortescue near to collapse in 2012, and since then it has been devoting enormous effort into making itself more financially stable. In 2012 its basic production costs were as high as US$50 a tonne, but they have since fallen substantially, and are now among the lowest in the world. It maintains an active exploration and development program at its Pilbara properties. It plans a major boost to capital spending in the June 2021 year, to as much as US$3.4 billion, compared with US$2 billion in June 2020. Its massive US$1.3 billion Eliwana Mine and Rail project is expected to begin production of iron ore from December 2020. Its other major development is the US$2.6 billion Iron Bridge Magnetite project, which is targeted to begin production in mid 2022. The company is optimistic that Chinese demand will remain strong, thanks to continuing programs of urbanisation and industrialisation. Nevertheless, its fortunes are tied intimately to the price of iron ore, which can be volatile, and it is also influenced by currency fluctuations. In addition, its ore tends to be of a lower grade than that being produced by some rivals. It forecasts iron ore shipments in the June 2021 year of 175 million tonnes to 180 million tonnes.

Year to 30 June	2019	2020
Revenues ($mn)	13 840.3	18 579.7
EBIT ($mn)	6 697.2	10 017.4
EBIT margin (%)	48.4	53.9
Gross margin (%)	48.7	55.2
Profit before tax ($mn)	6 345.8	9 695.7
Profit after tax ($mn)	4 426.4	6 862.3
Earnings per share (c)	143.23	223.00
Cash flow per share (c)	196.98	288.13
Dividend (c)	43	176
Percentage franked	100	100
Net tangible assets per share ($)	4.91	6.22
Interest cover (times)	19.1	31.1
Return on equity (%)	31.3	40.0
Debt-to-equity ratio (%)	19.6	1.9
Current ratio	1.4	2.3

GUD Holdings Limited

ASX code: GUD www.gud.com.au

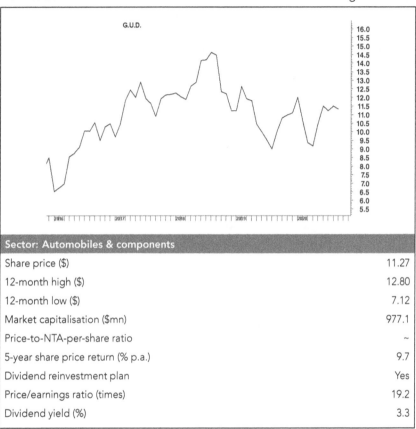

G.U.D.

Sector: Automobiles & components	
Share price ($)	11.27
12-month high ($)	12.80
12-month low ($)	7.12
Market capitalisation ($mn)	977.1
Price-to-NTA-per-share ratio	~
5-year share price return (% p.a.)	9.7
Dividend reinvestment plan	Yes
Price/earnings ratio (times)	19.2
Dividend yield (%)	3.3

GUD, based in Melbourne and founded in 1940, is a manufacturer and distributor of a diversified range of auto and industrial products. Its main automotive brands include Ryco, Wesfil, Goss, BWI — incorporating the Narva and Projecta brands — Griffiths Equipment, IM Group, AA Gaskets and Disc Brakes Australia. The company also manufactures and distributes Davey water pumps and water treatment products.

Latest business results (June 2020, full year)

Revenues edged up but profits were down as a second-half slowdown in demand boosted operating costs. New Zealand represents about 10 per cent of company turnover, and sales were hit especially severely by the hard lockdown imposed in that country. The core Automotive division saw sales steady for the year, with underlying EBIT down 7 per cent. This division contributes about three-quarters of company sales, but is responsible for around 90 per cent of profit. Wesfil filters enjoyed another year of strong growth, while Ryco filters saw demand roughly in line with the previous year. However, the BWI business — which includes automotive electrical accessories and power products — was hurt by the second-half slowdown and sales were down. The Davey water products business reported a 3 per cent rise in sales — the same increase as in the previous year, with underlying EBIT down 7 per cent. Domestic sales of Davey water products grew strongly, with bushfires generating solid demand for pumping equipment, but this was in large part offset by a decline in New Zealand and European business.

Outlook

Having divested itself of a series of businesses, GUD is now focused on the steadily growing Australian automotive after-market sector. It continues to broaden the product ranges for its various brands and it is also seeking to expand exports. It hopes to secure further acquisitions and has developed a set of acquisition criteria that it believes will boost profitability. Since June 2020 it has been experiencing a recovery in demand, though it has been cautious about whether this would be sustained. Nevertheless, it viewed the prospects for a weakening economy as a long-term positive for its business, with car owners holding onto their vehicles for longer, boosting demand for spare parts. The company also expects more use of cars as Australians avoid public transport and as they opt for domestic tourism rather than overseas travel. GUD is working to boost profits for its low-margin Davey business, and has been spending heavily on restructuring this business and on the development of new products.

Year to 30 June	2019	2020
Revenues ($mn)	434.1	438.0
Automotive (%)	76	76
Davey (%)	24	24
EBIT ($mn)	89.4	80.7
EBIT margin (%)	20.6	18.4
Gross margin (%)	48.6	46.1
Profit before tax ($mn)	82.1	71.1
Profit after tax ($mn)	60.9	50.9
Earnings per share (c)	70.39	58.72
Cash flow per share (c)	74.21	76.02
Dividend (c)	56	37
Percentage franked	100	100
Net tangible assets per share ($)	~	~
Interest cover (times)	12.2	8.4
Return on equity (%)	22.4	18.4
Debt-to-equity ratio (%)	47.6	51.7
Current ratio	2.9	2.7

GWA Group Limited

ASX code: GWA   www.gwagroup.com.au

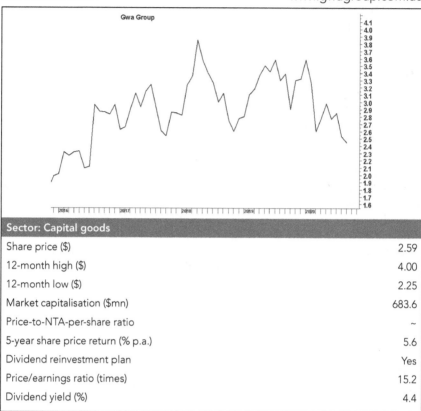

Sector: Capital goods	
Share price ($)	2.59
12-month high ($)	4.00
12-month low ($)	2.25
Market capitalisation ($mn)	683.6
Price-to-NTA-per-share ratio	~
5-year share price return (% p.a.)	5.6
Dividend reinvestment plan	Yes
Price/earnings ratio (times)	15.2
Dividend yield (%)	4.4

Brisbane-based GWA is a prominent designer, importer and distributor of residential and commercial bathroom and kitchen products, marketed under brands that include Caroma, Dorf, Fowler, Stylus and Clark. About 13 per cent of its sales are in New Zealand, with 7 per cent in the United Kingdom. In April 2019 it acquired the New Zealand company Methven, which designs and manufactures showers, taps and valves.

Latest business results (June 2020, full year)

In a challenging bathroom and fixtures market, revenues rose again but normalised profits fell for the first time in four years. The result included a first full year of business for the Methven acquisition. The company estimated that its Australian addressable market declined by about 10 per cent during the year, with detached house completions down by around 20 per cent, apartment construction falling 18 per cent, the renovation and replacement segment dropping by 8 per cent and commercial building activity down by approximately 4 per cent. The fourth quarter was especially weak, largely due to the COVID-19 pandemic. Altogether, the company estimated that the pandemic resulted in a drop of $22.2 million in sales and an $8.6 million hit to EBIT.

GWA continued its long-term cost-cutting program, with $5 million in savings during the year. Some additional short-term cost reductions in response to weakening market conditions delivered a further $10.5 million in savings. The integration of Methven generated cost synergies of some $3 million.

Outlook

After a long series of restructurings GWA is now almost completely exposed to a bathroom and kitchen fixtures market that in Australia is worth up to $1.4 billion annually. It claims market shares as high as 50 per cent for some of its products, with an overall share of about 23 per cent. It has targeted three sectors — renovations and replacements, commercial construction and detached housing — and is developing new, high-margin products specifically for these markets. It sees great potential for its Caroma Smart Command intelligent bathroom system, which enables the monitoring and management of water usage in commercial buildings. However, it has conceded that its addressable market is likely to decline further in the June 2021 year. Nevertheless, its commercial order book remains strong, thanks to solid demand related to aged care facilities and renovation and replacement activity. Its $112 million acquisition of Methven has helped broaden GWA's presence in several overseas countries. The acquisition is also expected to generate annual cost synergies of at least $6 million by June 2021.

Year to 30 June	2019	2020
Revenues ($mn)	381.7	398.7
EBIT ($mn)	78.1	71.8
EBIT margin (%)	20.5	18.0
Gross margin (%)	42.6	40.4
Profit before tax ($mn)	72.3	63.2
Profit after tax ($mn)	50.8	44.9
Earnings per share (c)	19.26	17.02
Cash flow per share (c)	21.14	19.83
Dividend (c)	18.5	11.5
Percentage franked	100	100
Net tangible assets per share ($)	~	~
Interest cover (times)	13.4	8.3
Return on equity (%)	19.0	15.9
Debt-to-equity ratio (%)	48.2	51.1
Current ratio	2.4	1.7

Hansen Technologies Limited

ASX code: HSN   www.hansencx.com

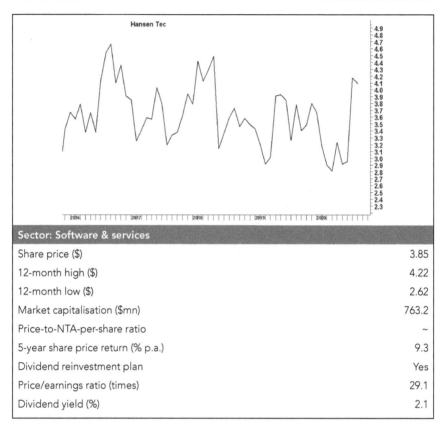

Sector: Software & services	
Share price ($)	3.85
12-month high ($)	4.22
12-month low ($)	2.62
Market capitalisation ($mn)	763.2
Price-to-NTA-per-share ratio	~
5-year share price return (% p.a.)	9.3
Dividend reinvestment plan	Yes
Price/earnings ratio (times)	29.1
Dividend yield (%)	2.1

Melbourne company Hansen Technologies dates back to an IT business launched in 1971. It later moved into the development of billing software systems and is today a significant global provider of these services, specialising in the electricity, gas, water, pay television and telecommunications sectors. Hansen has offices around the world, and services some 580 customers across 16 product lines in over 80 countries.

Latest business results (June 2020, full year)

Revenues and profits were up, in large part reflecting a full-year contribution from Hansen's biggest-ever acquisition, Toronto-based Sigma Systems, bought for $164 million in June 2019. However, the company also achieved growth from its existing customer base, with the completion of many successful upgrades and projects. During the year the company acquired 20 new customers, and these have committed more than $70 million in revenues over their initial contract terms. Its billing services business represents the bulk of the company's income. However, it also continues to receive a small amount from other legacy operations, notably its customer call centre. Hansen also reported what it called an underlying net profit after tax, excluding tax-effected amortisation of acquired intangibles, and on this basis its after-tax profit rose from $33.7 million in June 2019 to $47.4 million in June 2020.

Outlook

Though a small company, Hansen has developed a high reputation for its services. Once it does business with a customer it stands to benefit further from a long-term stream of recurring revenue. Its latest acquisition Sigma is a leading global provider of catalogue-driven software products for telecommunications, media and technology companies. Its successful integration into Hansen's operations has provided the company with further product innovation opportunities and has also helped it expand, reaching new markets in the Asia-Pacific and the Europe–Middle East sectors. Hansen has also been able to boost Sigma's operating margins, and expects further cross-selling opportunities and substantial synergy benefits. Hansen's particular strategy is growth by acquisition, and with the billing services industry still fragmented and largely regionalised, it expects further attractive acquisition opportunities to present themselves. In particular, it is aiming at assets that own intellectual property and with recurring revenue streams that will help Hansen move into new regions or market segments. It believes that economic upheavals caused by the COVID-19 pandemic could lead to further opportunities for expansion. To help reduce costs it has opened a development centre in Vietnam, and the Sigma acquisition has delivered another large development centre, in India.

Year to 30 June	2019	2020
Revenues ($mn)	231.3	301.4
EBIT ($mn)	29.8	39.5
EBIT margin (%)	12.9	13.1
Profit before tax ($mn)	27.8	30.3
Profit after tax ($mn)	21.5	26.2
Earnings per share (c)	10.91	13.23
Cash flow per share (c)	22.46	34.62
Dividend (c)	6	8
Percentage franked	93	23
Net tangible assets per share ($)	~	~
Interest cover (times)	15.0	4.3
Return on equity (%)	9.0	10.5
Debt-to-equity ratio (%)	59.3	45.1
Current ratio	1.7	1.6

Harvey Norman Holdings Limited

ASX code: HVN   www.harveynormanholdings.com.au

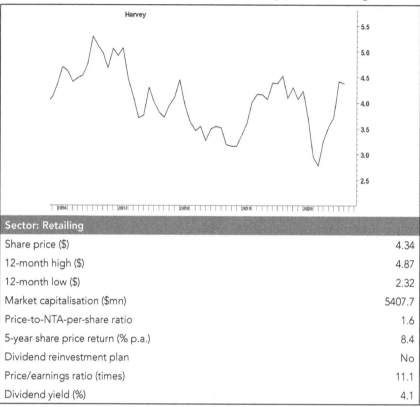

Sector: Retailing	
Share price ($)	4.34
12-month high ($)	4.87
12-month low ($)	2.32
Market capitalisation ($mn)	5407.7
Price-to-NTA-per-share ratio	1.6
5-year share price return (% p.a.)	8.4
Dividend reinvestment plan	No
Price/earnings ratio (times)	11.1
Dividend yield (%)	4.1

Sydney-based Harvey Norman, established in 1982, operates a chain of 290 retail stores specialising in electrical and electronic goods, home appliances, furniture, flooring, carpets and manchester items, throughout Australia, New Zealand, Ireland, Northern Ireland, Singapore, Malaysia, Slovenia and Croatia, under the Harvey Norman, Domayne and Joyce Mayne banners. The 194 Australian stores are independently held as part of a franchise operation, from which Harvey Norman receives income for advisory and advertising services. It also receives a considerable amount of income from its own stores, from its $3 billion property portfolio and from the provision of finance to franchisees and customers.

Latest business results (June 2020, full year)

Strong demand, generated by the COVID-19 pandemic, for home appliances, electronic goods and home furnishings at the company's stores around the world drove sales and profits higher. Total store sales — franchise and company-owned — rose 7.6 per cent to $8.23 billion. Sales by Harvey Norman's Australian franchisees rose 9 per cent to $6.16 billion, including same-store growth of 30.3 per cent in the June 2020 quarter.

Franchise income received by Harvey Norman rose 13 per cent to $949 million, with franchise pre-tax profit jumping by 40 per cent. Most of the Australian stores were able to remain open, despite the COVID-19 pandemic. However, many overseas stores were forced to close for varying periods. Total non-franchise retail revenues rose 3 per cent to $2.36 billion, with the pre-tax profit rising by 27 per cent. Irish sales were particularly strong, with profits more than doubling. New Zealand and Slovenia both recorded double-digit profit increases. The property business reported lower revenues and profits. During the year the company paid down much of its debt, and at June 2020 it had net cash holdings of more than $15 million.

Outlook

Harvey Norman has reported that buoyant sales have continued in the early months of the June 2021 financial year, as consumers continue to spend more time at home. With Australians unlikely to be able to travel much before 2021, the company is gearing up for a busy Christmas period. It has high fixed costs, so even modest increases in sales can translate to much larger increases in earnings. Nevertheless, its business is also highly exposed to economic conditions and consumer spending trends, and it could be affected by rising unemployment and growing economic weakness. It continues to expand, with plans to open 12 new company-owned stores overseas during the June 2021 year and one new franchise store in Australia.

Year to 30 June	2019	2020
Revenues ($mn)	3420.2	3545.8
Retail (%)	65	65
Franchising operations (%)	24	26
Property (%)	10	8
EBIT ($mn)	598.1	714.7
EBIT margin (%)	17.5	20.2
Gross margin (%)	32.4	32.2
Profit before tax ($mn)	574.6	661.3
Profit after tax ($mn)	402.3	480.5
Earnings per share (c)	34.70	39.19
Cash flow per share (c)	42.05	46.33
Dividend (c)	33	18
Percentage franked	100	100
Net tangible assets per share ($)	2.63	2.72
Interest cover (times)	25.4	13.4
Return on equity (%)	13.2	14.5
Debt-to-equity ratio (%)	19.6	~
Current ratio	1.6	1.7

IDP Education Limited

ASX code: IEL   www.idp.com

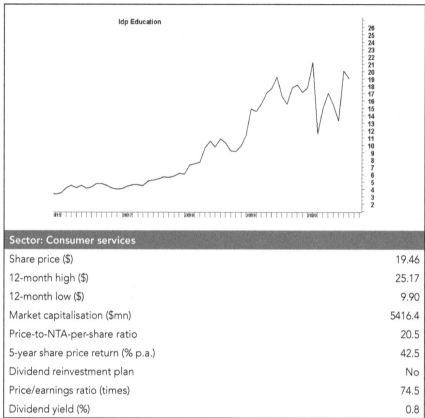

Sector: Consumer services	
Share price ($)	19.46
12-month high ($)	25.17
12-month low ($)	9.90
Market capitalisation ($mn)	5416.4
Price-to-NTA-per-share ratio	20.5
5-year share price return (% p.a.)	42.5
Dividend reinvestment plan	No
Price/earnings ratio (times)	74.5
Dividend yield (%)	0.8

Melbourne-based IDP Education dates back to 1969 and the launch of the Australian Asian Universities Cooperation Scheme, aimed at helping Asian students study in Australia. In 1981 it changed its name to the International Development Program (IDP), and opened a series of offices throughout Asia. It has since expanded through acquisition and organic growth, and today helps students from around the world find placements in higher education programs in English-speaking countries. It also works with University of Cambridge ESOL Examinations and the British Council to administer worldwide testing for the International English Language Testing System. About 40 per cent of IDP's equity is held by Education Australia, which is a company owned by 38 Australian universities.

Latest business results (June 2020, full year)

IDP overcame the COVID-19 pandemic to post a small increase in profits, despite a decline in revenues. The company reported revenue growth of 19 per cent during the first nine months of the financial year, followed by a 64 per cent crash in the final quarter. In response to the pandemic, the company introduced a range of measures that delivered a sharp reduction in its costs for the year. More than half the company's turnover derives from its English-language testing services, and revenues fell 9 per cent, as most testing centres were forced to close due to social distancing requirements. Much of the remainder of the company's turnover comes from its student placement services, and revenues for this business rose 12 per cent, with a 3 per cent increase in placement numbers to 51 000.

Outlook

IDP faces challenges while the COVID-19 pandemic restricts international travel. Around two-thirds of its revenues and three-quarters of its profits come from Asia, and particularly from China and India, which the company has noted are the key engines of growth for the international education industry more broadly. Demand for international education services remains high in both countries. However, the company's largest study destination by volume is Australia, and it is possible that many foreign students will not be able to enter the country again until some period in 2021. Other prominent study destinations for the company include the United Kingdom and Canada, where varying degrees of travel restrictions have been imposed. After most of its English-language testing centres were forced to close, IDP reported in August 2020 that they had reopened in 53 of the 55 countries in which it operates. At June 2020 IDP had net cash holdings of more than $247 million.

Year to 30 June	2019	2020
Revenues ($mn)	598.1	587.1
Asia (%)	66	66
Rest of World (%)	24	24
Australasia (%)	10	10
EBIT ($mn)	97.1	107.8
EBIT margin (%)	16.2	18.4
Profit before tax ($mn)	95.4	102.6
Profit after tax ($mn)	66.6	67.9
Earnings per share (c)	26.26	26.14
Cash flow per share (c)	33.32	41.88
Dividend (c)	19.5	16.5
Percentage franked	48	17
Net tangible assets per share ($)	0.08	0.95
Interest cover (times)	55.7	20.8
Return on equity (%)	52.3	24.9
Debt-to-equity ratio (%)	2.9	~
Current ratio	1.3	2.5

Infomedia Limited

ASX code: IFM   www.infomedia.com.au

Sector: Software & services	
Share price ($)	1.66
12-month high ($)	2.48
12-month low ($)	1.20
Market capitalisation ($mn)	621.6
Price-to-NTA-per-share ratio	7.2
5-year share price return (% p.a.)	16.6
Dividend reinvestment plan	No
Price/earnings ratio (times)	29.2
Dividend yield (%)	2.6

Sydney electronic data company Infomedia was formed in 1990, and has grown into a world leader in the development of specialised electronic catalogues. Its main product is the Microcat electronic parts catalogue for the automotive industry, with versions for most leading car companies. Sold to customers in 186 countries, the catalogue enables service personnel in a motor dealership to identify the correct replacement parts for a vehicle. The company also produces the Superservice data management product, which provides automotive dealers with a range of service, repair and warranty management tools.

Latest business results (June 2020, full year)

Infomedia overcame COVID-19 pandemic–related interruptions to post another excellent result, with double-digit gains in sales and profits. With the rise in earnings outstripping revenue gains, the company achieved a further boost to its profit margins. The first half saw a successful completion to the rollout of the company's major global electronic parts contract with Nissan, along with sales growth in many regions. However, increasing travel restrictions in the second half led to a series of delays to contract signings and project launches, before a big rebound in business in June 2020.

The best result came from the Asia-Pacific region, with double-digit rises in sales and profits. The other two regions, Americas and Europe/Middle East/Africa, both saw revenues up by 6 per cent.

Outlook

In a fiercely competitive global automobile market, car dealerships now often make more profit from the supply of parts and service than they do from actual car sales. It is this fast-growing after-sales sector that is the target market for Infomedia. With recurring revenues representing more than 95 per cent of turnover, it has a consistent and highly predictable revenue stream. It continues to invest heavily in research and development, and has a pipeline of new products for gradual release. It has begun trials of its Next Gen parts and services platforms, one of the largest development projects in its history. It believes the Next Gen electronics part catalogues will provide dealerships with innovative tools, including a major data analytics capability, that will enable them significantly to boost sales and productivity. Following a capital raising during the year, at June 2020 Infomedia had no debt and cash holdings of more than $100 million, and it plans to use this to execute its growth strategies. In particular, it hopes to access new markets and customers through acquisitions. With more than 80 per cent of its sales abroad, the company is highly exposed to currency fluctuations.

Year to 30 June	2019	2020
Revenues ($mn)	84.6	94.6
EBIT ($mn)	22.2	25.5
EBIT margin (%)	26.2	27.0
Profit before tax ($mn)	21.1	25.0
Profit after tax ($mn)	16.1	18.6
Earnings per share (c)	5.19	5.69
Cash flow per share (c)	10.60	12.08
Dividend (c)	3.9	4.3
Percentage franked	0	70
Net tangible assets per share ($)	0.01	0.23
Interest cover (times)	20.2	46.1
Return on equity (%)	27.3	17.0
Debt-to-equity ratio (%)	~	~
Current ratio	1.5	5.8

Integral Diagnostics Limited

ASX code: IDX   www.integraldiagnostics.com.au

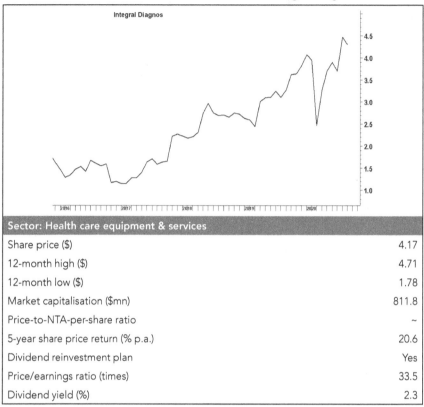

Sector: Health care equipment & services	
Share price ($)	4.17
12-month high ($)	4.71
12-month low ($)	1.78
Market capitalisation ($mn)	811.8
Price-to-NTA-per-share ratio	~
5-year share price return (% p.a.)	20.6
Dividend reinvestment plan	Yes
Price/earnings ratio (times)	33.5
Dividend yield (%)	2.3

Melbourne-based healthcare services company Integral Diagnostics got its start in 2002 with the formation of its Lake Imaging brand in Ballarat. It has since grown through acquisition and is today one of Australia's largest radiology providers, with operations in Victoria, Queensland and Western Australia. It is also active in New Zealand. Its services include x-ray, ultrasound, computed tomography (CT), magnetic resonance imaging (MRI) and nuclear medicine. In November 2019 it acquired Imaging Queensland and in September 2020 it acquired Ascot Radiology in New Zealand.

Latest business results (June 2020, full year)

New sites, investment in new equipment and the Imaging Queensland acquisition combined to deliver higher revenues and profits, despite a significant slowdown in business resulting from the COVID-19 pandemic. Underlying like-for-like revenue growth for the year was 2.4 per cent in Australia, though with a 1.6 per cent decline in New Zealand. The company invested $26 million in organic growth projects, including major upgrades to the equipment at some of its sites. Average fees per examination rose 1.7 per cent, reflecting a move within the industry to higher-end and more expensive scans, including MRIs and high-speed cardiac CTs. Imaging Queensland contributed revenues of $38.7 million. The company received $6.1 million in pandemic-related support payments from the Australian and New Zealand governments.

Outlook

Integral Diagnostics operates through a variety of brands. These include Lake Imaging in Victoria, Imaging Queensland and South Coast Radiology in Queensland, Global Diagnostics in Western Australia and Specialist Radiology Group and Trinity MRI in New Zealand. At June 2020 it operated from 64 sites, including 20 hospital sites, and with a total of 28 MRI machines. With growing and ageing populations in both Australia and New Zealand, the company believes that long-term industry fundamentals are strong. It says that it is becoming increasingly recognised that the use of diagnostic imaging in the early detection of disease can facilitate earlier and less invasive treatment options, which can ultimately lower overall healthcare costs. The industry remains quite fragmented, presenting many opportunities for further consolidation. The company expects its NZ$50 million acquisition of Ascot Radiology to be highly complementary to its existing New Zealand business, with cost and revenue synergy benefits and high growth opportunities. Integral Diagnostics also has solid expectations for its new North Melbourne Specialist and Research Centre, intended as a leading provider of advanced MRI and cardiac CT services to specialist referrers in Victoria's premier medical precinct around the Royal Melbourne Hospital.

Year to 30 June	2019	2020
Revenues ($mn)	232.4	275.6
EBIT ($mn)	36.5	43.6
EBIT margin (%)	15.7	15.8
Profit before tax ($mn)	30.6	35.3
Profit after tax ($mn)	21.0	23.0
Earnings per share (c)	13.53	12.43
Cash flow per share (c)	22.24	26.29
Dividend (c)	10	9.5
Percentage franked	100	100
Net tangible assets per share ($)	~	~
Interest cover (times)	6.2	5.3
Return on equity (%)	19.0	13.0
Debt-to-equity ratio (%)	92.8	54.2
Current ratio	0.9	1.1

Integrated Research Limited

ASX code: IRI　　　　　　　　　　　　　　　　　www.ir.com

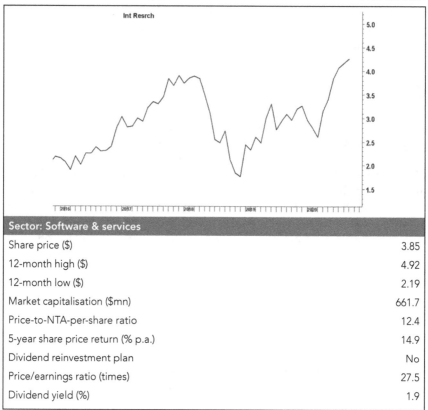

Sector: Software & services	
Share price ($)	3.85
12-month high ($)	4.92
12-month low ($)	2.19
Market capitalisation ($mn)	661.7
Price-to-NTA-per-share ratio	12.4
5-year share price return (% p.a.)	14.9
Dividend reinvestment plan	No
Price/earnings ratio (times)	27.5
Dividend yield (%)	1.9

Sydney-based Integrated Research, founded in 1988, is a software developer. Its main product, Prognosis, provides performance monitoring, diagnostics and reporting functions for an organisation's IT systems. It has particular application for high-volume environments, including ATM and EFTPOS systems, telecommunications networks, IT server infrastructure and internet services such as online banking and travel booking services. The company maintains offices in Australia, Britain, Germany, Singapore and the United States, and exports to more than 60 countries, with overseas business accounting for more than 95 per cent of company turnover. Customers include many of the world's largest organisations, such as stock exchanges, banks, credit card companies, airlines and universities, as well as government departments.

Latest business results (June 2020, full year)

In an excellent result, Integrated Research reported its seventh consecutive year of annual profit growth, driven by a 15 per cent increase in licence fees to $72 million. Maintenance fee revenues fell 4 per cent to $24 million, the second consecutive decline for this business. But testing services revenues bounced back with an 11 per cent rise to $5.5 million. The company segments its sales into three broad product lines. The largest of these, communications, saw sales up 17 per cent to $60 million, thanks to 29 new customers and new business licence sales of $5.8 million. Infrastructure revenues rose 9 per cent to $29 million, with a US$10 million, five-year contract with JP Morgan Chase — the largest contract in the company's history — one of the highlights. The payments business, which had seen revenues nearly double in the previous year, fell back 14 per cent to $14 million. The company reported that some of its significant contracts during the year came with major brands that included ANZ Banking, BT, DXC, GlaxoSmithKline, NTT and Woolworths.

Outlook

Integrated Research supplies software that monitors IT systems and thereby enables clients to improve customer service as well as avoid the risks associated with computer outages. Thanks to strong relationships with key hardware suppliers and the high reputation of its products, it is experiencing steady growth in demand, with a long-term recurring revenue base of licence fees. Renewal rates for its services remain very high. It is a potential beneficiary of accelerating moves around the world towards contactless payments and online video conferencing, which could boost demand for monitoring software. It has introduced a Software-as-a-Service business, with the launch of a cloud-based platform, and expects this to support the launch of a range of new products.

Year to 30 June	2019	2020
Revenues ($mn)	100.8	110.9
EBIT ($mn)	29.0	31.0
EBIT margin (%)	28.7	28.0
Profit before tax ($mn)	29.6	31.5
Profit after tax ($mn)	21.9	24.1
Earnings per share (c)	12.72	14.00
Cash flow per share (c)	19.32	21.01
Dividend (c)	7.25	7.25
Percentage franked	100	100
Net tangible assets per share ($)	0.27	0.31
Interest cover (times)	~	~
Return on equity (%)	34.2	31.6
Debt-to-equity ratio (%)	~	~
Current ratio	1.8	1.8

InvoCare Limited

ASX code: IVC

www.invocare.com.au

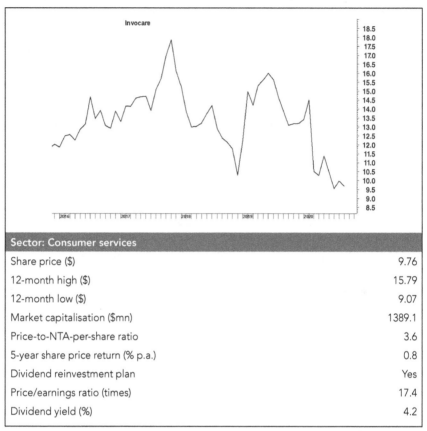

Sector: Consumer services	
Share price ($)	9.76
12-month high ($)	15.79
12-month low ($)	9.07
Market capitalisation ($mn)	1389.1
Price-to-NTA-per-share ratio	3.6
5-year share price return (% p.a.)	0.8
Dividend reinvestment plan	Yes
Price/earnings ratio (times)	17.4
Dividend yield (%)	4.2

Sydney-based funeral services provider InvoCare was formed in 2001 when the American funerals business Service Corporation International divested itself of its Australian interests, creating a new company. Today it operates funeral homes, cemeteries and crematoria throughout Australia, New Zealand and Singapore. In Australia it operates through three national brands — White Lady Funerals, Simplicity Funerals and Value Cremations — as well as more than 40 local brands. It operates more than 20 funeral home brands in New Zealand and two in Singapore. It also operates 14 cemeteries and crematoria in New South Wales and Queensland and two cemeteries in New Zealand.

Latest business results (June 2020, half year)

Revenues were down and profits crashed as the COVID-19 pandemic led to the imposition of severe restrictions on funeral services. The company also noted that, while precise data was not yet available, anecdotal feedback suggested that the number of deaths during the period had fallen, perhaps due to social distancing requirements leading to a decline in the number of people dying from the flu. Australian revenues fell by 8.5 per cent from the June 2019 half, mainly due to a decline in funeral service business, although memorial park revenues were also weak. The company reported a significant move away from expensive funerals and towards low-cost alternatives, including direct cremation services. New Zealand represents about 11 per cent of total turnover, and revenues fell 10.5 per cent. Singapore is just 5 per cent of company turnover, and revenues actually rose by 2.6 per cent, with an increase in the number of funerals and the receipt of some subsidies from the Singapore government.

Outlook

InvoCare occupies a central position in the Australian funeral sector, with a market share of around 29 per cent. Due to the combination of a growing population and an ageing population, the company forecasts that deaths in Australia over the coming decade will rise by about 2.3 per cent per year, giving its business a steady and predictable quality. It has initiated a $200 million refurbishment program aimed at modernising its facilities. This is intended in particular to meet what are seen as the demands of baby boomers for upbeat, celebratory funeral services with high-tech audio-visual equipment, rather than the more sombre traditional approach. The company also continues to seek out appropriate acquisition opportunities as a further means of growth. In 2018 it entered the pet cremation business, and although this represents just a tiny part of its business, it views it as another growth opportunity.

Year to 31 December	2018	2019
Revenues ($mn)	480.8	500.3
EBIT ($mn)	77.4	121.6
EBIT margin (%)	16.1	24.3
Gross margin (%)	100.0	100.0
Profit before tax ($mn)	57.7	97.2
Profit after tax ($mn)	41.4	63.9
Earnings per share (c)	37.95	55.95
Cash flow per share (c)	61.84	88.34
Dividend (c)	37	41
Percentage franked	100	100
Interest cover (times)	3.9	5.0
Return on equity (%)	17.6	26.3
Half year to 30 June	2019	2020
Revenues ($mn)	236.4	216.9
Profit before tax ($mn)	29.3	9.6
Profit after tax ($mn)	20.4	6.9
Earnings per share (c)	18.14	5.54
Dividend (c)	17.5	5.5
Percentage franked	100	100
Net tangible assets per share ($)	0.92	2.68
Debt-to-equity ratio (%)	116.4	12.1
Current ratio	1.3	2.0

IPH Limited

ASX code: IPH   www.iphltd.com.au

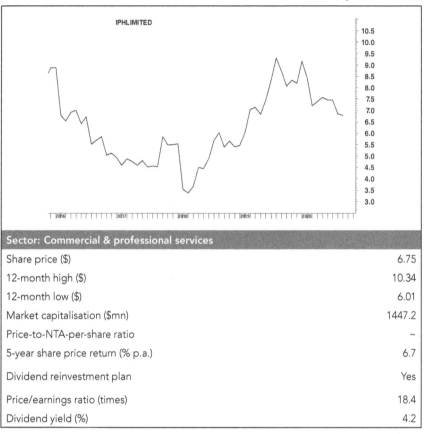

Sector: Commercial & professional services	
Share price ($)	6.75
12-month high ($)	10.34
12-month low ($)	6.01
Market capitalisation ($mn)	1447.2
Price-to-NTA-per-share ratio	~
5-year share price return (% p.a.)	6.7
Dividend reinvestment plan	Yes
Price/earnings ratio (times)	18.4
Dividend yield (%)	4.2

Sydney-based IPH, with roots that stretch back to 1887, is a holding company for a group of businesses offering a wide range of intellectual property services and products. These include the filing, prosecution, enforcement and management of patents, designs, trademarks and other intellectual property. The company also develops data analytics software through its subsidiary Practice Insight. IPH operates from offices in Australia, New Zealand, Singapore, Malaysia, China, Indonesia, Thailand and Hong Kong. In August 2019 it acquired its listed rival Xenith IP Group.

Latest business results (June 2020, full year)

The Xenith acquisition helped push revenues and underlying profits higher, and the company also enjoyed organic growth from existing businesses. For reporting purposes the company segments its operations into Australian and New Zealand businesses and Asian businesses. The former now represents nearly three-quarters of total turnover, with revenues up substantially, thanks to the addition of Xenith. However, on a like-for-like basis, revenues and profits edged down, with a reduction in client filings and a decline in legal business for the Spruson & Ferguson intellectual property subsidiary. By contrast, Asian operations saw revenues and profits increase on a like-for-like basis, and with higher profit margins, thanks to continuing growth in patent filing activity. The continuing integration of Xenith businesses into the group delivered cost synergies of $3.5 million.

Outlook

IPH has established itself as one of the leaders in Australia, New Zealand and South-East Asia in the intellectual property business. It has expanded steadily, through organic growth and acquisition. As it grows it achieves economies of scale that boost margins. It has become the largest filer of patents in Singapore, where it opened an office in 1997. It classifies the US, Western Europe, Japan and South Korea as the primary markets in its business, and its expressed aim is to establish itself in other regions. Its $192 million acquisition of Xenith has boosted its share of the domestic intellectual property market from around 20 per cent to more than 35 per cent and is also expected to deliver cost synergies over three years that will further boost margins. It is achieving success with its strategy of leveraging its network of companies, and domestic subsidiaries are now among the foremost clients of its trademark and patent operations in Beijing and Hong Kong. IPH has announced the planned NZ$7.9 million acquisition of Baldwins, a leading New Zealand intellectual property specialist, and has said it is actively seeking further acquisitions.

Year to 30 June	2019	2020
Revenues ($mn)	256.6	369.6
EBIT ($mn)	86.3	111.3
EBIT margin (%)	33.6	30.1
Profit before tax ($mn)	83.7	104.2
Profit after tax ($mn)	62.9	77.7
Earnings per share (c)	31.87	36.68
Cash flow per share (c)	38.29	52.96
Dividend (c)	25	28.5
Percentage franked	55	100
Net tangible assets per share ($)	0.15	~
Interest cover (times)	33.6	15.8
Return on equity (%)	22.8	22.0
Debt-to-equity ratio (%)	10.6	18.8
Current ratio	3.9	3.0

IRESS Limited

ASX code: IRE

www.iress.com.au

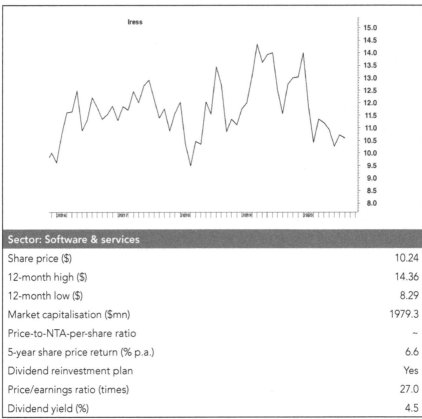

Sector: Software & services	
Share price ($)	10.24
12-month high ($)	14.36
12-month low ($)	8.29
Market capitalisation ($mn)	1979.3
Price-to-NTA-per-share ratio	~
5-year share price return (% p.a.)	6.6
Dividend reinvestment plan	Yes
Price/earnings ratio (times)	27.0
Dividend yield (%)	4.5

Melbourne-based IRESS was founded in 1993. It produces the IRESS (Integrated Real-time Equity System) share market information system, used widely throughout the Australian investment community. Within the IRESS system it offers a portfolio of information and trading products with numerous applications for stockbrokers, fund managers and other financial professionals. It is also active in wealth management services, with its Xplan financial planning software. A third activity is the Mortgages division, which provides mortgage processing software. The company has expanded its operations to New Zealand, Europe, North America, Singapore, Hong Kong and South Africa. In June 2020 it entered into a scheme of arrangement to acquire the ASX-listed financial technology company OneVue Holdings.

Latest business results (June 2020, half year)

Revenues rose, thanks to a strong performance in Australia and a full-year's contribution from the May 2019 acquisition of financial data specialist QuantHouse. A further contribution came from the acquisition in March 2020 of O&M Systems, a British supplier of market data to financial advisers. However, profits fell, reflecting losses in newly acquired businesses and increased staff costs due to the COVID-19 pandemic. The company also experienced weakness in its British mortgages business, due to project delays. South African operations grew a little in local currency, and the very small North American unit saw some strong growth.

Outlook

IRESS's businesses are strongly geared to levels of financial market activity, which can lead to volatility in its operations. It is also vulnerable to structural changes in the financial sector, with automated systems to a degree displacing active fund managers. Nevertheless, its products are widely used in Australia, and the company reports high levels of customer loyalty, with recurring revenues responsible for some 90 per cent of total turnover. It benefits from the steady growth of superannuation assets. It has been enjoying success with its Xplan Prime product for the financial planning industry. It also expects a rebound in its British mortgages business during the 2020 second half and 2021. Its acquisition of QuantHouse for 39 million euros has given it a highly complementary business. QuantHouse provides clients around the world with more than 145 data feeds of financial information, with an emphasis on Europe, North America and Asia. The $107 million bid to acquire OneVue will, if successful, give IRESS a strong position in the administration of funds, superannuation and investments. IRESS management believe it will also lead to the development of new software and services that bring greater efficiency and productivity for financial advisers.

Year to 31 December	2018	2019
Revenues ($mn)	464.6	508.9
EBIT ($mn)	91.1	96.6
EBIT margin (%)	19.6	19.0
Profit before tax ($mn)	85.0	88.5
Profit after tax ($mn)	64.1	65.1
Earnings per share (c)	37.60	37.87
Cash flow per share (c)	53.31	59.53
Dividend (c)	46	46
Percentage franked	47	30
Interest cover (times)	14.9	11.8
Return on equity (%)	15.5	15.2
Half year to 30 June	2019	2020
Revenues ($mn)	241.8	270.7
Profit before tax ($mn)	41.5	35.1
Profit after tax ($mn)	30.4	26.3
Earnings per share (c)	17.70	15.00
Dividend (c)	16	16
Percentage franked	10	35
Net tangible assets per share ($)	~	~
Debt-to-equity ratio (%)	47.4	8.7
Current ratio	1.1	1.7

JB Hi-Fi Limited

ASX code: JBH

investors.jbhifi.com.au

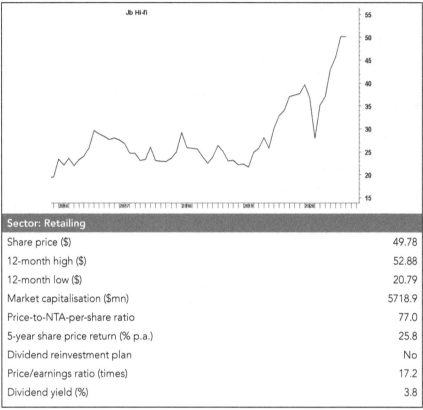

Sector: Retailing	
Share price ($)	49.78
12-month high ($)	52.88
12-month low ($)	20.79
Market capitalisation ($mn)	5718.9
Price-to-NTA-per-share ratio	77.0
5-year share price return (% p.a.)	25.8
Dividend reinvestment plan	No
Price/earnings ratio (times)	17.2
Dividend yield (%)	3.8

Melbourne-based JB Hi-Fi dates back to the opening in 1974 of a single recorded music store in the Melbourne suburb of East Keilor. It has since grown into a nationwide chain of home electronic and home appliance products outlets, and it has also expanded to New Zealand. In 2016 it acquired The Good Guys chain of home appliance stores. Its JB Hi-Fi Solutions division sells to the commercial, educational and insurance sectors. The company also maintains a growing online presence. At the end of June 2020 it operated 195 JB Hi-Fi and JB Hi-Fi Home stores in Australia, 14 JB Hi-Fi stores in New Zealand and 105 The Good Guys stores in Australia.

Latest business results (June 2020, full year)

In a volatile retail environment JB Hi-Fi posted an excellent result, with double-digit gains in sales and profits. At JB Hi-Fi Australia sales were up 12.5 per cent, as customers spent more time in their homes, generating strong demand for home entertainment hardware, computers and small appliances. Online sales grew by 57 per cent — including a 155 per cent surge in the fourth quarter — to a total of $404 million. By contrast, the small JB Hi-Fi New Zealand operation saw sales decline as lockdown measures forced the temporary closure of stores. This was only partially offset by a sharp rise in online business. The Good Guys division saw sales up 11.2 per cent, with strong demand for portable appliances, laundry and floorcare products, computers and televisions. Profits rose strongly at The Good Guys, though profit margins remained lower than those prevailing at the JB Hi-Fi Australia stores. During the year the company opened three new stores and closed four.

Outlook

JB Hi-Fi has a strong brand image throughout Australia and great customer loyalty. It has shown an impressive ability to contain costs. It continues to open new stores, though at a slower pace than in previous years. It is boosting floor space at its stores for growth categories such as mobile phones, gaming and connected technology. It is also working to strengthen its online operations, which surged during the June 2020 year to represent 7.5 per cent of total company turnover. It is in the process of consolidating and streamlining its supply chain, with a series of new home delivery centres. It believes its JB Hi-Fi Solutions division will eventually generate annual sales of around $500 million. It is working to turn around its underperforming New Zealand operations.

Year to 30 June	2019	2020
Revenues ($mn)	7095.3	7918.9
JB Australia (%)	67	67
The Good Guys (%)	30	30
JB New Zealand (%)	3	3
EBIT ($mn)	372.9	511.3
EBIT margin (%)	5.3	6.5
Gross margin (%)	21.5	21.4
Profit before tax ($mn)	359.3	476.0
Profit after tax ($mn)	249.8	332.7
Earnings per share (c)	217.41	289.56
Cash flow per share (c)	266.32	341.69
Dividend (c)	142	189
Percentage franked	100	100
Net tangible assets per share ($)	0.06	0.65
Interest cover (times)	27.4	14.5
Return on equity (%)	25.1	31.0
Debt-to-equity ratio (%)	30.6	~
Current ratio	1.4	0.9

Jumbo Interactive Limited

ASX code: JIN   www.jumbointeractive.com.au

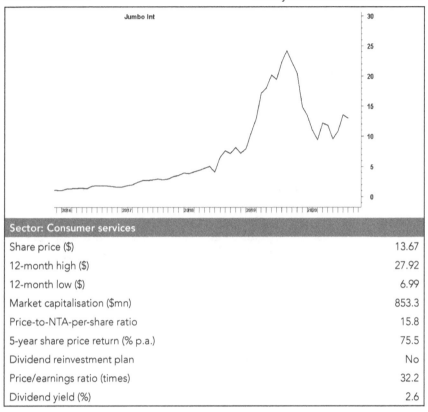

Sector: Consumer services	
Share price ($)	13.67
12-month high ($)	27.92
12-month low ($)	6.99
Market capitalisation ($mn)	853.3
Price-to-NTA-per-share ratio	15.8
5-year share price return (% p.a.)	75.5
Dividend reinvestment plan	No
Price/earnings ratio (times)	32.2
Dividend yield (%)	2.6

Jumbo Interactive was founded in Brisbane in 1995 as an internet service provider, but has since evolved into a major operator of internet services for lotteries. Its core business, Oz Lotteries, involves the sale of lottery services for Tabcorp at its ozlotteries.com website. These lotteries include OzLotto, Powerball, Lotto and Lucky Lotteries. It has introduced a Software-as-a-Service (SaaS) business, called Powered by Jumbo, that manages lotteries for charitable organisations. In November 2019 it entered the British market with the acquisition of lottery manager Gatherwell.

Latest business results (June 2020, full year)

Revenues rose, as the COVID-19 pandemic drove more lottery ticket buyers online, but profits marked time — having more than doubled in the previous year — as the company spent heavily on growth initiatives. Large Powerball jackpots are an important stimulus to increased sales, and there were 39 of these during the year, with an average value of $40.1 million, compared with 49, with an average value of $38.4

million, in the June 2019 year. Despite the smaller number of large jackpots — defined as a jackpot worth more than $15 million — the total transaction value during the year of all Jumbo's business was $348.6 million, up from $320.7 million in the previous year. This included a small contribution from the £3 million Gatherwell acquisition. The company reported that it had 827 411 active customers during the year, up from 761 863 in the previous year.

Outlook

Jumbo is a significant beneficiary of the Australian love of gambling. A new software platform and a vigorous marketing campaign have helped stimulate its recent growth. It is also enjoying success with new apps for mobile devices, and reports that these have succeeded in attracting a new demographic of younger customers. Consequently, 28 per cent of Australian lottery ticket sales are now online, up from 23.5 per cent in the June 2019 year. Jumbo has set itself an ambitious aspirational vision of annual ticket sales of $1 billion by the June 2022 year. It sees much of this growth coming from its new SaaS lottery software, and points to an addressable Australian market for charitable lotteries of $1 billion, with an additional $1.6 billion in the UK, where Gatherwell is one of the leaders in this business. However, it is the massive $22 billion American market that is the company's particular target, and it is seeking an acquisition or partnership opportunity there. Its target is that international sales will contribute at least half of company turnover by 2026.

Year to 30 June	2019	2020
Revenues ($mn)	65.2	71.2
EBIT ($mn)	36.8	37.2
EBIT margin (%)	56.4	52.3
Profit before tax ($mn)	38.2	38.0
Profit after tax ($mn)	26.4	26.5
Earnings per share (c)	43.86	42.47
Cash flow per share (c)	49.56	52.08
Dividend (c)	36.5	35.5
Percentage franked	100	100
Net tangible assets per share ($)	1.01	0.87
Interest cover (times)	~	~
Return on equity (%)	42.4	33.9
Debt-to-equity ratio (%)	~	~
Current ratio	3.6	3.2

Lifestyle Communities Limited

ASX code: LIC   www.lifestylecommunities.com.au

Sector: Real estate	
Share price ($)	9.22
12-month high ($)	9.87
12-month low ($)	4.53
Market capitalisation ($mn)	963.9
Price-to-NTA-per-share ratio	3.3
5-year share price return (% p.a.)	29.5
Dividend reinvestment plan	No
Price/earnings ratio (times)	22.5
Dividend yield (%)	0.6

Melbourne company Lifestyle Communities, founded in 2003, develops and maintains residential and retirement communities throughout Victoria, in growth areas of Melbourne and in regional centres. These are aimed at over-50s and retirees. At June 2020 it had completed 12 communities. Five more communities were under development and a further five were awaiting commencement. Altogether the company was managing more than 2500 homes.

Latest business results (June 2020, full year)

The COVID-19 pandemic hit Lifestyle Communities, with the lockdown of many of its facilities and a sharp slowing of business activity. This was compounded by planning delays and road access issues in the first half. Consequently, the company settled 253 new homes, below its target of 270 to 310 and down from 337 in the previous year. Profits were also hit by lower non-cash property revaluation gains. However, the growing number of homes under management and a 3.5 per cent rental fee increase meant that total rental fees received from the occupants of the company's homes rose from $18.9 million to $23 million. Deferred management fees, from the resale of existing homes, rose from $3.5 million to $5.2 million. During the year the company sold 280 new homes, up from 209 in the previous year, with an average price of $410 000, up from $401 000. At June 2020 it had 257 homes sold but not settled.

Outlook

Lifestyle Communities operates on a model that differs from many retirement facilities, in that its residents own their homes but pay a rental charge to the company for the land, on a 90-year lease. It thus has a growing annuity-style income as its business expands. It promotes its communities to active seniors, and the average age of new residents is around 67, which is about 10 years younger than the average age for new residents of retirement homes generally in Australia. Its goal has been to buy two new sites each year, focused on Melbourne's growth corridors and on key Victorian regional centres, although in the June 2020 year it actually acquired four new sites. These were at St Leonards, Pakenham, Clyde and Clyde North. It is actively developing new communities at Mount Duneed, Plumpton, Wollert, Kaduna Park and St Leonards, and expects to settle some 900 to 1100 homes over the three years to June 2023. As the company expands, its rental income will increase. In addition, the number of resales — sales of established homes — will also grow, boosting its deferred management fee income.

Year to 30 June	2019	2020
Revenues ($mn)	144.0	126.9
EBIT ($mn)	81.1	62.1
EBIT margin (%)	56.3	48.9
Gross margin (%)	24.8	21.7
Profit before tax ($mn)	79.7	61.1
Profit after tax ($mn)	55.1	42.8
Earnings per share (c)	52.67	40.96
Cash flow per share (c)	53.34	41.91
Dividend (c)	5.5	5.5
Percentage franked	100	100
Net tangible assets per share ($)	2.44	2.78
Interest cover (times)	57.9	62.1
Return on equity (%)	24.0	15.7
Debt-to-equity ratio (%)	37.3	44.1
Current ratio	1.1	1.8

Macquarie Group Limited

ASX code: MQG   www.macquarie.com

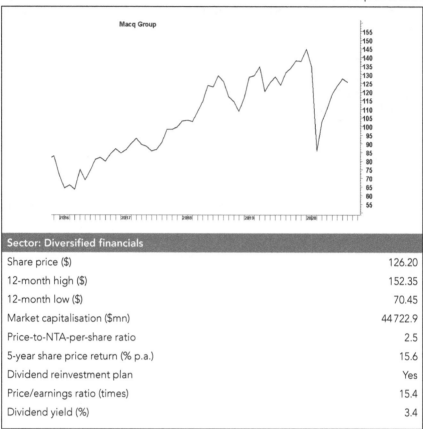

Sector: Diversified financials	
Share price ($)	126.20
12-month high ($)	152.35
12-month low ($)	70.45
Market capitalisation ($mn)	44 722.9
Price-to-NTA-per-share ratio	2.5
5-year share price return (% p.a.)	15.6
Dividend reinvestment plan	Yes
Price/earnings ratio (times)	15.4
Dividend yield (%)	3.4

Sydney-based Macquarie Group was established in 1969 as Hill Samuel Australia, a subsidiary of a British merchant bank. It is now Australia's leading locally owned investment bank, with a wide spread of activities and boasting special expertise in specific industries that include resources and commodities, energy, financial institutions, infrastructure and real estate. It has offices in 31 markets around the world, and international business accounts for around two-thirds of total company income.

Latest business results (March 2020, full year)

Profits fell after two straight years of double-digit rises. This reflected a high level of asset sales in the March 2019 year, along with the early impact of the COVID-19 pandemic. The bank now classifies its operations into four operating groups. Macquarie Asset Management, one of its core businesses, delivered an excellent result, with profits up 16 per cent, thanks to increased base and performance fees and higher investment income. At March 2020 this division held assets of $606 billion, up

10 per cent from a year earlier. A smaller division, Banking and Financial Services, which serves the Australian market, recorded a 2 per cent rise in profits, with growth in most areas of banking. The Commodities and Global Markets division saw profits flat from the previous year, with higher impairment charges and reduced trading revenues offset by strong global client contributions across all products and sectors. However, the Macquarie Capital division reported a sharp 57 per cent decline in profits, due in large part to strong asset realisations in the previous year, along with higher operating costs and impairment charges.

Outlook

At a time of global economic uncertainty, Macquarie is not prepared to make forecasts for the March 2021 year. More than 60 per cent of its profits are in the form of stable, annuity-style earnings, which reduces risk. Nevertheless, it expects costs to rise. It has been allowing personal and small business banking clients to defer a range of loan repayments. It also expects to be affected by subdued customer activity, especially in the commodities sector, and by delays in the timing of asset sales. In addition, profits are dampened by any appreciation in the value of the Australian dollar. But the longer-term outlook is rosy as the bank continues to push ahead with new projects. Its acquisition of Société Générale's energy commodities portfolio has boosted its strength in gas and power markets. It is also becoming a leader in green energy, with more than 250 projects under development or construction at March 2020.

Year to 31 March	2019	2020
Operating income ($mn)	12754.0	12325.0
Net interest income ($mn)	1760.0	1859.0
Operating expenses ($mn)	8887.0	8871.0
Profit before tax ($mn)	3867.0	3454.0
Profit after tax ($mn)	2982.0	2731.0
Earnings per share (c)	920.36	819.54
Dividend (c)	575	430
Percentage franked	45	40
Non-interest income to total income (%)	86.2	84.9
Net tangible assets per share ($)	46.21	50.21
Cost-to-income ratio (%)	69.7	72.0
Return on equity (%)	17.5	14.1
Return on assets (%)	1.5	1.2

Magellan Financial Group Limited

ASX code: MFG   www.magellangroup.com.au

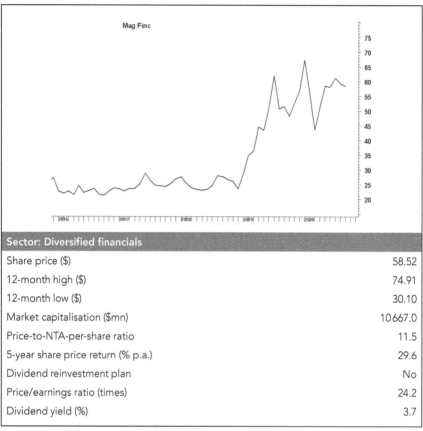

Sector: Diversified financials	
Share price ($)	58.52
12-month high ($)	74.91
12-month low ($)	30.10
Market capitalisation ($mn)	10667.0
Price-to-NTA-per-share ratio	11.5
5-year share price return (% p.a.)	29.6
Dividend reinvestment plan	No
Price/earnings ratio (times)	24.2
Dividend yield (%)	3.7

Sydney-based Magellan is a specialist investment management company that evolved in 2006 from the ASX-listed Pengana Hedgefunds Limited. Its main business is Magellan Asset Management, which offers managed funds to retail and institutional investors, with particular specialties in global equities, infrastructure, Australian equities — through Airlie Funds Management, which it acquired in 2018 — and sustainable asset investments.

Latest business results (June 2020, full year)

Magellan overcame a highly volatile second half to post another excellent result. Management and services fees rose 25 per cent to $592 million. However, performance fees edged down by 3 per cent to $81 million, having more than doubled in the previous year. Once again the company achieved success in containing its basic costs, and its cost-to-income ratio fell to an impressive 19.7 per cent, down from

21.3 per cent a year earlier. At June 2020 Magellan had funds under management of $97.2 billion, up from $86.7 billion a year earlier, thanks to a solid investment performance and net inflows of $5.7 billion. Note that the profits in the table in this book are underlying profits. On a statutory basis, the after-tax profit rose by 5 per cent to $396 million.

Outlook

Magellan continues to expand impressively, and funds under management exceed those of two rivals, Platinum Asset Management and Perpetual. It has a record of strong, long-term performance in global equities, and has become a significant beneficiary of moves by Australian investors to diversify into overseas markets. It also benefits from the reputation and stock-picking prowess of its Chairman and Chief Investment Officer Hamish Douglass. Nevertheless, it remains heavily dependent on the state of financial markets, and it would suffer from any big sell-off in equities, or from a prolonged bear market. In addition, as its funds swell in size it becomes increasingly difficult for its fund managers to find the new investments needed to continue outperforming its benchmarks. It plans to consolidate three global equities funds into a single trust with a market value of some $15 billion, making it the largest listed trust on the ASX. It is launching a low-fee family of funds called MFG Core, aimed at competing with passive fund managers. It has also developed a major new fund aimed at retirees seeking income from their assets, and is waiting for final regulatory approval. In another initiative, it sees great potential in investment in global sustainable assets, and plans to make its Magellan Sustainable Fund available to retail investors by the end of 2020.

Year to 30 June	2019	2020
Revenues ($mn)	556.1	672.6
EBIT ($mn)	470.7	570.6
EBIT margin (%)	84.6	84.8
Profit before tax ($mn)	473.2	573.2
Profit after tax ($mn)	364.2	438.3
Earnings per share (c)	205.92	241.46
Cash flow per share (c)	208.71	245.37
Dividend (c)	185.2	214.9
Percentage franked	75	75
Net tangible assets per share ($)	3.44	5.08
Interest cover (times)	~	~
Return on equity (%)	53.8	49.2
Debt-to-equity ratio (%)	~	~
Current ratio	6.2	9.8

McPherson's Limited

ASX code: MCP   www.mcphersons.com.au

Sector: Household & personal products	
Share price ($)	3.02
12-month high ($)	3.40
12-month low ($)	1.30
Market capitalisation ($mn)	323.9
Price-to-NTA-per-share ratio	12.7
5-year share price return (% p.a.)	40.5
Dividend reinvestment plan	Yes
Price/earnings ratio (times)	19.8
Dividend yield (%)	3.6

Melbourne-based McPherson's, established in 1860, is a supplier of health, wellness and beauty products. Its brands include Manicare, Lady Jayne, Dr. LeWinn's, A'kin, Glam by Manicare, Swisspers, Moosehead, Maseur and Multix. The company also distributes the products of some external manufacturers. It sells to major retail chains, independent stores and pharmacies, with extensive operations in both Australia and New Zealand. It also has a small business in Singapore, focused on personal care products and household consumables. A branch in Hong Kong manages contract manufacturing.

Latest business results (June 2020, full year)

Sales and profits rose in a solid result. Once again the main driver of growth was the skin, hair and body category, thanks especially to surging demand for Dr. LeWinn's products. This brand is growing in popularity in China, and export sales there soared by 130 per cent. Domestically the brand achieved 18 per cent growth. The company's largest market segment, household essentials, achieved 2 per cent sales growth, thanks to continuing good demand for the Multix range of products. The essential beauty segment recorded 1 per cent revenues growth, with a decline in demand for Lady Jayne products offset by strength in the Manicare line. Agency brands saw a sharp decline in business, following the termination of agency agreements with the Trilogy and Karen Murrell brands.

Outlook

Following a major restructuring of its operations, McPherson's is now focusing on three broad segments, health, wellness and beauty. It sees particular potential for its Dr. LeWinn's line of anti-ageing skincare products. Thanks to an agreement with a Chinese marketing agency, ABM, Dr. LeWinn's sales in China have grown from $0.5 million in the June 2017 year to $37.2 million in June 2020. The company maintains an extensive research and development capability to develop new products, with an emphasis on the high-growth skincare segment. A new partnership with Woolworths will provide increased visibility and scale for a range of A'kin natural beauty products. McPherson's hopes to move into new product areas in joint ventures with key retail partners. Recently launched new products are the Kotia range of deer milk cosmetics, Sugar Baby tanning and skincare products, and the Soulful range of dried fruit snacks, infused honey and adult milk powders. A review of the company's supply chain and distribution network is expected to generate annual savings of up to $2 million from the June 2022 year. McPherson's has expressed interest in further bolt-on acquisitions or merger opportunities that will extend its product offerings.

Year to 30 June	2019	2020
Revenues ($mn)	210.3	222.2
Household essentials & others (%)	30	29
Skin, hair & body (%)	19	29
Essential beauty (%)	27	26
Private label (%)	13	10
Agency brands (%)	11	6
EBIT ($mn)	19.9	25.1
EBIT margin (%)	9.4	11.3
Profit before tax ($mn)	19.0	24.0
Profit after tax ($mn)	13.7	16.3
Earnings per share (c)	13.02	15.29
Cash flow per share (c)	15.04	19.87
Dividend (c)	10	11
Percentage franked	100	100
Net tangible assets per share ($)	0.21	0.24
Interest cover (times)	22.4	21.8
Return on equity (%)	14.7	17.5
Debt-to-equity ratio (%)	7.7	10.2
Current ratio	1.9	1.5

Medibank Private Limited

ASX code: MPL   www.medibank.com.au

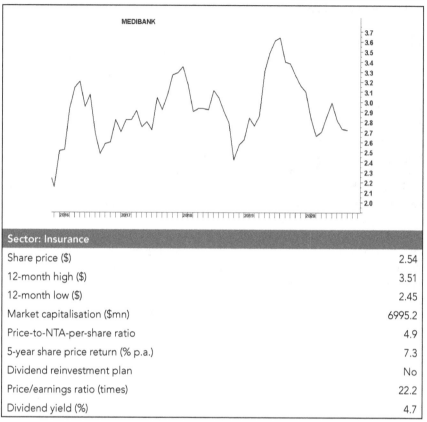

Sector: Insurance	
Share price ($)	2.54
12-month high ($)	3.51
12-month low ($)	2.45
Market capitalisation ($mn)	6995.2
Price-to-NTA-per-share ratio	4.9
5-year share price return (% p.a.)	7.3
Dividend reinvestment plan	No
Price/earnings ratio (times)	22.2
Dividend yield (%)	4.7

Melbourne-based Medibank Private was established by the Australian government in 1976 as a not-for-profit private health insurer under the Health Insurance Commission. It was privatised and listed on the ASX in 2014. Today it is Australia's largest private health insurer, with a market share of 27 per cent, operating under the Medibank and ahm brands. It has also branched into other areas, including travel insurance, pet insurance, life insurance, income protection and funeral insurance. Its Medibank Health division specialises in the provision of healthcare services over the phone, online or face-to-face.

Latest business results (June 2020, full year)

Revenues edged up, as member numbers continued to grow, but profits fell sharply. Total policyholder numbers grew by 10 600 during the year, although most of this increase was concentrated in the budget ahm health insurance brand. Premium revenues rose 1.3 per cent. The company also reported a pleasing 3 per cent decline in management expenses for the year. However, profits were hit by a combination of rising insurance claims, the COVID-19 pandemic and a low return from the company's investment portfolio. Medibank paid out $5.24 billion in claims from its members, up 3 per cent from the previous year, and despite a slowdown in claims during parts of 2020, when some elective surgery was postponed. It recognised a liability of $297.1 million related to these postponed claims. In addition, the pandemic led to the postponement of planned premium increases and the introduction of a $185 million support package for members. The very small Medibank Health division saw its profits up 26 per cent.

Outlook

Medibank occupies a central role in the national health sector. Nevertheless, its business is heavily regulated, and it is difficult to achieve significant growth. In addition, as the population ages, customer claim volumes have been growing, often faster than premium rises. Maintaining a tight control on expenses is important for the company, and it has a target of $50 million in annual productivity savings in the three years to June 2023. It has introduced new dental and optical networks, with reduced rates for members, along with an enhanced rewards program. It has significantly boosted its telehealth services, and it has launched pilot programs to reduce costs by providing medical and rehabilitation services at a patient's home. The company's target is for growth in member numbers of up to 1 per cent in the June 2021 year, with a market share gain of up to 1 per cent.

Year to 30 June	2019	2020
Revenues ($mn)	6655.8	6769.6
EBIT ($mn)	573.4	453.6
EBIT margin (%)	8.6	6.7
Profit before tax ($mn)	616.3	450.2
Profit after tax ($mn)	437.7	315.6
Earnings per share (c)	15.89	11.46
Cash flow per share (c)	19.67	16.07
Dividend (c)	13.1	12
Percentage franked	100	100
Net tangible assets per share ($)	0.56	0.52
Interest cover (times)	~	133.4
Return on equity (%)	23.3	16.8
Debt-to-equity ratio (%)	~	~
Current ratio	2.1	1.8

Mineral Resources Limited

ASX code: MIN   www.mineralresources.com.au

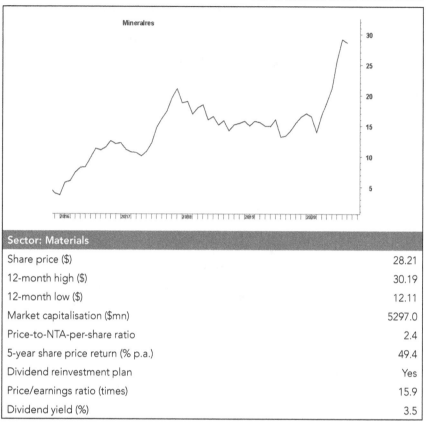

Sector: Materials	
Share price ($)	28.21
12-month high ($)	30.19
12-month low ($)	12.11
Market capitalisation ($mn)	5297.0
Price-to-NTA-per-share ratio	2.4
5-year share price return (% p.a.)	49.4
Dividend reinvestment plan	Yes
Price/earnings ratio (times)	15.9
Dividend yield (%)	3.5

Mineral Resources, based in Perth, was founded in 1993, and is a mining and mining services company. Its mining services side operates through a group of three subsidiaries. They are PIHA, a leader in specialist pipeline engineering and construction; CSI Mining Services, which provides contract crushing, screening and processing services to the resources sector; and Process Minerals International, a minerals processor and exporter, with a specialty in bringing new mines into production on behalf of owners. The company's mining side comprises iron ore production assets and holdings in the Wodgina lithium mine and the Mount Marion lithium project.

Latest business results (June 2020, full year)

Mineral Resources enjoyed an excellent year, with strong gains in revenues and profits. The key was the company's iron ore business, which benefited from increased production and higher prices. Total iron ore sales of 14.08 million tonnes were up 33 per cent from the previous year, thanks to a 134 per cent surge in sales from the company's Koolyanobbing mine. The average price received by the company of

$110.30 per tonne was up 22 per cent from the June 2019 year. By contrast, lithium operations remained weak. The company's mining services operations performed very well, with substantial increases in revenues and profits, thanks especially to work on ramping up the Koolyanobbing mine and growth in external haulage and mining contracts. In addition to the figures in this book, the company reported a $1.3 billion pre-tax profit from the sale to Albermarle Corporation of the United States of a 60 per cent stake in its Wodgina lithium mine.

Outlook

Mineral Resources is actively seeking to expand its iron ore exposure and believes it could boost annual sales to 40 million tonnes within two years and to 60 million tonnes within four years. However, this is dependent on it being allowed to build new shipping berths at Port Hedland, and it is engaged in talks on this matter with the West Australian government. It sees particularly strong potential for its Wodgina lithium mine, the world's largest known hard-rock lithium deposit, with a mine life of as much as 50 years. However, it has suspended operations there until lithium prices recover. It is experiencing strong growth in demand for its mining services activities, and believes this business could double in size by June 2022. Following the sale of a stake in its Wodgina lithium mine, Mineral Resources at June 2020 had net cash holdings of more than $230 million.

Year to 30 June	2019	2020
Revenues ($mn)	1512.0	2124.7
EBIT ($mn)	324.4	571.5
EBIT margin (%)	21.5	26.9
Profit before tax ($mn)	293.0	481.0
Profit after tax ($mn)	205.0	334.0
Earnings per share (c)	109.08	177.35
Cash flow per share (c)	166.89	280.15
Dividend (c)	44	100
Percentage franked	100	100
Net tangible assets per share ($)	6.81	11.81
Interest cover (times)	10.3	6.3
Return on equity (%)	15.5	18.4
Debt-to-equity ratio (%)	63.1	~
Current ratio	2.8	2.0

MNF Group Limited

ASX code: MNF

mnfgroup.limited

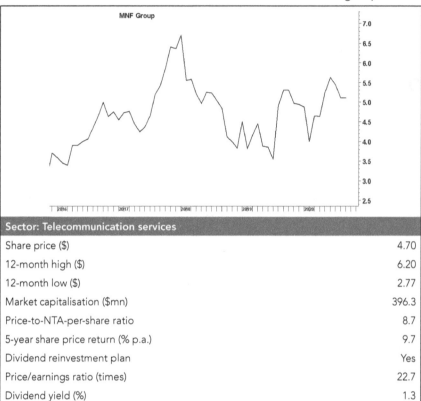

Sector: Telecommunication services	
Share price ($)	4.70
12-month high ($)	6.20
12-month low ($)	2.77
Market capitalisation ($mn)	396.3
Price-to-NTA-per-share ratio	8.7
5-year share price return (% p.a.)	9.7
Dividend reinvestment plan	Yes
Price/earnings ratio (times)	22.7
Dividend yield (%)	1.3

Sydney telecommunications services provider MNF Group, formerly known as My Net Fone, dates back to 2004. Its largest business, Global Wholesale, comprises the TNZI international voice traffic operation and the Tollshield and OpenCA toll fraud prevention brands. The Domestic Wholesale division includes the core Symbio and iBoss brands, providing retail service providers and IT companies in Australia and New Zealand with a range of telecommunications products and services. The Direct division incorporates many brands, including MNF Enterprise, Supernet, Connexus, Express Virtual Meetings, Pennytel and MyNetFone, and provides telecommunications services to residential, business and government customers in Australia, New Zealand and Singapore.

Latest business results (June 2020, full year)

Revenues and profits rose as MNF became a beneficiary of the COVID-19 pandemic, thanks to its role in providing the phone numbers needed in voice communication technology. All the growth came in the company's Domestic Wholesale division, with sales up 32 per cent to $90 million and the gross profit jumping 41 per cent. This business benefited strongly from fast-growing demand during the pandemic for phone numbers and voice minutes. The Global Wholesale division saw a 4 per cent decline in revenues, with gross profit down 11 per cent. The Direct division recorded a 7 per cent decline in sales, with gross profit down 23 per cent. This partially reflected the divestiture in May 2019 of some of the company's residential customer base. During the year MNF's high-margin recurring revenues rose 27 per cent to $101.5 million.

Outlook

One of MNF's key businesses is providing connectivity for companies like Zoom, so that people can access a video conference from their own telephones. It provides temporary phone numbers for this purpose. This business has seen strong growth due to the COVID-19 pandemic, and there are many indications that teleconferencing is set to continue growing. In the June 2020 year the company issued 4.5 million phone numbers, a 17 per cent increase from the previous year. MNF believes its Global Wholesale division offers the best potential for long-term growth, through building a strong business in the Asia-Pacific region. Its 2018 acquisition of the niche Singapore telecommunications company SuperInternet Group was part of this strategy, and it expects to begin trials in Singapore in December 2020 of a range of its services, with a full production launch in March 2021. A second growth strategy is an expansion of the company's portfolio of communications software products and services. It is also working to strengthen long-term relationships with wholesale customers.

Year to 30 June	2019	2020
Revenues ($mn)	215.6	230.9
Global wholesale (%)	52	46
Domestic wholesale (%)	31	39
Direct (%)	17	15
EBIT ($mn)	20.3	24.1
EBIT margin (%)	9.4	10.4
Gross margin (%)	38.3	41.8
Profit before tax ($mn)	18.6	21.3
Profit after tax ($mn)	14.1	16.6
Earnings per share (c)	19.23	20.68
Cash flow per share (c)	31.47	40.75
Dividend (c)	6.1	6.1
Percentage franked	100	100
Net tangible assets per share ($)	~	0.54
Interest cover (times)	11.6	8.7
Return on equity (%)	17.5	15.0
Debt-to-equity ratio (%)	47.5	~
Current ratio	1.6	2.2

Money3 Corporation Limited

ASX code: MNY   investors.money3.com.au

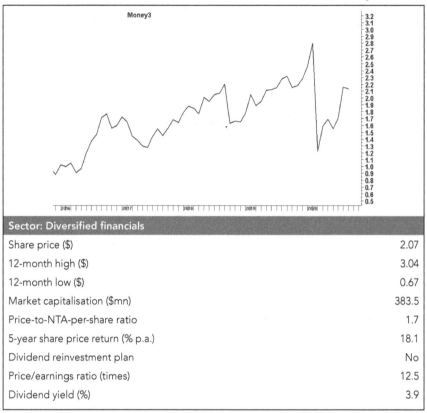

Sector: Diversified financials	
Share price ($)	2.07
12-month high ($)	3.04
12-month low ($)	0.67
Market capitalisation ($mn)	383.5
Price-to-NTA-per-share ratio	1.7
5-year share price return (% p.a.)	18.1
Dividend reinvestment plan	No
Price/earnings ratio (times)	12.5
Dividend yield (%)	3.9

Melbourne-based moneylender Money3 was formally established in 2005 through the consolidation of nine separate loans businesses operating in Melbourne and Geelong. In 2019 it sold its online and branch-based small-loans business, and now specialises in vehicle loans of up to $75 000 and personal loans up to $12 000. It has entered the New Zealand car loans business with the acquisition in March 2019 of Go Car Finance.

Latest business results (June 2020, full year)

A full year's contribution from Go Car Finance and continuing strong business in Australia generated a good result, despite the impact of the COVID-19 pandemic. Australian revenues rose 21 per cent to $102.8 million, with New Zealand revenues more than trebling to $21.3 million and a big jump in profits. Nevertheless, New Zealand profit margins were substantially lower than those in Australia. During the year the company advanced $247.7 million in loans and collected $277.2 million. The company reported that at a time of uncertainty many customers made efforts to increase their loan repayments, and in some cases even pay out their loans. At June

2020 the gross loan book of $433.8 million was up from $372.8 million a year earlier. Virtually all the growth in the loan book occurred in the first half.

Outlook

With its origins as a provider of short-term unsecured loans, also known as payday lending, Money3 had come under some government and social pressures, with questions raised about the ethics of its activities. Consequently, it had been working to transform itself into a diversified financial services company. It is now mainly a specialist provider of vehicle finance. The Australian market for consumer vehicle financing is estimated at around $20 billion annually, with $6.3 billion for used vehicles, and Money3 sees substantial scope for growth. It is investing in new digital systems to lower operating costs and is introducing new products. It has established a team that aims at lifting the number of returning customers. With the exit from the short-term loans business, the company's quality of earnings has been enhanced, and it expects that this will reduce its costs of funding. It sees significant scope for growth in the buoyant New Zealand used car sector, and is considering initiatives that include the introduction of profit-sharing agreements with vehicle dealers. It has also expressed a willingness to consider further acquisitions. Its target is for a loan book of $500 million by June 2021, rising to $1 billion by June 2024.

Year to 30 June	2019	2020
Revenues ($mn)	91.7	124.0
EBIT ($mn)	46.9	58.3
EBIT margin (%)	51.1	47.0
Profit before tax ($mn)	35.3	43.7
Profit after tax ($mn)	24.2	30.3
Earnings per share (c)	13.48	16.50
Cash flow per share (c)	13.82	17.52
Dividend (c)	10	8
Percentage franked	100	100
Net tangible assets per share ($)	1.19	1.23
Interest cover (times)	4.1	4.0
Return on equity (%)	10.5	12.4
Debt-to-equity ratio (%)	41.4	50.1
Current ratio	12.8	10.8

Mortgage Choice Limited

ASX code: MOC

www.mortgagechoice.com.au

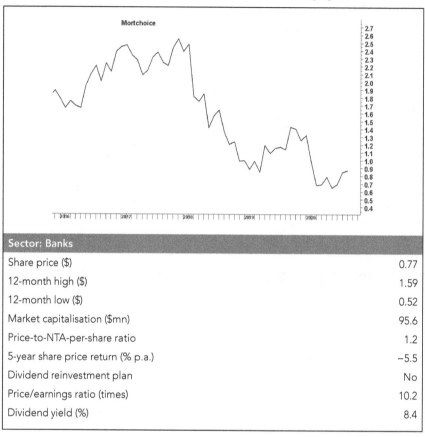

Sector: Banks	
Share price ($)	0.77
12-month high ($)	1.59
12-month low ($)	0.52
Market capitalisation ($mn)	95.6
Price-to-NTA-per-share ratio	1.2
5-year share price return (% p.a.)	−5.5
Dividend reinvestment plan	No
Price/earnings ratio (times)	10.2
Dividend yield (%)	8.4

Sydney company Mortgage Choice, established in 1992, is today one of the country's largest mortgage brokers. It works through a national network of hundreds of franchises and loan consultants, supported by its own offices and providing advice on mortgages, personal loans, commercial loans, equipment finance and insurance products. The company also operates the FinChoice financial planning business.

Latest business results (June 2020, full year)

Continuing weakness in the housing mortgage business — due in part to bushfires and the COVID-19 pandemic — sent revenues and profits lower for another year. Profits were also affected by the impact of a new broker remuneration model, introduced in August 2018, and by an increase in operating expenses. During the year the company settled home loans worth $10 billion, up 7 per cent from the previous year. At June 2020 the loan book totalled $54 billion, down from $54.3 billion. Its share of the national home loans market held steady at 3.4 per cent. FinChoice — the new name for the Mortgage Choice Financial Planning operation — represented about 5 per cent of total company income. It saw revenues down and it reported a loss for the year. However, FinChoice's underlying business continued to grow, with funds under advice at June 2020 of $1.1 billion, up 15 per cent from the previous year. Mortgage Choice also reported what it called a cash-adjusted financial result, and on this basis its after-tax profit fell from $12.9 million in June 2019 to $12.4 million. At June 2020 the company managed a mortgage broking network of 385 franchisees, down from 391 a year earlier.

Outlook

Mortgage Choice is well established throughout Australia, at a time when the use of mortgage brokers represents about 55 per cent of the housing market. It was a beneficiary of a buoyant housing environment lasting many years, thanks especially to low interest rates and a firm economy. It has reported a steady improvement in market conditions, with settlements in the June 2020 quarter up by 18 per cent over the June 2019 quarter. It has been investing heavily in new technology, and has considerably streamlined and automated many aspects of its loan processing and client communication procedures. A strategic review conducted during the June 2020 year is expected to lead to further technological innovations. It is endeavouring to boost its broking network, with the recruitment of new franchisees. It is also working to build its financial planning business, investing in technology that enables advisers to deliver cost-effective advice.

Year to 30 June	2019	2020
Revenues ($mn)	174.4	172.8
EBIT ($mn)	19.3	13.1
EBIT margin (%)	11.1	7.6
Profit before tax ($mn)	19.9	13.6
Profit after tax ($mn)	13.7	9.4
Earnings per share (c)	10.98	7.54
Cash flow per share (c)	12.69	10.70
Dividend (c)	6	6.5
Percentage franked	100	100
Net tangible assets per share ($)	0.62	0.63
Interest cover (times)	~	~
Return on equity (%)	15.9	10.7
Debt-to-equity ratio (%)	0.7	~
Current ratio	1.3	1.3

NIB Holdings Limited

ASX code: NHF www.nib.com.au

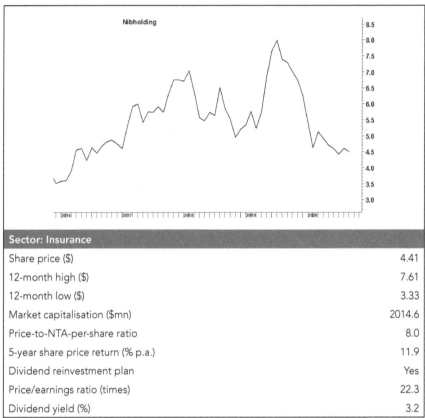

Sector: Insurance	
Share price ($)	4.41
12-month high ($)	7.61
12-month low ($)	3.33
Market capitalisation ($mn)	2014.6
Price-to-NTA-per-share ratio	8.0
5-year share price return (% p.a.)	11.9
Dividend reinvestment plan	Yes
Price/earnings ratio (times)	22.3
Dividend yield (%)	3.2

Newcastle private health insurer NIB Holdings was established as the Newcastle Industrial Benefits Hospital Fund in 1952 by workers at the BHP steelworks. It subsequently demutualised and became the first private health insurer to list on the ASX. It is also active in New Zealand. Other businesses are travel insurance and the provision of specialist insurance services to international students and workers in Australia.

Latest business results (June 2020, full year)

Revenues rose but profits crashed as the company was hit by rising claims from its members and by losses in its travel insurance business. The company's flagship Australian Residents Health Insurance (ARHI) saw premium revenues increase by 2.9 per cent to $2.1 billion. This growth would have been higher but for the postponement of planned price rises. Policyholder numbers grew by 1.9 per cent, compared with industry growth of just 0.4 per cent. However, these figures were outstripped by net claims expenses, up 5.3 per cent, and profits for this business fell. ARHI represents about 85 per cent of company revenues and 80 per cent of company profit. New Zealand health insurance represents a further 10 per cent of company turnover. This business enjoyed a strong year, with double-digit increases in revenues and profits. The company's high-margin health insurance program for international students and workers in Australia was hit by border closures. Nevertheless, revenues continued to grow, although profits fell sharply. But the tiny travel insurance business, representing less than 0.5 per cent of company turnover, generated a large loss.

Outlook

NIB continues to see its policyholder base grow faster than the industry average. It benefits from its New Zealand exposure, where it is the country's second-largest health insurer. It has expressed the belief that the COVID-19 pandemic has heightened community awareness of the risk of disease and the need for insurance protection. Nevertheless, as the population ages, it faces growing numbers of claims from its members, at a time when healthcare costs are rising rapidly. As a regulated industry it faces restrictions in how much it can raise its premiums in response. Further, as premiums rise a process of member attrition sets in, with younger members especially likely to exit. It is working to cut costs and branch into new areas of business. It has launched a new joint venture company, Honeysuckle Health, aimed at using data analytics to deliver healthcare programs. It has also formed a partnership with Chinese pharmaceuticals company Tasly to enter the Chinese health insurance market.

Year to 30 June	2019	2020
Premium revenues ($mn)	2372.6	2473.1
EBIT ($mn)	211.5	129.1
EBIT margin (%)	8.9	5.2
Profit before tax ($mn)	213.0	125.0
Profit after tax ($mn)	149.8	90.1
Earnings per share (c)	32.89	19.75
Cash flow per share (c)	38.34	25.83
Dividend (c)	23	14
Percentage franked	100	100
Net tangible assets per share ($)	0.59	0.55
Interest cover (times)	~	31.5
Return on equity (%)	25.6	15.0
Debt-to-equity ratio (%)	15.7	5.8
Current ratio	1.9	1.7

Nick Scali Limited

ASX code: NCK www.nickscali.com.au

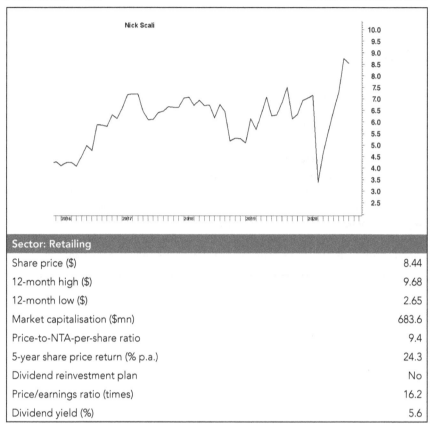

Sector: Retailing	
Share price ($)	8.44
12-month high ($)	9.68
12-month low ($)	2.65
Market capitalisation ($mn)	683.6
Price-to-NTA-per-share ratio	9.4
5-year share price return (% p.a.)	24.3
Dividend reinvestment plan	No
Price/earnings ratio (times)	16.2
Dividend yield (%)	5.6

Sydney-based Nick Scali is one of Australia's largest furniture importers and retailers, with a history dating back more than 50 years. It specialises in leather and fabric lounge suites along with dining room and bedroom furniture. It has six distribution centres and at June 2020 operated 58 Nick Scali Furniture stores, including three in New Zealand, and five Nick Scali Clearance stores.

Latest business results (June 2020, full year)

Revenues edged down and profits were generally flat in a challenging retail environment. The company estimated that it lost $9 million to $11 million in sales due to store closures during COVID-19-related lockdowns in Australia and New Zealand, and on a same-store basis sales fell by nearly 7 per cent. It was the third straight year for same-store sales to decline. It also experienced delays of up to four weeks in its supply chain from Asia. However, it was able to boost profit margins through reductions in full-time staff numbers, negotiated rental concessions and the receipt of government wage subsidies. In April 2020 it responded to the pandemic with the launch of an online store, and this generated $3 million in revenues in the three months to June 2020. During the year the company opened one new store, in New Zealand.

Outlook

Nick Scali is directly affected by trends in consumer spending, interest rates, currency movements, housing sales and renovation activity, and the general economy. It has reported that from April to July 2020 it experienced monthly order inflow growth of more than 70 per cent, compared with April to July 2019. With around two-thirds of the company's products made to order, and with delivery times of up to three months, this sharp increase in business is expected to generate a 50 per cent to 60 per cent rise in profits for the December 2020 half. Nick Scali continues to grow, with an eventual target of 80 to 85 stores throughout Australia and New Zealand. It expects to open two new stores during the December 2020 half, one in Auckland and one in Bennetts Green, New South Wales. In addition, it has purchased a retail property in Adelaide that will become its flagship store in that city, replacing an existing store. It is also working to expand its new online store, with the target of a $4 million EBIT contribution for the June 2021 year. At June 2020 Nick Scali had net cash holdings of more than $29 million.

Year to 30 June	2019	2020
Revenues ($mn)	268.0	262.5
EBIT ($mn)	59.9	67.1
EBIT margin (%)	22.3	25.6
Gross margin (%)	62.9	62.7
Profit before tax ($mn)	59.7	60.2
Profit after tax ($mn)	42.1	42.1
Earnings per share (c)	52.00	51.95
Cash flow per share (c)	57.25	88.97
Dividend (c)	45	47.5
Percentage franked	100	100
Net tangible assets per share ($)	1.02	0.90
Interest cover (times)	264.9	9.7
Return on equity (%)	49.9	52.4
Debt-to-equity ratio (%)	~	~
Current ratio	1.3	1.1

Northern Star Resources Limited

ASX code: NST   www.nsrltd.com

Sector: Materials	
Share price ($)	13.15
12-month high ($)	16.77
12-month low ($)	8.85
Market capitalisation ($mn)	9733.0
Price-to-NTA-per-share ratio	4.6
5-year share price return (% p.a.)	47.8
Dividend reinvestment plan	No
Price/earnings ratio (times)	35.3
Dividend yield (%)	1.3

Perth-based Northern Star Resources, one of Australia's largest gold producers, was founded in 2000. It mines gold deposits at its Jundee and Kalgoorlie sites in Western Australia. In 2018 it acquired the Pogo gold mine in Alaska, the eighth-largest gold mine in the US. In December 2019 it acquired Echo Resources, operator of the Bronzewing gold project in Western Australia. In January 2020 it acquired a 50 per cent interest in the Kalgoorlie Super Pit. It has an active exploration program in Western Australia and the Northern Territory.

Latest business results (June 2020, full year)

Rising production and a surging gold price helped Northern Star to a big rise in revenues and profits. Gold sales of 900 388 ounces were up from 840 580 ounces in the previous year, thanks to the Kalgoorlie Super Pit acquisition and a full year's contribution from Pogo. The average price received of $2208 per ounce was up from $1764. Average costs rose from $1296 per ounce to $1496, in large part because of the addition of Pogo, which incurs substantially higher expenses than Northern Star's Australian mines. Pogo was also hit by a COVID-19 outbreak among some of its workers.

Outlook

Northern Star is a low-cost producer by global standards and is actively working to boost its output. In August 2020 it said that, thanks to acquisitions, its gold reserves had doubled during the year to 10.8 million ounces, with mineral resources of 32 million ounces. During the June 2021 year it plans to spend $198 million on growth projects — most of this at Pogo and the Kalgoorlie Super Pit — and a further $101 million for exploration work. At Pogo it has already succeeded in cutting costs and boosting output, and believes this mine will eventually be producing more than 300 000 ounces of gold annually, compared with 174 000 ounces in June 2020. At the Kalgoorlie Super Pit, which it operates in a joint venture with Saracen Mineral Holdings, it also sees great potential. It expects this mine to produce up to 480 000 ounces in the June 2021 year — split between Northern Star and Saracen — rising to as much as 675 000 ounces by June 2028. The company also sees solid prospects for its Tanami exploration projects in Western Australia and the Northern Territory. Its June 2021 forecast is for production of 940 000 ounces to 1.06 million ounces of gold, and it believes that it could be producing as much as 1.3 million ounces annually by the June 2027 year.

Year to 30 June	2019	2020
Revenues ($mn)	1401.2	1971.7
EBIT ($mn)	222.3	362.3
EBIT margin (%)	15.9	18.4
Gross margin (%)	21.4	26.6
Profit before tax ($mn)	214.8	344.6
Profit after tax ($mn)	154.7	258.3
Earnings per share (c)	24.38	37.30
Cash flow per share (c)	63.02	87.98
Dividend (c)	13.5	17
Percentage franked	100	100
Net tangible assets per share ($)	1.72	2.88
Interest cover (times)	29.5	20.5
Return on equity (%)	16.0	15.9
Debt-to-equity ratio (%)	~	6.2
Current ratio	2.1	1.7

Objective Corporation Limited

ASX code: OCL　　　　　　　　　　　　　　www.objective.com

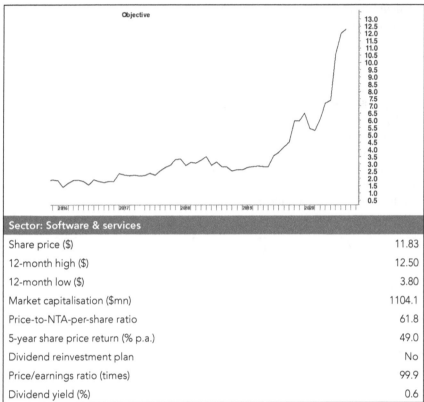

Sector: Software & services	
Share price ($)	11.83
12-month high ($)	12.50
12-month low ($)	3.80
Market capitalisation ($mn)	1104.1
Price-to-NTA-per-share ratio	61.8
5-year share price return (% p.a.)	49.0
Dividend reinvestment plan	No
Price/earnings ratio (times)	99.9
Dividend yield (%)	0.6

Sydney-based Objective, founded in 1987, provides information technology software and services. Its particular specialty is working with federal, state and local governments, as well as government agencies and regulated industries, and it has operations in Australia, New Zealand and the United Kingdom. It operates under many product categories. Objective Enterprise Connect Management (ECM) allows a public or private body to manage all its physical and electronic records. Objective Connect allows organisations to exchange content securely and easily. Objective Keystone helps organisations create and publish new content. Objective Trapeze assists the digitisation process for complex files and documents. Objective Redact removes sensitive information from a document.

Latest business results (June 2020, full year)

In an excellent result, Objective reported double-digit increases in revenues and profits. For reporting purposes the company divides its businesses into four broad segments. The largest of these, Objective Content Solutions — essentially the Object ECM business — represents 72 per cent of company turnover, and saw revenues up by 5 per cent, thanks to new customers and a big jump in subscription software contracts. Revenues soared by 148 per cent for Objective Planning Solutions — incorporating Objective Trapeze and Objective Redact products — thanks especially to the addition of two acquisitions, Master Business Systems and Alpha Group. Objective Keystone, representing about 10 per cent of turnover, saw revenues fall, reflecting the conclusion of a large project in the previous year. The very small Objective Connect business achieved a 34 per cent jump in revenues, thanks in part to the COVID-19 pandemic, with many employees working remotely.

Outlook

Objective is a small company working in niche businesses but with a solid reputation and a high level of profitability in its domestic operations. It is working to move its businesses, as much as possible, to a subscription model, which will make revenues and earnings more predictable each year. Recurring revenues rose by 22 per cent in the June 2020 year, to represent 75 per cent of total income. The company's particular goal is to help customers streamline the processes of compliance, accountability and governance. Its products share a common interface, and as the product range grows it is increasingly able to cross-sell to its existing customer base. The company continues to expand, and in July 2020 announced its biggest-ever acquisition, Itree, a developer of software for government agencies and regulators in Australia and New Zealand. Acquired for $18.5 million, Itree is expected to provide a significant boost to Objective's June 2021 earnings.

Year to 30 June	2019	2020
Revenues ($mn)	62.1	70.0
EBIT ($mn)	10.8	13.7
EBIT margin (%)	17.3	19.5
Profit before tax ($mn)	10.8	13.6
Profit after tax ($mn)	9.1	11.0
Earnings per share (c)	9.77	11.84
Cash flow per share (c)	13.39	15.61
Dividend (c)	5	7
Percentage franked	100	100
Net tangible assets per share ($)	0.18	0.19
Interest cover (times)	~	160.9
Return on equity (%)	33.0	33.7
Debt-to-equity ratio (%)	~	~
Current ratio	1.3	1.2

OFX Group Limited

ASX code: OFX   www.ofx.com

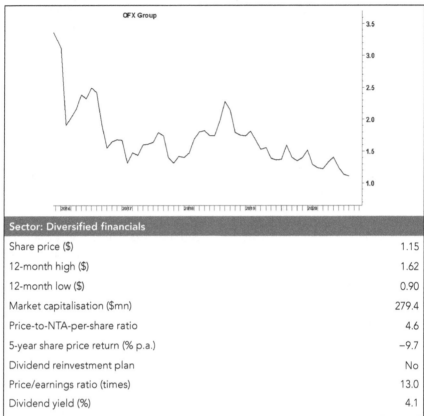

OFX Group

Sector: Diversified financials	
Share price ($)	1.15
12-month high ($)	1.62
12-month low ($)	0.90
Market capitalisation ($mn)	279.4
Price-to-NTA-per-share ratio	4.6
5-year share price return (% p.a.)	−9.7
Dividend reinvestment plan	No
Price/earnings ratio (times)	13.0
Dividend yield (%)	4.1

Sydney-based foreign exchange specialist OFX Group, formerly known as OzForex, was launched in 1998 as a currency information website. It provides international payments services in 55 currencies to more than 190 countries, with offices in Sydney, London, Hong Kong, Singapore, Toronto, Auckland and San Francisco.

Latest business results (March 2020, full year)

OFX enjoyed another solid year, with revenues and profits again moving higher. In particular, it benefited from a strong fourth quarter, with the onset of the COVID-19 pandemic sparking a big jump in trading activity. The company was also a beneficiary of its drive into overseas markets. Australian and New Zealand business — which contributes about 50 per cent of company turnover — saw revenues up by 4 per cent, but profits fell as the company invested heavily in new technology. North American revenues jumped 24 per cent, and now represent about a quarter of company turnover. More impressively, profits from the region, which had fallen sharply in the previous year, more than doubled. European profits rose 20 per cent and the small Asian segment saw profits up by 6 per cent. The total number of the company's active clients fell by 2 per cent to 152 700, but the number of transactions per active client rose by nearly 9 per cent to 7.3. The total transaction turnover for the year was $24.7 billion, up 4 per cent from the previous year.

Outlook

OFX occupies a small position in the huge global foreign currency market. This is a highly competitive business, and much of the company's success derives from developing strong relationships with its clients and from offering them personalised service and more attractive rates than competitors like the big banks. It is also highly dependent on new technologies in order to help it maintain a cost advantage. The foreign exchange business appears to offer low barriers to entry, and with interest rates low it has been attracting many new entrants. However, levels of profitability are low for many of these companies, and OFX expects market consolidation to increase. In 2020 it launched a new partnership with Link Market Services, making it easier for offshore investors who hold investments in listed Australian companies, and who use Link as their register, to transfer their funds internationally. This is expected to generate income of approximately $5 million annually for OFX. The company continues to build its overseas businesses, and has restructured its Asian and its Australia/New Zealand operations, with expectations of firm growth.

Year to 31 March	2019	2020
Revenues ($mn)	128.7	137.2
EBIT ($mn)	25.6	26.6
EBIT margin (%)	19.9	19.4
Profit before tax ($mn)	25.9	26.1
Profit after tax ($mn)	20.4	21.4
Earnings per share (c)	8.44	8.81
Cash flow per share (c)	12.12	13.15
Dividend (c)	5.92	4.7
Percentage franked	100	35
Net tangible assets per share ($)	0.24	0.25
Interest cover (times)	~	49.2
Return on equity (%)	30.8	29.4
Debt-to-equity ratio (%)	~	~

Orica Limited

ASX code: ORI www.orica.com

Sector: Materials	
Share price ($)	17.04
12-month high ($)	24.27
12-month low ($)	13.25
Market capitalisation ($mn)	6912.0
Price-to-NTA-per-share ratio	3.7
5-year share price return (% p.a.)	5.8
Dividend reinvestment plan	Yes
Price/earnings ratio (times)	17.4
Dividend yield (%)	3.2

Melbourne-based Orica was founded in 1874 as a supplier of explosives to the Victorian gold mining industry, and for many years it was a subsidiary of Britain's Imperial Chemical Industries. It is today a global leader in commercial explosives for the mining, quarrying, oil and gas, infrastructure and construction sectors. It is also a leading supplier of sodium cyanide for gold extraction. Its Minova business provides support equipment for underground mining and tunnelling operations. It has customers in more than 100 countries, and overseas sales represent more than 70 per cent of total income.

Latest business results (March 2020, half year)

Revenues and EBIT were a little higher, but a jump in net interest payments meant that the after-tax profit was down. Business was helped by a continuing series of cost efficiencies and some foreign exchange gains, although the company took a $7 million EBIT hit from COVID-19 lockdowns in March 2020. The Australia/Pacific/Asia segment saw firm growth in sales, especially in Australia, though profits were dented by bushfires and by higher gas prices. In addition, Orica continued to incur costs with its new $800 million joint venture Burrup ammonium nitrate unit in Western Australia, which reduced EBIT by $7 million. North American volume sales were flat on the

March 2019 half, though profits edged up. Latin America recorded a double-digit increase in profits, despite just a small rise in sales revenues, thanks to growing demand for higher-margin products and increased cyanide volumes. The smallest regional segment, Europe/Middle East/Africa, enjoyed the best result for the second consecutive year, thanks to continuing strong growth in demand for explosives and cyanide. The small Minova business continued its recovery, with a big jump in profits, despite reduced sales.

Outlook

With most of its business geared towards the mining industry, Orica's fortunes will rise or fall accordingly. It expects COVID-19 lockdowns to reduce previously expected sales by 10 per cent to 15 per cent in the September 2020 half. Demand from the gold industry represents around 20 per cent of sales, and the company will benefit from any increase in gold activity. It is working on upgrading and rationalising its production facilities, and expects to see a continuing stream of cost efficiencies. It has achieved success in turning around its underperforming Minova unit, which is now back in profit. The Burrup plant is now operational and is expected to build production to commercial levels during the September 2020 half. However, the company is vulnerable to rising energy prices.

Year to 30 September	2018	2019
Revenues ($mn)	5373.8	5878.0
EBIT ($mn)	618.1	664.8
EBIT margin (%)	11.5	11.3
Profit before tax ($mn)	496.8	555.1
Profit after tax ($mn)	324.2	372.0
Earnings per share (c)	85.72	97.90
Cash flow per share (c)	156.29	170.65
Dividend (c)	51.5	55
Percentage franked	0	9
Interest cover (times)	5.1	6.1
Return on equity (%)	11.1	12.7
Half year to 31 March	2019	2020
Revenues ($mn)	2828.9	2880.3
Profit before tax ($mn)	244.9	245.6
Profit after tax ($mn)	166.7	165.2
Earnings per share (c)	43.91	42.90
Dividend (c)	22	16.5
Percentage franked	0	0
Net tangible assets per share ($)	2.97	4.67
Debt-to-equity ratio (%)	61.6	50.9
Current ratio	1.3	1.4

Pacific Smiles Group Limited

ASX code: PSQ   investors.pacificsmilesgroup.com.au

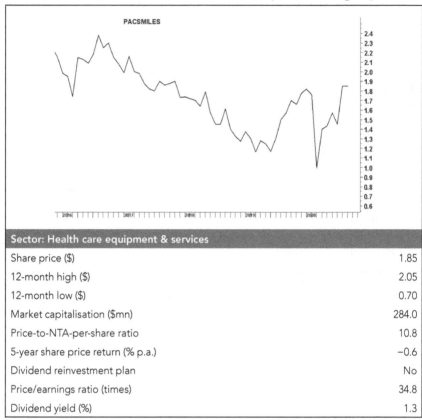

Sector: Health care equipment & services	
Share price ($)	1.85
12-month high ($)	2.05
12-month low ($)	0.70
Market capitalisation ($mn)	284.0
Price-to-NTA-per-share ratio	10.8
5-year share price return (% p.a.)	−0.6
Dividend reinvestment plan	No
Price/earnings ratio (times)	34.8
Dividend yield (%)	1.3

Based in Maitland, New South Wales, Pacific Smiles was formally established in 2003 from a group of dental partnerships. Today it provides its dental practices with a wide array of support staff and back-office services that allow the dentists to retain their independence and their clinical autonomy while focusing on their clinical services. It operates in New South Wales, Victoria, Queensland and Canberra under the Pacific Smiles Dental and the nib Dental Care brands.

Latest business results (June 2020, full year)

The COVID-19 pandemic hit the company, with many of its dental practices obliged to close down for varying periods, and forcing revenues and profits down for the year. This was despite a strong start, with patient fees and underlying profits up by around 14 per cent during the eight months to February 2020. For the full year, total patient fees of $186.3 million were slightly down from $187.4 million in the previous year. On a same-centre basis, fees were down by 4.5 per cent. During the year the company added five new centres — at Robina and Mitchelton in Queensland and at Epping, Ocean Grove and Narre Warren in Victoria — bringing the total number of centres at June 2020 to 94, with 383 chairs, up from 351. The company said that during the year it had negotiated around $1 million in rental savings and deferrals with its landlords. It also received $8.4 million from the government's JobKeeper program.

Outlook

The dental business in Australia is fragmented, with around 70 per cent of dentists working in their own private practices or in small partnerships, and some companies — including the ASX-listed 1300SMILES — are now working to consolidate them. Pacific Smiles has a long-term target of 250 centres, 800 dental chairs and a dental industry market share of more than 5 per cent. It finds that as it grows it is able to introduce efficiencies to its practices, boosting business and reducing operating costs, although start-up expenses for new practices can be high. In July 2020 it announced plans to enter the Western Australian market, through a 10-year agreement with HBF, the state's largest private health fund. HBF will build a minimum of five dental clinics over 18 months, with Pacific Smiles the exclusive operator of these. The company's early forecast for the June 2021 year is for approximately 15 per cent growth in patient fees and in underlying profits. It expects to add about 10 new dental centres to its network during the year.

Year to 30 June	2019	2020
Revenues ($mn)	122.2	120.6
EBIT ($mn)	12.9	12.5
EBIT margin (%)	10.6	10.3
Profit before tax ($mn)	12.2	11.8
Profit after tax ($mn)	8.9	8.1
Earnings per share (c)	5.87	5.32
Cash flow per share (c)	12.06	18.48
Dividend (c)	5.8	2.4
Percentage franked	100	100
Net tangible assets per share ($)	0.20	0.17
Interest cover (times)	19.5	18.7
Return on equity (%)	21.5	20.8
Debt-to-equity ratio (%)	24.5	18.2
Current ratio	0.7	0.8

Pendal Group Limited

ASX code: PDL   www.pendalgroup.com

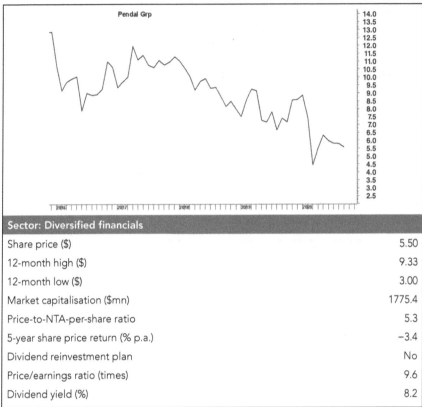

Sector: Diversified financials	
Share price ($)	5.50
12-month high ($)	9.33
12-month low ($)	3.00
Market capitalisation ($mn)	1775.4
Price-to-NTA-per-share ratio	5.3
5-year share price return (% p.a.)	−3.4
Dividend reinvestment plan	No
Price/earnings ratio (times)	9.6
Dividend yield (%)	8.2

Sydney-based funds management company Pendal Group started life as part of Ord-BT, an investment banking firm established in 1969. Ord-BT, later renamed as BT Financial Group, was subsequently acquired by Westpac Banking Corporation, which added to it some other funds management businesses, then created BT Investment Management as a new entity to be listed on the ASX. It was later renamed as Pendal Group. Today Pendal actively manages a wide range of investments in Australian equities, listed property and fixed interest, in international fixed interest, in multi-asset portfolios and in alternative investments. Its London-based subsidiary J O Hambro Capital Management, with offices in Singapore and the US, manages international funds. Other Pendal international funds are managed by external firms.

Latest business results (March 2020, half year)

Revenues were little changed from the March 2019 half and the cash after-tax profit rose, in a good result during a period of market volatility. Base management fees edged up 1 per cent to $240.9 million, but performance fees crashed from $4.4 million to just $0.6 million. For comparison, in the March 2018 half, performance fees were $47.6 million. Funds under management at March 2020 of $86 billion were down from $100.9 billion a year earlier, although the company said that 70 per cent of its funds had outperformed their benchmarks over the preceding one-year period. A higher wage bill helped push expenses up by 2 per cent. Note that the cash profit factors out certain non-cash items. On a statutory basis the company's after-tax profit fell from $69.6 million to $54.8 million.

Outlook

Pendal is heavily dependent on market activity and investor sentiment. Its business can also be buffeted by its own performance, which helps determine levels of performance fees. In addition, with 74 per cent of its equities funds under management held in foreign currencies it is heavily influenced by currency fluctuations. However, it benefits from moves by Australian investors into overseas equities and from its drive to diversify its sources of fund inflows. Overseas clients are now responsible for more than half the funds under management and Pendal's overseas business generates some 85 per cent of company profit. The company sees great potential in providing advice on a form of socially responsible investing known as environmental, social and governance (ESG) investing. Its subsidiary Regnan, an ESG specialist, plans a series of socially responsible funds and products that are aligned with the 17 sustainable development goals of the United Nations.

Year to 30 September	2018	2019
Revenues ($mn)	558.5	491.3
EBIT ($mn)	241.3	200.7
EBIT margin (%)	43.2	40.8
Profit before tax ($mn)	241.6	201.0
Profit after tax ($mn)	201.6	163.5
Earnings per share (c)	72.07	57.57
Cash flow per share (c)	75.93	60.81
Dividend (c)	52	45
Percentage franked	15	10
Interest cover (times)	~	~
Return on equity (%)	23.9	18.1
Half year to 31 March	2019	2020
Revenues ($mn)	243.1	243.3
Profit before tax ($mn)	103.0	100.2
Profit after tax ($mn)	84.5	86.6
Earnings per share (c)	29.60	26.80
Dividend (c)	20	15
Percentage franked	10	10
Net tangible assets per share ($)	1.02	1.03
Debt-to-equity ratio (%)	~	~
Current ratio	1.5	1.8

Perpetual Limited

ASX code: PPT   www.perpetual.com.au

Sector: Diversified financials	
Share price ($)	29.59
12-month high ($)	47.47
12-month low ($)	19.65
Market capitalisation ($mn)	1622.8
Price-to-NTA-per-share ratio	6.6
5-year share price return (% p.a.)	1.2
Dividend reinvestment plan	Yes
Price/earnings ratio (times)	16.8
Dividend yield (%)	5.2

Sydney-based financial services company Perpetual was established in 1886 as Perpetual Trustees. It divides its operations into three broad areas. Perpetual Investments is a funds management business offering a range of managed investment products to the retail, wholesale and institutional markets. Perpetual Private is a specialist boutique financial services business aimed at high-net-worth individuals, and providing its clients with access to tailored financial, tax, legal and estate planning advice. The Perpetual Corporate Trust division is a leading provider of corporate trustee and transaction support services to the financial services industry. In June 2020 Perpetual acquired the American specialist investment firm Trillium Asset Management, and in July 2020 it announced plans to buy a 75 per cent stake in the United States investment management company Barrow Hanley.

Latest business results (June 2020, full year)

Another poor performance from the Perpetual Investments division sent revenues and profits lower. This business saw revenues down 16 per cent, with profits tumbling 31 per cent, largely the result of continuing net outflows from its funds. It was the fifth consecutive year of lower profits for this division. Funds under management of $28.4 billion were up from $27.2 billion in the previous year, thanks to the Trillium acquisition. Excluding this, funds under management fell to $22.8 billion. The Perpetual Private division saw revenues edge down, with profits falling 27 per cent as the company boosted its spending to support future business growth. This division was also hit by the economic slowdown in the second half and the sustained low interest rate, which hurt non-market revenues. The Perpetual Corporate Trust division again saw revenues and profits up, thanks to growth from existing clients and a series of new business wins.

Outlook

Perpetual's funds management business is set to be transformed by its $64 million Trillium acquisition and its $465 million Barrow Hanley acquisition. These will triple funds under management to more than $90 billion and are expected to provide significant growth opportunities in the Australian market as well as a platform for international expansion. Trillium has a specialty in ethical funds that incorporate environmental, social and governance (ESG) considerations into the investment process. Such funds are growing in popularity, and Perpetual is launching Trillium ESG funds in Australia. The Perpetual Private division continues to invest in building up its network of advisers, leading to a steady increase in client numbers. The well-regarded Perpetual Corporate Trust division continues to grow, and now provides the highest profit margins of the three divisions.

Year to 30 June	2019	2020
Revenues ($mn)	508.9	483.9
Perpetual Private (%)	37	38
Perpetual Investments (%)	41	36
Perpetual Corporate Trust (%)	22	26
EBIT ($mn)	164.5	120.4
EBIT margin (%)	32.3	24.9
Profit before tax ($mn)	162.2	116.6
Profit after tax ($mn)	115.9	82.0
Earnings per share (c)	250.89	176.26
Cash flow per share (c)	294.23	245.45
Dividend (c)	250	155
Percentage franked	100	100
Net tangible assets per share ($)	6.85	4.49
Interest cover (times)	70.3	31.5
Return on equity (%)	17.5	12.5
Debt-to-equity ratio (%)	6.0	11.0
Current ratio	1.9	1.3

Pinnacle Investment Management Group Limited

ASX code: PNI   www.pinnacleinvestment.com

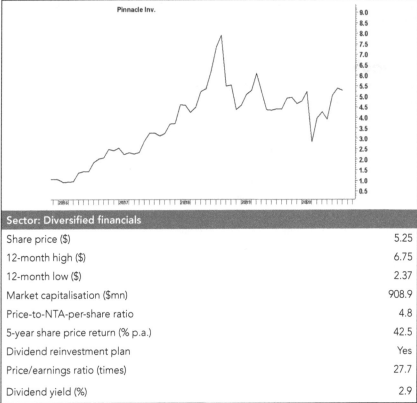

Pinnacle Inv.

Sector: Diversified financials	
Share price ($)	5.25
12-month high ($)	6.75
12-month low ($)	2.37
Market capitalisation ($mn)	908.9
Price-to-NTA-per-share ratio	4.8
5-year share price return (% p.a.)	42.5
Dividend reinvestment plan	Yes
Price/earnings ratio (times)	27.7
Dividend yield (%)	2.9

Sydney-based Pinnacle Investment Management started life in 2006 as a boutique funds management company that was majority-owned by Wilson HTM Investment Group. In 2016 it was fully acquired by Wilson Group, with Wilson Group changing its own name to Pinnacle. Today it is a prominent adviser to small funds management groups, providing them with distribution services, business support and responsible entity services, while also holding an equity stake in these companies.

Latest business results (June 2020, full year)

In a volatile environment for financial markets, Pinnacle was able to achieve increases in revenues and profits. At June 2020 the company comprised 16 fund management affiliates, and it held shareholdings in these that ranged from 23.5 per cent to 49.9 per cent. Total revenues during the year for the 16 fund managers of $291.1 million was up from $236.8 million in the previous year. Of this amount, $26.7 million came from performance fees, up from $15.3 million. Total funds under management for the 16 fund manager affiliates reached $58.7 billion at June 2020, up 8.1 per cent from a year earlier. Excluding the funds that were added when Coolabah Capital joined the group in December 2019, funds grew by 2.6 per cent for the year.

Outlook

Pinnacle's initial role is to provide its fund manager affiliates with equity, seed capital and working capital. It then allows its managers to focus on investment performance by providing them with marketing and other support services. Pinnacle's own revenues and profits derive from the revenues it receives from its affiliates for its services, together with its share of their profits, so performance is important. It has achieved success with the fund management companies it has chosen to join its group, reporting that 90 per cent of funds with a five-year track record had by June 2020 outperformed their benchmarks during this period. It is seeking to diversify into new asset classes, and in 2020 Aikya Investment Management, which specialises in managing emerging markets equity portfolios, joined the group. Pinnacle has also been steadily boosting its exposure to retail funds, which provide higher margins than institutional funds, and these now represent 23 per cent of total funds under management. The company has been working to boost its marketing strength with the hiring of additional staff. In particular, it has been expanding its overseas marketing efforts. Nevertheless, with its business directly tied to trends in global financial markets, Pinnacle would suffer in any prolonged market downturn.

Year to 30 June	2019	2020
Revenues ($mn)	54.3	60.4
EBIT ($mn)	30.4	32.8
EBIT margin (%)	56.0	54.4
Profit before tax ($mn)	30.5	32.4
Profit after tax ($mn)	30.5	32.4
Earnings per share (c)	18.29	18.93
Cash flow per share (c)	18.34	19.38
Dividend (c)	15.4	15.4
Percentage franked	100	100
Net tangible assets per share ($)	1.04	1.08
Interest cover (times)	~	69.5
Return on equity (%)	22.2	17.7
Debt-to-equity ratio (%)	~	7.4
Current ratio	7.2	3.8

Platinum Asset Management Limited

ASX code: PTM www.platinum.com.au

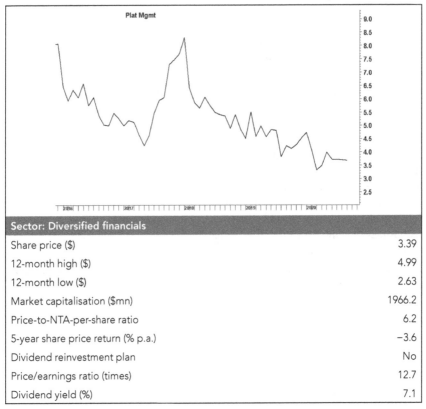

Sector: Diversified financials	
Share price ($)	3.39
12-month high ($)	4.99
12-month low ($)	2.63
Market capitalisation ($mn)	1966.2
Price-to-NTA-per-share ratio	6.2
5-year share price return (% p.a.)	−3.6
Dividend reinvestment plan	No
Price/earnings ratio (times)	12.7
Dividend yield (%)	7.1

Sydney funds management company Platinum Asset Management was established in 1994 by former chief executive Kerr Neilson. It has developed a specialty in managing portfolios of international equities. Its primary product is the $8.4 billion Platinum International Fund. Other funds specialise in Europe, Asia, Japan, health care, technology and international brands. Much of the company equity is held by Platinum directors and staff members and by Kerr Neilson and his former wife.

Latest business results (June 2020, full year)

Revenues and profits again fell. Average funds under management for the year declined for a second straight year, down 6.3 per cent to $23.7 billion, driven by net fund outflows of $3 billion. This was due especially to underperformance in the flagship Platinum International Fund. Consequently, management fee revenues dropped 6.5 per cent to $275.9 million. However, performance fee revenues jumped to $9.1 million, compared with just $30 000 in the previous year, thanks mainly to strong performances from the company's Asian and healthcare funds. Staff costs were down, but more than offset by rising rents and office fit-out costs, and total expenses for the year rose. At June 2020 the company held funds under management of $21.4 billion, down from $24.8 billion in June 2019 and $25.7 billion in June 2018.

Outlook

Platinum has gained a degree of renown among Australian investors for an impressive long-term period of outperformance for its international equity funds, thanks to its stock-picking skills, and this has sparked some solid growth in funds under management. However, during the June 2020 year only two of its eight leading funds outperformed their benchmarks. The company has attributed this to its preference for value stocks, at a time when growth stocks were leading global markets higher. In a letter to investors, the Platinum managing director in August 2020 said that, with value stocks so out-of-favour among investors, he saw all the signs of a fully-fledged investment mania. Platinum is working to boost its business with international clients. In 2018 it opened an office in London with three staff members who, despite COVID-19 pandemic restrictions, have been actively seeking to develop relationships with prospective clients. It is working to build a client base in the United States through a partnership with the financial advisory and distribution services specialist AccessAlpha Worldwide. It is also actively seeking out further new markets and innovative new products. At June 2020 Platinum had no debt and cash holdings of more than $105 million.

Year to 30 June	2019	2020
Revenues ($mn)	295.2	285.0
EBIT ($mn)	219.4	219.3
EBIT margin (%)	74.3	77.0
Profit before tax ($mn)	222.9	220.8
Profit after tax ($mn)	157.7	155.6
Earnings per share (c)	27.03	26.76
Cash flow per share (c)	27.16	27.41
Dividend (c)	27	24
Percentage franked	100	100
Net tangible assets per share ($)	0.55	0.55
Interest cover (times)	~	~
Return on equity (%)	48.0	48.6
Debt-to-equity ratio (%)	~	~
Current ratio	13.1	8.7

Pro Medicus Limited

ASX code: PME   www.promed.com.au

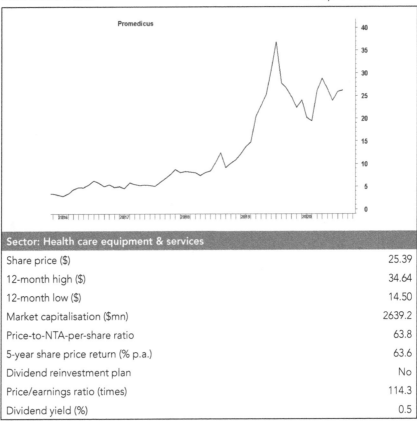

Sector: Health care equipment & services	
Share price ($)	25.39
12-month high ($)	34.64
12-month low ($)	14.50
Market capitalisation ($mn)	2639.2
Price-to-NTA-per-share ratio	63.8
5-year share price return (% p.a.)	63.6
Dividend reinvestment plan	No
Price/earnings ratio (times)	114.3
Dividend yield (%)	0.5

Melbourne-based Pro Medicus, established in 1983, provides software and internet products and services to the medical profession. Its Visage 7.0 medical imaging software provides radiologists and clinicians with advanced visualisation capability for the rapid viewing of medical images. Its Radiology Information Systems (RIS) product provides proprietary medical software for practice management. In Australia it operates the Promedicus.net online network for doctors. It has extensive business operations throughout Australia, Europe and North America, and overseas sales represent more than 80 per cent of total turnover.

Latest business results (June 2020, full year)

Pro Medicus enjoyed another year of double-digit revenues and profits growth, thanks to strong business in North America and Australia. North America has grown to represent around three-quarters of total company turnover, and sales and EBIT were both up by 24 per cent. This was attributable to growing transaction-based revenues from the sale of Visage technology. Australian sales rose 19 per cent, with EBIT up 29 per cent, thanks mainly to RIS contracts with Healius and I-MED Radiology

Network. By contrast, European sales, which more than doubled in the previous year, fell by 38 per cent, with EBIT crashing 86 per cent, due to a one-off $3 million capital sale to the German government in the previous year. Though the bulk of the company's sales derive from North America, around 95 per cent of EBIT came from Australian operations.

Outlook

Pro Medicus has been enjoying some outstanding success in America for its Visage 7 software, which has the speed and functionality to meet the requirements of many different kinds of users. The company is now one of the market leaders in this business, and it is making a substantial investment in research and development activities aimed at new products and enhancements to existing products, including artificial intelligence–based products and cloud-based systems. It also benefits from a new emphasis on telehealth engendered by the COVID-19 pandemic. It has a growing amount of recurring income. During the June 2020 year the company continued to make strong inroads into the American market, with three new contracts, each extending over five years. The largest, worth $22 million, was with Northwestern Memorial HealthCare in Chicago. The other two were a $9 million contract with Ohio State University and a $6 million deal with the Palo Alto teleradiology company Nines. Pro Medicus has said that it has a very strong pipeline of new business opportunities, in terms of both quantity and quality, that will support future growth. In September 2020 it announced a seven-year $25 million contract with NYU Langone Health, a leading New York healthcare provider.

Year to 30 June	2019	2020
Revenues ($mn)	50.1	56.8
EBIT ($mn)	25.9	29.8
EBIT margin (%)	51.6	52.5
Profit before tax ($mn)	26.1	30.0
Profit after tax ($mn)	19.1	23.1
Earnings per share (c)	18.46	22.21
Cash flow per share (c)	24.34	29.61
Dividend (c)	8	12
Percentage franked	100	100
Net tangible assets per share ($)	0.30	0.40
Interest cover (times)	~	~
Return on equity (%)	45.3	42.2
Debt-to-equity ratio (%)	~	~
Current ratio	3.8	4.8

PWR Holdings Limited

ASX code: PWH   www.pwr.com.au

Pwr Holdings

Sector: Automobiles & components	
Share price ($)	4.91
12-month high ($)	5.16
12-month low ($)	2.50
Market capitalisation ($mn)	491.4
Price-to-NTA-per-share ratio	12.5
5-year share price return (% p.a.)	12.6
Dividend reinvestment plan	No
Price/earnings ratio (times)	37.6
Dividend yield (%)	1.2

Based on the Gold Coast, automotive products company PWR got its start in 1987. It specialises in cooling systems, including aluminium radiators, intercoolers and oil coolers. It has a particular specialty in the supply of cooling systems to racing car teams. Other customers include the automotive original equipment manufacturing sector and the automotive after-market sector. It operates from manufacturing and distribution facilities in Australia and the United States, with a European distribution centre in the United Kingdom. It owns the American cooling products manufacturer C&R Racing. More than 85 per cent of company sales are to customers overseas, mainly in Europe and North America.

Latest business results (June 2020, full year)

In a challenging year for the company, revenues edged up but profits were down, as a strong first half was upturned by the COVID-19 pandemic, which forced a shutdown of motor sport around the world. In fact, the revenue gain was attributable to favourable foreign currency movements, and actual sales for the year declined a little. The company's core PWR Performance Products division, which supplies the company's products to non-USA markets, saw revenues down by 4 per cent, with domestic demand higher but European sales down by 10 per cent. By contrast, C&R Racing enjoyed a relatively good year, despite the motor sport shutdown, with revenues up 21 per cent and profits also higher. The company said it had received job-support payments from both the Australian and American governments.

Outlook

PWR supplies its cooling systems to most Formula One racing teams, as well as to teams in other leading motor sports around the world, including Nascar and Indycar. It stands to gain as these sports resume. It spends heavily on research and development in order to maintain its market-leading position. It is also working to move into other market areas with high growth potential. In particular, it is achieving success as an original equipment manufacturer supplying bespoke cooling systems to high-performance automobile companies that include Porsche, Pagani and Aston Martin. In the June 2020 year this business grew 60 per cent to represent 15 per cent of total company turnover. The company also sees strong growth prospects through diversifying into cooling technologies for applications such as storage batteries in the energy sector, high-powered drones, electric cars and aerospace. In June 2020 sales of products based on these emerging technologies grew 62 per cent, to represent 6 per cent of company turnover. At June 2020 PWR had net cash holdings of nearly $12 million.

Year to 30 June	2019	2020
Revenues ($mn)	65.4	65.7
PWR performance products (%)	80	76
C&R Racing (%)	20	24
EBIT ($mn)	19.3	18.4
EBIT margin (%)	29.5	28.0
Profit before tax ($mn)	19.8	18.2
Profit after tax ($mn)	14.2	13.0
Earnings per share (c)	14.21	13.05
Cash flow per share (c)	16.68	17.75
Dividend (c)	8.5	5.9
Percentage franked	100	100
Net tangible assets per share ($)	0.38	0.39
Interest cover (times)	~	110.8
Return on equity (%)	28.6	24.3
Debt-to-equity ratio (%)	~	~
Current ratio	4.1	3.4

Ramsay Health Care Limited

ASX code: RHC   www.ramsayhealth.com

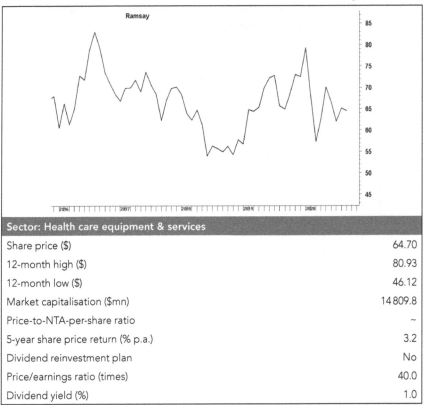

Ramsay

Sector: Health care equipment & services	
Share price ($)	64.70
12-month high ($)	80.93
12-month low ($)	46.12
Market capitalisation ($mn)	14 809.8
Price-to-NTA-per-share ratio	~
5-year share price return (% p.a.)	3.2
Dividend reinvestment plan	No
Price/earnings ratio (times)	40.0
Dividend yield (%)	1.0

Ramsay Health Care, based in Sydney, was established in 1964 and has grown to become Australia's largest operator of private hospitals, with 72 hospitals and day surgery units. It has also expanded globally. Ramsay United Kingdom has become one of the leading providers of independent hospital services in England, with a network of 34 acute hospitals and day procedure centres. A French subsidiary, Ramsay Santé, is a market leader in France, and also operates facilities in Germany, Italy, Denmark, Sweden and Norway. A joint venture company, Ramsay Sime Darby Health Care, manages facilities in Malaysia, Indonesia and Hong Kong.

Latest business results (June 2020, full year)

Revenues rose but profits fell sharply as the COVID-19 pandemic quite dramatically hit second-half operations. Until February 2020 the company had been forecasting full-year like-for-like profit growth of 2 per cent to 4 per cent. However, the pandemic led to a postponement of elective surgery in many regions, along with inflated costs. In addition, the company entered into agreements with various national and state governments to make its facilities available for COVID-19 patients. In England,

France, Italy and Sweden in particular, the company's facilities were at the forefront of the pandemic. Profits tumbled in all regions except for Europe, where they actually rose, but this reflected the addition of a large acquisition in the previous year.

Outlook

Ramsay is a beneficiary of an ageing population, which is driving a steady growth in demand for healthcare services in Australia and many other countries. Nevertheless, while COVID-19 remains a problem the company views the short-term outlook as quite uncertain. It is also vulnerable to a slowdown in growth in the number of Australians choosing to take out private health insurance. It notes that waiting lists for elective surgery have grown in each of its markets, and it believes that this could be a boost to business. In the United Kingdom it will participate in a tender process for medical facility operators able to assist for four years in reducing public waiting lists. It also sees potential from the deepened relationship it has developed during the pandemic with Britain's National Health Service. Following a $1.5 billion capital raising in 2020 the company has said it is seeking new opportunities to expand its business, both in Australia and overseas. During the June 2020 year it approved $196 million in spending domestically on new projects, including 209 new beds, seven operating theatres, 13 consulting suites and a new emergency department.

Year to 30 June	2019	2020
Revenues ($mn)	11 552.8	12 160.3
EBIT ($mn)	1 108.0	952.3
EBIT margin (%)	9.6	7.8
Profit before tax ($mn)	938.8	541.0
Profit after tax ($mn)	590.9	336.9
Earnings per share (c)	288.95	161.89
Cash flow per share (c)	526.41	591.11
Dividend (c)	151.5	62.5
Percentage franked	100	100
Net tangible assets per share ($)	~	~
Interest cover (times)	6.5	2.3
Return on equity (%)	24.1	10.7
Debt-to-equity ratio (%)	148.8	64.3
Current ratio	1.1	1.1

REA Group Limited

ASX code: REA   www.rea-group.com

Sector: Media & entertainment	
Share price ($)	112.81
12-month high ($)	121.89
12-month low ($)	62.05
Market capitalisation ($mn)	14858.7
Price-to-NTA-per-share ratio	69.5
5-year share price return (% p.a.)	23.2
Dividend reinvestment plan	No
Price/earnings ratio (times)	55.3
Dividend yield (%)	1.0

Melbourne-based REA was founded in 1995. Through its websites realestate.com.au and realcommercial.com.au it is a leader in the provision of online real estate advertising services in Australia, with roughly a 60 per cent market share. It also owns Flatmates.com.au, the residential property data company Hometrack Australia, the short-term co-working property website Spacely and the mortgage broking franchise group Smartline Home Loans. It operates property websites throughout Asia, and has a 20 per cent shareholding in the Move online property marketing company in the US. News Corp owns more than 60 per cent of REA's equity.

Latest business results (June 2020, full year)

Revenues and profits were down in a challenging business environment. The first half was affected by significant declines in residential listings and new project commencements. This was largely due to an increase in lending restrictions from banks and other financial institutions as a result of the 2019 Banking Royal Commission. Then a recovery in early 2020 was stalled by the COVID-19 pandemic. The company responded with some sharp cuts to its operating expenses, which helped limit the impact. Australian revenues fell 7 per cent for the year, driven by a 27 per cent slump in new project commencements. The company's small mortgage business rebounded from the previous year with a small gain in profits. Asian operations contributed revenues of $47.9 million, down slightly from a year earlier, but with profits higher. American losses continued. For the second straight year some substantial non-cash, one-off impairment charges for its Asian operations meant that on a statutory basis the company's after-tax profit actually rose 7 per cent to $112.4 million.

Outlook

REA is heavily geared to trends in the domestic housing market, and it is wary about the near-term outlook, despite some early signs of a pick-up in growth. It is also concerned about continuing weakness in new project developments. However, it has some flexibility in how it manages its cost base, and this will help limit the impact of declines in its businesses. It has postponed price increases due to take effect from July 2020, but expects to implement them once a sustained residential market recovery is evident. It sees great potential in its Asian strategy, with the continuing introduction of new products, although it is concerned about political upheavals in Hong Kong. REA's 20 per cent holding of Move, one of the largest real estate websites in the US, has given the company a foothold in the vast American property market.

Year to 30 June	2019	2020
Revenues ($mn)	874.9	820.3
EBIT ($mn)	441.6	397.0
EBIT margin (%)	50.5	48.4
Profit before tax ($mn)	432.9	392.3
Profit after tax ($mn)	295.5	268.9
Earnings per share (c)	224.34	204.13
Cash flow per share (c)	269.57	263.82
Dividend (c)	118	110
Percentage franked	100	100
Net tangible assets per share ($)	0.93	1.62
Interest cover (times)	50.7	84.3
Return on equity (%)	32.0	30.4
Debt-to-equity ratio (%)	19.0	12.1
Current ratio	0.7	1.2

Regis Resources Limited

ASX code: RRL www.regisresources.com.au

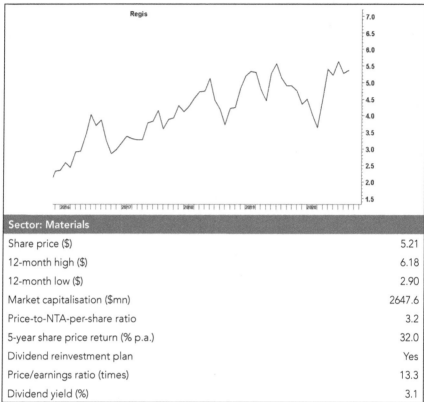

Sector: Materials	
Share price ($)	5.21
12-month high ($)	6.18
12-month low ($)	2.90
Market capitalisation ($mn)	2647.6
Price-to-NTA-per-share ratio	3.2
5-year share price return (% p.a.)	32.0
Dividend reinvestment plan	Yes
Price/earnings ratio (times)	13.3
Dividend yield (%)	3.1

Perth-based Regis Resources is a gold exploration and production company. Its core business is the Duketon Gold Project in the north-eastern goldfields region of Western Australia. Since operations started at Duketon in 2010 the company has been steadily expanding the size of the project and extending mine life. In 2012 Regis acquired the McPhillamys Gold Project in western New South Wales.

Latest business results (June 2020, full year)

The rising gold price generated a big jump in revenues and profits. During the year the company produced 352 042 ounces of gold, down from 363 418 ounces in the previous year, and sold 353 182 ounces, down from 369 721 ounces. The average sales price of $2200 per ounce was up from $1765. The average production all-in sustaining cost of $1246 per ounce jumped 21 per cent from $1029 in the previous year, with harder ore at Duketon North raising expenses and an increase in drill and blast costs at Duketon South. For reporting purposes the company groups its various mines into two segments. Duketon South comprises the Garden Well, Rosemont, Erlistoun, Tooheys Well and Baneygo mines. Revenues for this segment rose 12.4 per cent, with the pre-tax profit up 16.2 per cent. The smaller Duketon North operation comprises the Moolart Well, Gloster, Anchor, Dogbolter and Petra mines, with revenues up 26.3 per cent and the pre-tax profit jumping by 36.2 per cent.

Outlook

Regis has an estimated seven to 10 years of reserves at its mines, although the company's costs could begin to rise as it works to exploit this resource base. In August 2020 it announced the acquisition of the Ben Hur mineral resources from Stone Resources Australia, which will add further life to its Duketon operations. The company plans a new exploration program for this asset. It has developed an underground mining operation at its Rosemont open pit mine, with the first ore in July 2019 and commercial production launched in June 2020. It is now considering a new underground project at its Garden Well mine. The McPhillamys Gold Project in New South Wales contains an estimated 2.02 million ounces of gold, sufficient for a 10-year life, and Regis is in the process of seeking formal regulatory approval for development work to begin. The company's June 2021 forecast is for gold production of between 355 000 ounces and 380 000 ounces, at a cost of between $1230 and $1300 per ounce. At June 2020 Regis had no debt and cash holdings of more than $192 million.

Year to 30 June	2019	2020
Revenues ($mn)	652.5	755.8
Duketon South operations (%)	75	73
Duketon North operations (%)	25	27
EBIT ($mn)	232.6	285.8
EBIT margin (%)	35.6	37.8
Gross margin (%)	38.4	40.2
Profit before tax ($mn)	233.5	284.7
Profit after tax ($mn)	163.2	199.5
Earnings per share (c)	32.18	39.26
Cash flow per share (c)	46.86	60.64
Dividend (c)	16	16
Percentage franked	100	100
Net tangible assets per share ($)	1.41	1.64
Interest cover (times)	~	246.8
Return on equity (%)	24.1	25.7
Debt-to-equity ratio (%)	~	~
Current ratio	3.0	2.7

Rio Tinto Limited

ASX code: RIO   www.riotinto.com

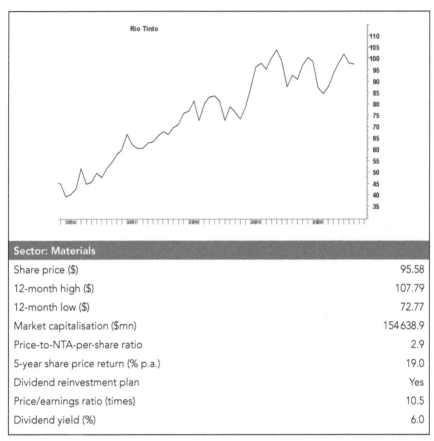

Rio Tinto

Sector: Materials	
Share price ($)	95.58
12-month high ($)	107.79
12-month low ($)	72.77
Market capitalisation ($mn)	154 638.9
Price-to-NTA-per-share ratio	2.9
5-year share price return (% p.a.)	19.0
Dividend reinvestment plan	Yes
Price/earnings ratio (times)	10.5
Dividend yield (%)	6.0

British-based Rio Tinto, one of the world's largest mining companies, was founded by European investors in 1873 in order to reopen some ancient copper mines at the Tinto River in Spain. It maintains an ASX presence in a dual-listing structure and continues to pay franked dividends to Australian shareholders. Its products include iron ore, copper, gold, industrial minerals, diamonds and aluminium. Subsidiaries include the 68-per-cent-owned uranium miner Energy Resources of Australia.

Latest business results (June 2020, half year)

Rio Tinto's iron ore business helped power it to another strong result, with growing Chinese demand more than offsetting weakness in other markets. The average iron ore price was little changed from the June 2019 half, but lower operating costs and a 3 per cent uptick in shipments helped generate an increase in profits. Iron ore generates about 55 per cent of company revenues, but in June 2020 was responsible for more than 80 per cent of profit. The Aluminium division represents 22 per cent of company turnover, and this business was hit by the COVID-19 pandemic. Demand was lower, particularly from the automobile sector, and prices fell, forcing revenues and profits down. The Copper and Diamonds division experienced a particularly sharp decline in revenues and profits, with demand and prices falling as a result of the pandemic. This business was also hurt by an earthquake at the company's Kennecott copper operations in the US. Lower prices sent revenues and profits lower for the Energy and Minerals division. Note that Rio Tinto reports its results in US dollars. The tables in this book are based on Australian dollar figures and exchange rates supplied by the company.

Outlook

Rio Tinto maintains a substantial portfolio of well-run assets across many countries, and with generally low operating costs. For the time being its fortunes are heavily dependent on trends in the global iron ore market, and these in turn are strongly influenced by Chinese economic developments. The company believes that rising infrastructure spending in China will keep iron ore demand strong in 2021. It maintains a high level of capital expenditure, with spending of around US$6 billion during 2020, rising to US$7 billion annually in 2021 and 2022. Major growth projects include the Oyu Tolgoi copper mine development in Mongolia, which is destined eventually to become the world's largest copper mine, the Zulti South industrial minerals mine in South Africa, the Winu copper-gold project in Western Australia and the Koodaideri iron ore mine in Western Australia.

Year to 31 December	2018	2019
Revenues ($mn)	54 029.0	61 664.0
EBIT ($mn)	18 154.0	22 520.9
EBIT margin (%)	33.6	36.5
Profit before tax ($mn)	17 750.0	22 158.0
Profit after tax ($mn)	11 744.0	14 819.0
Earnings per share (c)	683.07	909.09
Cash flow per share (c)	994.44	1 293.29
Dividend (c)	421.73	568.82
Percentage franked	100	100
Interest cover (times)	44.9	62.1
Return on equity (%)	19.6	24.6
Half year to 30 June	2019	2020
Revenues ($mn)	29 341.0	29 418.0
Profit before tax ($mn)	7 343.0	8 021.0
Profit after tax ($mn)	6 983.0	7 217.0
Earnings per share (c)	427.00	446.20
Dividend (c)	219.08	216.47
Percentage franked	100	100
Net tangible assets per share ($)	31.44	32.89
Debt-to-equity ratio (%)	19.1	18.0
Current ratio	1.5	1.6

Sandfire Resources NL

ASX code: SFR   www.sandfire.com.au

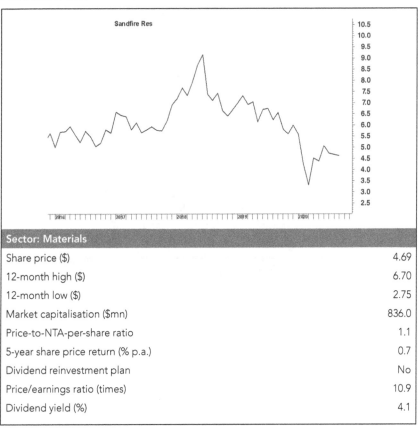

Sector: Materials	
Share price ($)	4.69
12-month high ($)	6.70
12-month low ($)	2.75
Market capitalisation ($mn)	836.0
Price-to-NTA-per-share ratio	1.1
5-year share price return (% p.a.)	0.7
Dividend reinvestment plan	No
Price/earnings ratio (times)	10.9
Dividend yield (%)	4.1

Perth-based Sandfire Resources dates back to 2004 when geologist Graeme Hutton listed the company on the ASX, with a portfolio of exploration projects. In 2009 the company discovered a significant copper and gold resource, and today it is a major copper and gold producer at its DeGrussa mine in Western Australia and also at the nearby Monty mine, which it acquired in 2018. It maintains an active exploration program in Australia and abroad. In October 2019 it acquired copper exploration company MOD Resources.

Latest business results (June 2020, full year)

Higher copper production at its mines boosted revenues, but increased depreciation and amortisation charges pushed down profits. During the year the company produced 72 238 tonnes of copper, up from 69 394 tonnes in the previous year, and 42 263 ounces of gold, down from 44 455 ounces. This included a full year of production from the satellite Monty mine. The average operating cost of US$0.72 per pound was down from US$0.83 per pound in the previous year. At the EBITDA level profits rose from $293.9 million in June 2019 to $315.3 million. However, the acquisition in 2018 of the Monty mine led to a substantially higher depreciation and amortisation charge — $201.4 million, compared with $140.8 million in June 2019 — and pre-tax and after-tax profits were down.

Outlook

Despite some copper price weakness in 2020, the company is optimistic about long-term trends, particularly given the tight balance between supply and demand as well as the underlying strength of demand from China. The company also believes the price will benefit from major new infrastructure initiatives throughout Asia and the rapid rise of new sources of demand from the electric vehicle and energy storage industries. However, its DeGrussa mine has an estimated life of only several more years. Sandfire's forecast for the June 2021 year is for production of between 67 000 tonnes and 70 000 tonnes of copper and between 36 000 ounces and 40 000 ounces of gold, at an average cost of between US$0.90 and US$0.95 per pound. Its acquisition of MOD Resources has delivered substantial copper-silver assets in Botswana and consequently the company is in the process of deciding whether to initiate a major mining program. Sandfire owns an 85 per cent stake in the Black Butte Copper Project in Montana, USA, and it has also been evaluating this resource with a view to starting construction of an underground mine. However, it faces legal challenges from groups opposed to resource development in the region.

Year to 30 June	2019	2020
Revenues ($mn)	592.2	656.8
EBIT ($mn)	153.1	113.8
EBIT margin (%)	25.8	17.3
Profit before tax ($mn)	158.6	111.1
Profit after tax ($mn)	106.5	74.1
Earnings per share (c)	66.76	42.88
Cash flow per share (c)	155.06	159.50
Dividend (c)	23	19
Percentage franked	100	100
Net tangible assets per share ($)	3.77	4.20
Interest cover (times)	~	42.5
Return on equity (%)	18.8	11.0
Debt-to-equity ratio (%)	~	~
Current ratio	5.0	5.4

Schaffer Corporation Limited

ASX code: SFC

schaffer.com.au

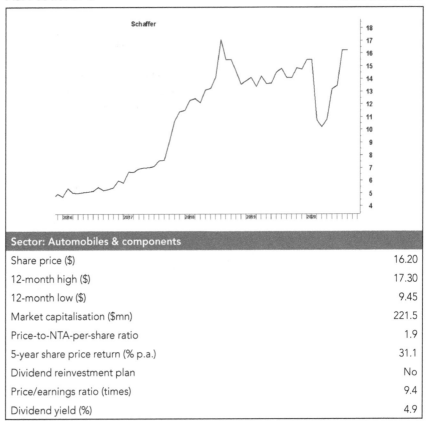

Sector: Automobiles & components	
Share price ($)	16.20
12-month high ($)	17.30
12-month low ($)	9.45
Market capitalisation ($mn)	221.5
Price-to-NTA-per-share ratio	1.9
5-year share price return (% p.a.)	31.1
Dividend reinvestment plan	No
Price/earnings ratio (times)	9.4
Dividend yield (%)	4.9

Perth company Schaffer was founded in 1955 to manufacture sand-lime bricks for the construction industry. Today its Delta Corporation subsidiary produces precast and prestressed concrete floors, beams and wall products, aimed mainly at the Western Australian construction market. However, its primary business now is the manufacture of leather goods, with a particular emphasis on products for the automotive industry, through its 83-per-cent-owned subsidiary Automotive Leather. This business operates from facilities in Australia, China and Slovakia, and supplies leading auto makers around the world. A third business for Schaffer is investments and property development, and it owns a growing portfolio of rental and development sites, mainly in Western Australia.

Latest business results (June 2020, full year)

Revenues fell as the company's leather business was hit by the weakness of the global automobile industry. However, the after-tax profit edged up, thanks to gains in the company's investment portfolio. Leather revenues dropped 26 per cent to $130 million, with profits also falling sharply. For two months from late January the

COVID-19 pandemic hit Chinese demand, then from March to late May European demand also slumped. Company efforts to reduce expenses were successful in limiting the damage to earnings. The company's concrete products business also struggled in a challenging Western Australian construction market, where it faced high levels of competition and project delays. This division saw revenues down 9 per cent to $17.8 million, and it fell back into the red. By contrast, Schaffer's investment portfolio enjoyed an excellent year, contributing $10.8 million to after-tax profit, compared with $1.8 million in the previous year. This included a $7.7 million non-cash gain, primarily in the value of an investment in the ASX-listed Harvest Technology Group.

Outlook

The company's core automotive leathergoods business is highly dependent on trends in the global car-making sector. Though a recovery from the depths of the COVID-19 pandemic is likely, the longer-term outlook seems subdued as global economies remain weak. However, the company expects to benefit during the June 2021 year from the start of new vehicle programs in both Europe and China, and an expanded investment in computer numerical controlled cutting machines at its plants is reducing costs. The company also sees signs of a recovery in its construction operations, thanks to a number of large pending infrastructure projects in Western Australia along with the possibility of some government stimulus schemes aimed at boosting the economy. The company's investment portfolio continues to grow, worth $163 million at June 2020, up 21 per cent from a year earlier.

Year to 30 June	2019	2020
Revenues ($mn)	202.9	155.1
EBIT ($mn)	40.3	40.7
EBIT margin (%)	19.9	26.2
Gross margin (%)	29.2	28.0
Profit before tax ($mn)	38.6	38.5
Profit after tax ($mn)	22.9	23.6
Earnings per share (c)	165.61	171.91
Cash flow per share (c)	199.39	228.80
Dividend (c)	70	80
Percentage franked	100	100
Net tangible assets per share ($)	7.55	8.37
Interest cover (times)	23.0	19.1
Return on equity (%)	23.3	21.3
Debt-to-equity ratio (%)	10.2	14.8
Current ratio	1.9	2.4

SeaLink Travel Group Limited

ASX code: SLK   www.sealinktravelgroup.com.au

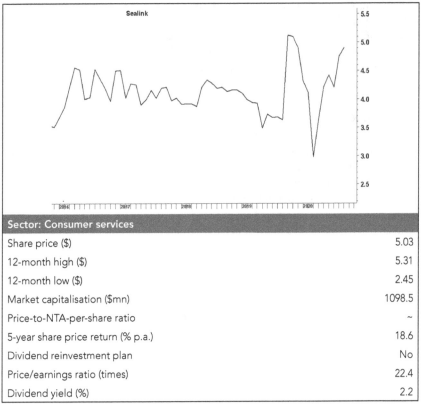

Sector: Consumer services	
Share price ($)	5.03
12-month high ($)	5.31
12-month low ($)	2.45
Market capitalisation ($mn)	1098.5
Price-to-NTA-per-share ratio	~
5-year share price return (% p.a.)	18.6
Dividend reinvestment plan	No
Price/earnings ratio (times)	22.4
Dividend yield (%)	2.2

Adelaide tourism and transport company SeaLink has its roots in the launch of a Kangaroo Island ferry service, Philanderer Ferries, in the 1970s. It has since expanded considerably, and today provides a wide range of bus, ferry, resort and tourism services under more than 20 brands. Since the $635 million acquisition in January 2020 of bus operator Transit Systems Group (TSG) it has divided its operations into three broad segments. The Australian Bus division operates metropolitan public bus services in Australian cities. The International Bus division operates metropolitan public bus services in London and Singapore. The Marine and Tourism division manages all the company's legacy operations. These include ferry services, packaged holidays and other travel activities, the Captain Cook Cruises business in Sydney and Perth, and the Kingfisher Bay Resort Group on Fraser Island in Queensland.

Latest business results (June 2020, full year)

A five-and-a-half-month contribution from the TSG acquisition sent revenues soaring, with profits also higher, and comparisons with the previous year have little meaning. When many regions entered into various degrees of lockdown due to the COVID-19 pandemic, the company's newly acquired bus services were deemed an essential facility, and continued to operate. By contrast, some of SeaLink's tourism businesses were, after a positive first half, forced to limit or suspend operations. These affected businesses included the Kangaroo Island ferry service — which was hit by both bushfires and then the pandemic — and Captain Cook Cruises. Consequently, revenues for the Marine and Tourism division fell 14 per cent to $214 million, with profits down 22 per cent. The company also announced significant one-off costs relating to the TSG acquisition, as well as impairment charges on some of its tourism assets, and at the statutory level it fell into the red.

Outlook

SeaLink has been transformed by its TSG acquisition, which has delivered more than 3400 buses operating more than 1000 bus routes. Bus operations will now be responsible for up to 80 per cent of company income. SeaLink also expects at least $4.6 million in annual cost synergies. Thanks to the acquisition, some 87 per cent of SeaLink's revenue is now contracted to government clients, and it sees a solid pipeline of growth opportunities. Many of its other operations are geared towards levels of tourism, and it is hopeful of a recovery as travel restrictions between states are eased and, with Australians largely unable to travel abroad, domestic tourism enjoys a boom. It will promote this through a new brand, Brilliant Travels.

Year to 30 June	2019	2020
Revenues ($mn)	248.8	623.7
Australian bus (%)	0	45
Marine & tourism (%)	100	34
International bus (%)	0	21
EBIT ($mn)	32.7	52.7
EBIT margin (%)	13.2	8.5
Profit before tax ($mn)	28.8	43.4
Profit after tax ($mn)	25.3	37.2
Earnings per share (c)	24.95	22.48
Cash flow per share (c)	41.09	53.90
Dividend (c)	15	11
Percentage franked	100	100
Net tangible assets per share ($)	1.03	~
Interest cover (times)	8.3	5.7
Return on equity (%)	16.3	10.0
Debt-to-equity ratio (%)	52.6	31.7
Current ratio	1.1	0.7

Select Harvests Limited

ASX code: SHV   www.selectharvests.com.au

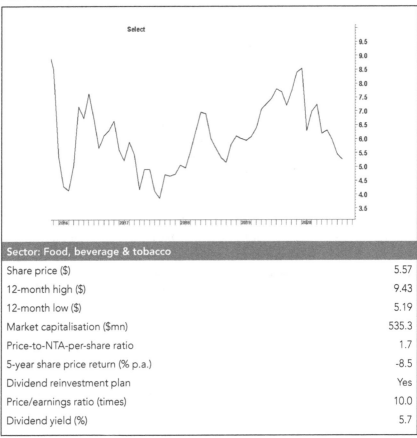

Sector: Food, beverage & tobacco	
Share price ($)	5.57
12-month high ($)	9.43
12-month low ($)	5.19
Market capitalisation ($mn)	535.3
Price-to-NTA-per-share ratio	1.7
5-year share price return (% p.a.)	-8.5
Dividend reinvestment plan	Yes
Price/earnings ratio (times)	10.0
Dividend yield (%)	5.7

Melbourne-based Select Harvests, founded in 1978, is one of Australia's biggest almond growers and processors and also one of the largest growers in the world. It owns and leases around 7700 hectares of almond orchards in Victoria, New South Wales and South Australia, and also operates two almond-processing facilities in Victoria. The company's Food division markets almonds and other nuts, as well as health mixes and muesli, to customers in Australia and abroad that include supermarkets, health food stores, other retailers and food manufacturers. Its main brands are Lucky, Sunsol, NuVitality, Renshaw and Allinga Farms.

Latest business results (March 2020, half year)

Sales and profits fell, as the company was hit by a combination of weaker global almond prices and COVID-19 disruptions to distribution channels. The average almond price of around $8.20 per kilogram was nearly 5 per cent less than the price of a year earlier, partly due to market expectations of a record 2020 crop in the US. The company also faced higher costs, including a big increase in the price of water, which is its main expense. The Food division achieved strong sales, but with continual profit margin erosion due to competitive pressures, particularly from major retailer house brands. Though the Food division generates about three-quarters of total company turnover, it contributes less than 10 per cent of company profit. Please note that Select Harvests has changed its reporting period from a June year-end to a September year-end. The September 2018 figures in this book are unofficial estimates only, calculated from figures supplied by the company for the 12 months to June 2018 and the three months to September 2018.

Outlook

Select Harvests announced in July 2020 that the 2020 almond harvest had been completed, with a crop volume of approximately 23 000 tonnes, slightly up from 22 690 tonnes in 2019. The company had sales contracts for more than 80 per cent of its output, at prices from $7.25 to $7.75 per kilogram. In the September 2019 year it received an average of $8.60 per kilogram. On a longer-term view, the company's outlook is positive. It is a beneficiary of a steady rise in global demand for almonds, in recognition of their health benefits. In 2013 it began a program of new tree plantings, and as almond trees take seven years to reach maturity it now expects crop volumes to grow. It has also been investing in infrastructure such as frost fans, and has been successful in boosting production yields.

Year to 30 September	2018*	2019
Revenues ($mn)	222.3	298.5
EBIT ($mn)	27.1	80.0
EBIT margin (%)	12.2	26.8
Profit before tax ($mn)	21.9	76.1
Profit after tax ($mn)	15.1	53.0
Earnings per share (c)	15.82	55.50
Cash flow per share (c)	32.64	71.34
Dividend (c)	12	32
Percentage franked	100	100
Interest cover (times)	5.2	20.5
Return on equity (%)	4.0	13.5
* September 2018 figures are estimates only		

Half year to 31 March	2019	2020
Revenues ($mn)	100.0	93.5
Profit before tax ($mn)	28.9	24.7
Profit after tax ($mn)	20.0	17.4
Earnings per share (c)	21.00	18.10
Dividend (c)	12	9
Percentage franked	100	100
Net tangible assets per share ($)	3.42	3.33
Debt-to-equity ratio (%)	23.8	17.6
Current ratio	3.3	2.1

Servcorp Limited

ASX code: SRV   www.servcorp.com.au

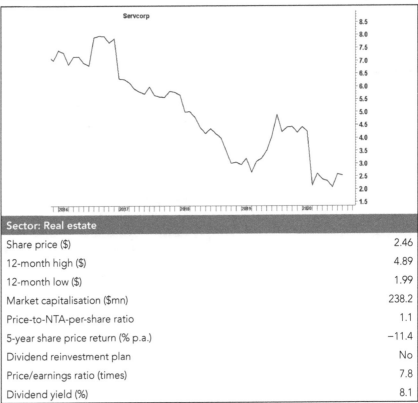

Sector: Real estate	
Share price ($)	2.46
12-month high ($)	4.89
12-month low ($)	1.99
Market capitalisation ($mn)	238.2
Price-to-NTA-per-share ratio	1.1
5-year share price return (% p.a.)	−11.4
Dividend reinvestment plan	No
Price/earnings ratio (times)	7.8
Dividend yield (%)	8.1

Sydney-based Servcorp was founded in 1978 to provide serviced office space to small businesses. It has expanded to provide advanced corporate infrastructure, including IT and telecommunications services, and office support services. It also offers what it terms virtual offices, providing a prestigious address and a range of services — such as message forwarding and access to meeting rooms — for people or businesses not needing a physical office. About 40 per cent of the company's business is in North Asia, with more than a quarter in Europe and the Middle East. In June 2020 it was operating 126 floors of offices in 43 cities across 21 countries.

Latest business results (June 2020, full year)

In a challenging environment, Servcorp achieved a good result, thanks to its strength in North Asia, and improved business in the Middle East and the United Kingdom, though partially offset by a continuing underperformance in the United States. On a like-for-like basis, the total occupancy rate was 69 per cent at June 2020, down from

73 per cent a year earlier. The big North Asian segment enjoyed another strong year, with double-digit increases in revenues and cash earnings, despite weakness in China and Hong Kong. The next-largest segment, Europe and the Middle East, also reported a good year, with cash earnings almost doubling, thanks in particular to significant contributions from Saudi Arabia, Qatar and the UAE. The Australia/New Zealand/South-East Asia segment saw its profits rise, despite disruptions to business from the COVID-19 pandemic. However, the troubled United States segment saw revenues down, with a sharply expanded loss. During the year the company opened new floors in New York and Shanghai and closed 29 others.

Outlook

Servcorp is a world leader in its business, with good market shares and a reputation for quality. However, its business is being affected by the COVID-19 pandemic, which in the longer term could lead to reduced demand for the company's prestige inner-city office space as increasing numbers of people work from home. Conversely, the work-from-home trend is boosting demand for the company's virtual offices. In the shorter term, the pandemic has hit demand in some regions and is also obliging the company to negotiate rent relief with both its tenants and its own landlords. It continues to expand, but is also working to address its poorly performing American operations. In June it announced the closure of its office space in eight US cities, leaving it to concentrate on operations in New York, Chicago, Houston and Washington DC.

Year to 30 June	2019	2020
Revenues ($mn)	334.9	349.1
EBIT ($mn)	29.9	36.2
EBIT margin (%)	8.9	10.4
Profit before tax ($mn)	32.0	37.5
Profit after tax ($mn)	29.2	30.6
Earnings per share (c)	30.16	31.61
Cash flow per share (c)	58.65	63.84
Dividend (c)	23	20
Percentage franked	49	14
Net tangible assets per share ($)	2.32	2.14
Interest cover (times)	~	~
Return on equity (%)	11.9	13.3
Debt-to-equity ratio (%)	~	~
Current ratio	1.3	0.8

Service Stream Limited

ASX code: SSM   www.servicestream.com.au

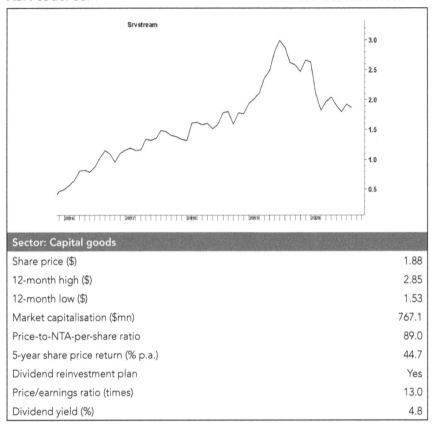

Sector: Capital goods	
Share price ($)	1.88
12-month high ($)	2.85
12-month low ($)	1.53
Market capitalisation ($mn)	767.1
Price-to-NTA-per-share ratio	89.0
5-year share price return (% p.a.)	44.7
Dividend reinvestment plan	Yes
Price/earnings ratio (times)	13.0
Dividend yield (%)	4.8

Melbourne-based contractor Service Stream provides a variety of engineering services to the telecommunication, electricity, gas, water and new energy industries. It segments its operations into four divisions. The Fixed Communications division offers construction and maintenance services for fixed-line communications networks, with Telstra and the National Broadband Network (NBN) among its major customers. The Network Construction division is engaged in the design, construction and engineering of infrastructure projects, mainly in the telecommunications sector. The Energy and Water division is involved in a range of specialist metering and other services to the electricity, gas and water sectors. A fourth division is based on the acquisition in January 2019 of Comdain Infrastructure, and provides engineering and asset management services to owners and operators of gas and water networks.

Latest business results (June 2020, full year)

A full year's contribution from Comdain boosted revenues, with profits also edging up. The telecommunications segment — incorporating the Fixed Communications and the Network Construction divisions — reported a fall in revenues, following the conclusion of some NBN-related work. This business was also affected by delays in some wireless projects due to the COVID-19 pandemic. However, higher margins actually led to a rise in telecommunications profits. The utilities segment — comprising the Energy and Water division and Comdain Infrastructure — enjoyed a 45 per cent jump in sales thanks to the addition of Comdain. Revenues would have been higher but for a series of pandemic-related delays. Utilities profits also rose strongly, although profit margins were below those for telecommunications work.

Outlook

Service Stream has been transformed by the Comdain acquisition. It was previously heavily dependent on the telecommunications sector, which contributed more than 80 per cent of its revenues. Comdain's engineering and asset management services, mainly in east coast markets, combine well with Service Stream's own core capabilities of design, construction, operations and maintenance. The company believes it is now able to offer a greatly enhanced service to clients, and with the potential for expansion to new markets. It also expects continuing synergy benefits. However, on the telecommunications side, the company's big NBN projects are set to end, although it expects continuing demand for NBN maintenance work, leading to a growing amount of annuity-style revenue. It has also secured contracts relating to the roll-out of 5G telecommunications networks in Australia, and this business has the potential for solid growth. At June 2020 Service Stream had net cash holdings of more than $19 million, and it continues to seek further complementary acquisitions.

Year to 30 June	2019	2020
Revenues ($mn)	851.0	928.0
Telecommunications (%)	68	59
Utilities (%)	32	41
EBIT ($mn)	84.5	87.4
EBIT margin (%)	9.9	9.4
Profit before tax ($mn)	83.3	84.0
Profit after tax ($mn)	57.7	58.8
Earnings per share (c)	15.15	14.46
Cash flow per share (c)	19.41	22.25
Dividend (c)	9	9
Percentage franked	100	100
Net tangible assets per share ($)	~	0.02
Interest cover (times)	70.3	25.4
Return on equity (%)	22.4	18.7
Debt-to-equity ratio (%)	~	~
Current ratio	1.2	1.4

SG Fleet Group Limited

ASX code: SGF

investors.sgfleet.com

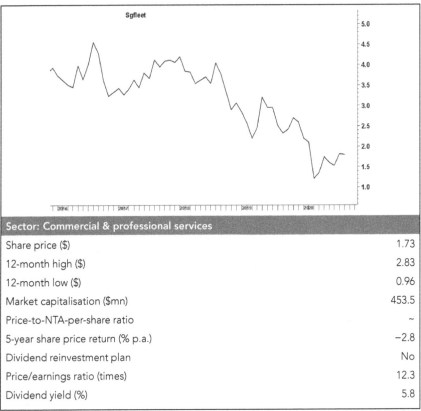

Sector: Commercial & professional services	
Share price ($)	1.73
12-month high ($)	2.83
12-month low ($)	0.96
Market capitalisation ($mn)	453.5
Price-to-NTA-per-share ratio	~
5-year share price return (% p.a.)	−2.8
Dividend reinvestment plan	No
Price/earnings ratio (times)	12.3
Dividend yield (%)	5.8

SG Fleet, based in Sydney, has its roots in the formation in 1986 of Leaseway Transportation, a specialist fleet management company. Leaseway was later sold to the Commonwealth Bank, which in turn sold it in 2004 to a South African company, Super Group, who renamed it FleetAustralia. In 2014 it was listed on the ASX as SG Fleet Group. Today it offers a range of fleet management services in Australia, New Zealand and the United Kingdom. It also provides salary packaging services. It operates under the brand SG Fleet and, in the UK, Fleet Hire. In addition, it operates the nlc vehicle financing business in Australia. South Africa's Super Group continues to hold a 60 per cent equity stake in the company.

Latest business results (June 2020, full year)

The COVID-19 pandemic hit SG Fleet, which saw revenues and profits fall. The company reported that in the fourth quarter its revenues fell by 42 per cent, and it was also hit by the continuing decline in new car sales in Australia. Australian sales revenues fell 11 per cent with pre-tax profit crashing by 39 per cent. British business represents around 20 per cent of total company turnover. The UK general election of December 2019 appeared to bring a new level of consumer confidence, and the company was able to pursue a significant number of new opportunities. But new vehicle registrations fell sharply after the COVID-19 lockdown at the end of March, and total British sales revenues for the year fell 8 per cent, with the pre-tax profit nearly halving. The company's total fleet size grew from 139 945 vehicles in June 2019 to 143 278 in June 2020.

Outlook

SG Fleet occupies a solid position in a competitive industry. It generates good profit margins, and as it grows it achieves significant economies of scale that boost margins higher. However, its business is influenced to a degree by the state of the economy, and in particular the level of new car sales. Nevertheless, it enjoys a large amount of annuity-style income, with many long-term clients, as it is costly for a car fleet customer to switch providers. It expects a series of new products to solidify relationships with existing customers and attract new ones. Already, the majority of its largest customers take up at least three of its products. Among recent initiatives, it has invested in the DingGo digital portal for private car repairs and in the Carly short-term car hire company.

Year to 30 June	2019	2020
Revenues ($mn)	508.1	451.6
EBIT ($mn)	93.7	59.2
EBIT margin (%)	18.4	13.1
Profit before tax ($mn)	85.8	52.4
Profit after tax ($mn)	60.5	36.7
Earnings per share (c)	23.20	14.01
Cash flow per share (c)	35.33	26.33
Dividend (c)	17.69	10.00
Percentage franked	100	100
Net tangible assets per share ($)	~	~
Interest cover (times)	11.8	8.6
Return on equity (%)	22.8	13.3
Debt-to-equity ratio (%)	8.9	5.2

Smartgroup Corporation Limited

ASX code: SIQ   www.smartgroup.com.au

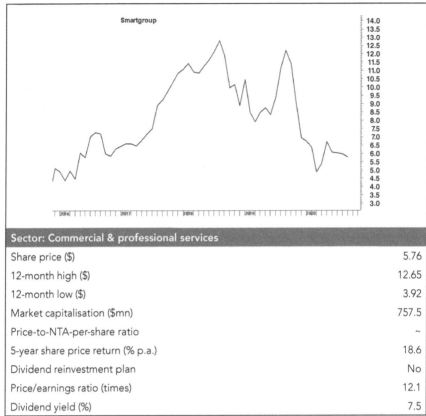

Sector: Commercial & professional services	
Share price ($)	5.76
12-month high ($)	12.65
12-month low ($)	3.92
Market capitalisation ($mn)	757.5
Price-to-NTA-per-share ratio	~
5-year share price return (% p.a.)	18.6
Dividend reinvestment plan	No
Price/earnings ratio (times)	12.1
Dividend yield (%)	7.5

Sydney-based Smartgroup got its start in 1999 as Smartsalary, a salary packaging specialist. It later branched into other businesses, and has grown significantly, both organically and through acquisition. It is now engaged in salary packaging services, as well as vehicle novated leasing, fleet management, payroll administration, share plan administration and workforce optimisation consulting services.

Latest business results (June 2020, half year)

Revenues and profits fell by double-digit amounts as the company took a hit from the COVID-19 pandemic. The fall in revenues was due mainly to a 15 per cent reduction from the June 2019 half in novated lease settlement volumes. This followed a 19 per cent drop in Australian private new vehicle sales during this period. Salary packages of 355 500 during the half were roughly in line with June 2019. However, packaging revenue was down, due to lower interest earned on client accounts. In response to the pandemic, the company introduced temporary cost-cutting measures, and this reduced expenses for the half by $4 million. Smartgroup operates two smaller businesses, software services and fleet management services, together representing a little more than 20 per cent of company turnover, and they both held up fairly well, with revenues edging up and profits slightly down.

Outlook

Smartgroup is one of Australia's two largest companies involved in the salary packaging and novated leasing businesses. The other is McMillan Shakespeare. Essentially this business involves taking advantage of complex legislation to provide tax deductions for employees, mainly those working in charities or in the public sector. Smartgroup has grown considerably through a series of acquisitions, and at June 2020 it had around 4000 clients. As it grows it achieves economies of scale, and profit margins increase. The company is also working to boost cross-selling of its various products among existing clients, and at June 2020 there were 200 clients using two or more of its products, up from 180 clients a year earlier. Smartgroup sells some insurance products, and changes to the terms of these products from the company's underwriting partner, from July 2020, will hurt profits. This business is also under threat from reviews being undertaken by the Treasury Department and the Australian Securities and Investments Commission. In addition, the company is vulnerable to weakness in the economy and in employment trends. Its business is also affected by trends in new car sales, and these have recently been weak in Australia, as some companies choose to cut costs by retaining and refinancing existing staff cars, rather than buying new ones.

Year to 31 December	2018	2019
Revenues ($mn)	242.3	249.8
EBIT ($mn)	89.0	91.7
EBIT margin (%)	36.7	36.7
Profit before tax ($mn)	84.3	88.7
Profit after tax ($mn)	59.3	61.4
Earnings per share (c)	46.65	47.58
Cash flow per share (c)	66.33	67.10
Dividend (c)	41.5	43
Percentage franked	100	100
Interest cover (times)	19.0	30.4
Return on equity (%)	23.9	21.6
Half year to 30 June	2019	2020
Revenues ($mn)	125.8	111.4
Profit before tax ($mn)	44.2	33.0
Profit after tax ($mn)	30.9	22.9
Earnings per share (c)	23.90	19.60
Dividend (c)	21.5	17
Percentage franked	100	100
Net tangible assets per share ($)	~	~
Debt-to-equity ratio (%)	7.6	4.8
Current ratio	1.1	1.5

Super Retail Group Limited

ASX code: SUL   www.superretailgroup.com.au

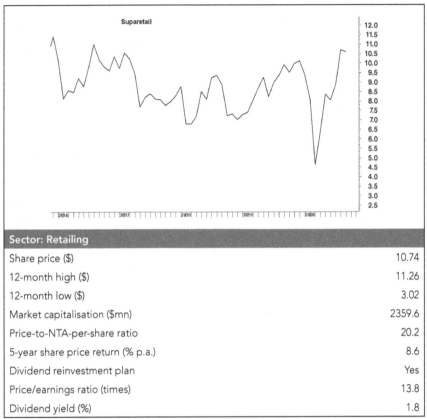

Sector: Retailing	
Share price ($)	10.74
12-month high ($)	11.26
12-month low ($)	3.02
Market capitalisation ($mn)	2359.6
Price-to-NTA-per-share ratio	20.2
5-year share price return (% p.a.)	8.6
Dividend reinvestment plan	Yes
Price/earnings ratio (times)	13.8
Dividend yield (%)	1.8

Specialist retail chain Super Retail Group was established as a mail-order business in 1972 and has its headquarters in Strathpine, north of Brisbane. It now comprises a number of key retail brands, with nearly 700 stores throughout Australia and New Zealand. Supercheap Auto is a retailer of automotive spare parts and related products. Rebel is a prominent sporting goods chain. BCF is a retailer of boating, camping and fishing products. Macpac is an outdoor adventure and activity specialist retailer.

Latest business results (June 2020, full year)

Revenues and profits rose in a mixed year for the company, with strength at Supercheap Auto and Rebel, but weakness at BCF and Macpac. Group sales were up 3.6 per cent on a same-store basis, and online sales of $290.5 million were a 44 per cent jump from the previous year. Supercheap Auto enjoyed an excellent year, with growth in all categories and a double-digit increase in profits. Rebel benefited from strong demand for home fitness products as a result of the COVID-19 pandemic. BCF actually saw sales rise, but this business was disrupted by bushfires, travel restrictions and increased competition, and profits fell. Macpac too was hit by bushfires and travel restrictions, along with store closures in New Zealand, and sales and profits fell.

Outlook

Having restructured its operations, including the 2018 acquisition of Macpac, Super Retail now controls four prominent brands with strong positions in their respective markets. It is working to build these businesses with a variety of strategies. It plans a steady rollout of new stores. It is also boosting its digital capacity and expects online sales to continue their strong growth. It is increasing its range of higher-margin own-brand and exclusive products at its stores, and is harnessing customer loyalty through the promotion of members' clubs. The company believes that it stands to be a significant beneficiary of a post-pandemic world, as Australian consumers, unable or unwilling to travel abroad, boost spending on domestic leisure and recreation. The company also benefits from rising demand for health and wellbeing products and services. Nevertheless, despite Super Retail's strengths, it operates in a challenging retail environment, with online businesses like Amazon a competitor for many of its products. With much of its product range imported, it is also vulnerable to currency fluctuations. Having raised capital during the year, the company at June 2020 had more than $37 million in net cash holdings. It expects to open at least 10 new stores during the June 2021 year.

Year to 27 June*	2019	2020
Revenues ($mn)	2710.4	2825.2
Supercheap Auto (%)	38	39
Rebel (%)	38	37
BCF (%)	19	19
Macpac (%)	5	5
EBIT ($mn)	228.0	273.4
EBIT margin (%)	8.4	9.7
Gross margin (%)	45.1	45.0
Profit before tax ($mn)	206.7	218.3
Profit after tax ($mn)	152.5	154.1
Earnings per share (c)	77.28	77.98
Cash flow per share (c)	121.16	124.54
Dividend (c)	50	19.5
Percentage franked	100	100
Net tangible assets per share ($)	~	0.53
Interest cover (times)	10.7	5.0
Return on equity (%)	19.2	17.1
Debt-to-equity ratio (%)	47.4	~
Current ratio	1.3	1.1

* 29 June 2019

Supply Network Limited

ASX code: SNL   www.supplynetwork.com.au

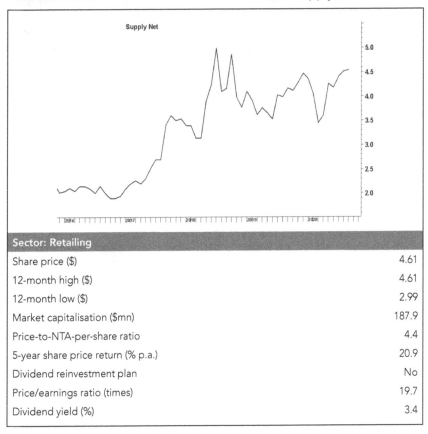

Sector: Retailing	
Share price ($)	4.61
12-month high ($)	4.61
12-month low ($)	2.99
Market capitalisation ($mn)	187.9
Price-to-NTA-per-share ratio	4.4
5-year share price return (% p.a.)	20.9
Dividend reinvestment plan	No
Price/earnings ratio (times)	19.7
Dividend yield (%)	3.4

Sydney-based Supply Network is a supplier of bus and truck parts in the commercial vehicle aftermarket, operating under the brand name Multispares, which was established in 1976. It manages offices, distribution centres and workshops at 16 locations throughout Australia and five in New Zealand.

Latest business results (June 2020, full year)

Supply Network reported another solid result, with higher sales and profits, despite some impact from the COVID-19 pandemic. This led to flat sales for about six weeks from mid March in Australia and declining sales in New Zealand. Australian business comprises more than 80 per cent of total company turnover, and sales were up 11 per cent, although the pre-tax profit edged down. During the year the company opened a new branch at Eagle Farm, an industrial precinct near Brisbane Airport, and this has been performing above expectations. New Zealand operations achieved a 7 per cent increase in sales, and profits rebounded from their decline of the previous year.

Outlook

Supply Network is one of the leaders in the competitive Australian market for the supply of truck and bus parts. With a great diversity of vehicle makes and models, and with a considerable difference in requirements between various regions of the country, the company has established a decentralised management structure with a strong regional focus. Its core activity in recent years has become the supply of truck components, with this business growing at a faster pace than the supply of bus components. In part, this results from large numbers of newer bus fleets around the country, reducing demand for replacement parts. Consequently, nearly 80 per cent of company sales now are to the trucking sector. Company fleets are the largest customer group, and these are sophisticated buyers of parts with a focus on costs, making this business highly competitive. Independent repair workshops are the next-largest customer group. The company has set itself a target of $150 million in sales in the June 2022 year, growing eventually to $200 million. To achieve this goal it is working to streamline operations at its distribution centres and is deploying new technologies to improve the accuracy and speed of product transactions. It is also investigating options to expand its existing distribution centre in Hamilton, New Zealand, and is reviewing proposals for a new distribution centre in Melbourne. It has secured an option for additional warehouse space at its Darra branch, in Brisbane's south-west freight corridor. It is also investigating ways to add a series of smaller distribution centres to its network.

Year to 30 June	2019	2020
Revenues ($mn)	123.9	136.8
EBIT ($mn)	12.8	15.3
EBIT margin (%)	10.3	11.2
Profit before tax ($mn)	12.3	13.6
Profit after tax ($mn)	8.7	9.5
Earnings per share (c)	21.32	23.42
Cash flow per share (c)	24.61	37.36
Dividend (c)	14.5	15.5
Percentage franked	100	100
Net tangible assets per share ($)	0.94	1.04
Interest cover (times)	28.8	9.0
Return on equity (%)	23.8	23.7
Debt-to-equity ratio (%)	20.4	18.8
Current ratio	2.6	2.4

Technology One Limited

ASX code: TNE   www.technologyonecorp.com

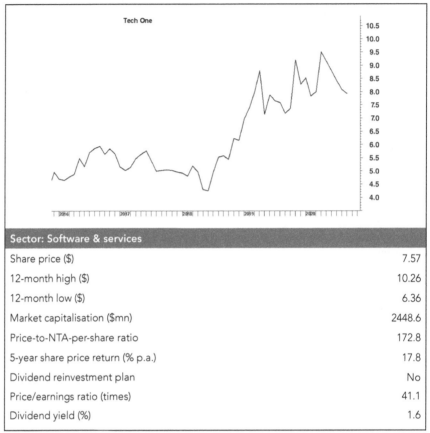

Tech One

Sector: Software & services	
Share price ($)	7.57
12-month high ($)	10.26
12-month low ($)	6.36
Market capitalisation ($mn)	2448.6
Price-to-NTA-per-share ratio	172.8
5-year share price return (% p.a.)	17.8
Dividend reinvestment plan	No
Price/earnings ratio (times)	41.1
Dividend yield (%)	1.6

Brisbane-based Technology One, founded in 1987, designs, develops, implements and supports a wide range of financial management, accounting and business software. It enjoys particular strength in local government. Its software is also used by educational institutions, including many Australian universities. Other key markets are financial services, central government, and health and community services. It derives revenues not only from the supply of its products but also from annual licence fees. It operates from offices in Australia, New Zealand, Malaysia and the UK. It has opened research and development centres in Indonesia and Vietnam.

Latest business results (March 2020, half year)

Revenues and profits rose by single-digit amounts, in another satisfactory result for the company. Once again Technology One enjoyed success in moving its customers onto its Software as a Service (SaaS) cloud platforms. The number of large-scale enterprise SaaS customers rose to 475, up from 389 a year earlier. SaaS annual recurring revenue of $110 million was a 33 per cent jump from a year before. There was a particularly strong result from consulting services — essentially the business of implementing the company's software — with a 49 per cent jump in pre-tax profit on just a small increase in revenues. But British operations remained in the red. The company maintained its high level of research and development spending, up 10 per cent to $30.5 million. It reported that COVID-19 had had just a minimal impact on its business. Note that it has restated its September 2018 results, due to new accounting standards.

Outlook

Technology One has become a star among Australian high-tech companies, with growing profits and regular dividend increases. In large part this reflects a strong product line, a solid flow of recurring income, and a heavy investment in new products and services. It is achieving great success with its SaaS offerings, which put software in the cloud, rather than on the customers' own computers, meaning that the customers always have the latest software versions, giving them greater flexibility than previously. Technology One expects profits to rise 8 per cent to 12 per cent in the September 2020 year, and it believes the company will continue to double in size every four to five years. In mid 2020 the media reported claims from a Hong Kong–based research group that Technology One has been using accounting tricks to inflate its revenues and profits. The company has firmly denied this and said it would refer the matter to the Australian Securities and Investment Commission.

Year to 30 September	2018	2019
Revenues ($mn)	253.0	285.0
EBIT ($mn)	24.5	75.8
EBIT margin (%)	9.7	26.6
Profit before tax ($mn)	24.8	76.4
Profit after tax ($mn)	21.7	58.5
Earnings per share (c)	6.87	18.43
Cash flow per share (c)	8.48	20.36
Dividend (c)	9.02	11.93
Percentage franked	80	64
Interest cover (times)	~	~
Return on equity (%)	12.9	63.4
Half year to 31 March	2019	2020
Revenues ($mn)	128.5	138.0
Profit before tax ($mn)	24.5	25.9
Profit after tax ($mn)	17.9	19.1
Earnings per share (c)	5.65	5.98
Dividend (c)	3.15	3.47
Percentage franked	75	60
Net tangible assets per share ($)	0.03	0.04
Debt-to-equity ratio (%)	~	~
Current ratio	0.8	0.9

Vita Group Limited

ASX code: VTG www.vitagroup.com.au

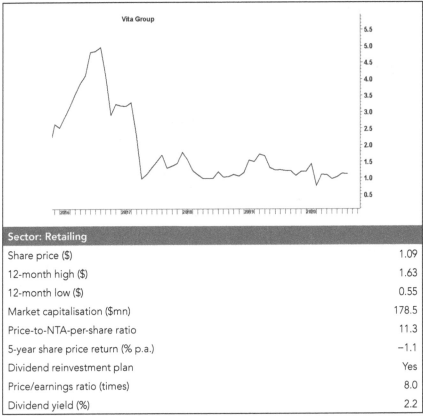

Sector: Retailing	
Share price ($)	1.09
12-month high ($)	1.63
12-month low ($)	0.55
Market capitalisation ($mn)	178.5
Price-to-NTA-per-share ratio	11.3
5-year share price return (% p.a.)	−1.1
Dividend reinvestment plan	Yes
Price/earnings ratio (times)	8.0
Dividend yield (%)	2.2

Brisbane-based Vita, founded in 1995 as a single store, is a specialist retailer of technology and communication products and services, such as mobile phones and related products and services, along with third-party voice and data services. It also manages service and rental contracts, as well as selling voice and data services. In the business field it operates under the Telstra Business Centre and Vita Enterprise Solutions brands. It sells mobile accessories under its own Sprout brand. Since 2016 it has been moving into the health and wellness sector, with the Artisan Aesthetics chain of skincare clinics. It has sold its SQDAthletica men's lifestyle products business.

Latest business results (June 2020, full year)

Revenues rose but profits fell in a challenging year for the company. Its core information and communications technology business saw revenues up 2 per cent, thanks especially to firm growth in sales of retail products and services, although with a pandemic-related slowing of business in the fourth quarter and some disruption from changes in Telstra's remuneration policies. The company's own Sprout brand continued to make a positive contribution, with its revenues up by 14 per cent.

However, business-related activities saw revenues down as the company placed a greater focus on more profitable customer segments. The Skin-Health and Wellness division recorded a 47 per cent increase in revenues to $20.1 million, despite store closures during the period of the pandemic, and this business remained in the red. During the year the number of skincare clinics rose from 13 to 21. The company reported $10.2 million in JobKeeper payments from the government, as well as rent assistance from landlords.

Outlook

Vita Group has grown to occupy a prominent position in the sale of telecommunications products to retail consumers and is a significant beneficiary of the continuing strong demand in Australia for the latest devices. However, it is highly dependent on Telstra, which can cause a degree of volatility in its operations. In order to lessen this dependence, it has been moving into the health and wellness sector, and has been developing its own network of skincare clinics. It has ambitious plans for these, and believes it could become one of Australia's leading providers of skincare services, with an eventual nationwide chain of 70 to 90 stores. To complement this business, it has also acquired a training organisation and specialist software. At June 2020 Vita had net cash holdings of more than $24 million, and it has expressed a desire to grow further through acquisition.

Year to 30 June	2019	2020
Revenues ($mn)	753.7	773.1
EBIT ($mn)	34.7	37.2
EBIT margin (%)	4.6	4.8
Profit before tax ($mn)	34.1	33.8
Profit after tax ($mn)	24.3	22.4
Earnings per share (c)	15.04	13.71
Cash flow per share (c)	21.86	31.21
Dividend (c)	9.2	2.4
Percentage franked	100	100
Net tangible assets per share ($)	0.02	0.10
Interest cover (times)	52.7	10.8
Return on equity (%)	23.5	19.0
Debt-to-equity ratio (%)	~	~
Current ratio	0.8	0.8

Wesfarmers Limited

ASX code: WES

www.wesfarmers.com.au

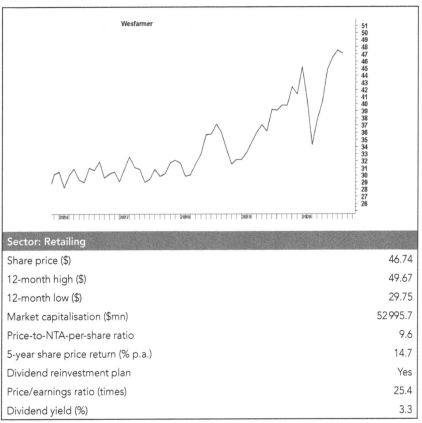

Sector: Retailing	
Share price ($)	46.74
12-month high ($)	49.67
12-month low ($)	29.75
Market capitalisation ($mn)	52995.7
Price-to-NTA-per-share ratio	9.6
5-year share price return (% p.a.)	14.7
Dividend reinvestment plan	Yes
Price/earnings ratio (times)	25.4
Dividend yield (%)	3.3

Perth-based Wesfarmers, founded in 1914 as a farmers' cooperative, is now a conglomerate with many areas of operation. Having divested itself of its Coles supermarket operations, its primary business now is the Bunnings network of hardware stores. Other retail businesses include the Officeworks, Kmart and Target chains and the Catch online operation. In addition, it produces fertilisers, chemicals and industrial safety products. It has retained a 5 per cent equity stake in Coles, holds 50 per cent of the Flybuys loyalty card business, owns a 25 per cent interest in the ASX-listed BWP property trust — which owns many Bunnings warehouses — and holds half the equity in both the financial services business Gresham Partners and the timber business Wespine Industries. At June 2020 it operated 996 Bunnings, Kmart, Target and Officeworks stores throughout Australia and 71 Bunnings and Kmart stores in New Zealand.

Latest business results (June 2020, full year)

Solid growth in retail sales generated a positive result for Wesfarmers. The core Bunnings operation did best, with sales up 14 per cent and underlying EBIT up 18 per cent. The Kmart Group division, incorporating Kmart, Target and Catch, saw sales up by 7 per cent but underlying EBIT fell 22 per cent, as good business at Kmart was more than offset by a dismal performance at Target, which fell into the red. Officeworks enjoyed double-digit increases in sales and profits. Total group online sales reached $2.1 billion. The COVID-19 pandemic forced the company to spend heavily on protective measures for its stores, and it also experienced significant volatility in sales along with some supply chain interruptions. Among its industrial businesses, the Chemicals, Energy and Fertilisers division recorded flat sales, with profits hit by some higher costs and lower margins. The Blackwoods safety products business had another poor year, and the company's Workwear Group was also weak.

Outlook

Wesfarmers expects continuing steady growth from Bunnings, driven by new stores, new sales categories, product innovation and the rollout of a full online offering. It also remains optimistic about the long-term prospects for Officeworks. It sees great potential for Catch — acquired in August 2019 — as online sales surge. However, Target stores remain a problem and the company plans a major restructuring, including the conversion of 27 Target stores to Kmart stores. It is also taking steps to address weakness at its Blackwoods and Workwear businesses. It expects its Chemicals, Energy and Fertilisers division to be hurt by weaker energy prices and lower margins.

Year to 30 June	2019	2020
Revenues ($mn)	27 920.0	30 846.0
Bunnings (%)	47	49
Kmart Group (%)	31	30
Industrials (%)	14	12
Officeworks (%)	8	9
EBIT ($mn)	2 948.0	2 942.0
EBIT margin (%)	10.6	9.5
Profit before tax ($mn)	2 799.0	2 819.0
Profit after tax ($mn)	1 940.0	2 083.0
Earnings per share (c)	171.68	184.17
Cash flow per share (c)	219.20	319.27
Dividend (c)	178	152
Percentage franked	100	100
Net tangible assets per share ($)	5.20	4.88
Interest cover (times)	19.8	23.9
Return on equity (%)	11.9	21.6
Debt-to-equity ratio (%)	22.4	~
Current ratio	1.2	1.1

Westpac Banking Corporation

ASX code: WBC www.westpac.com.au

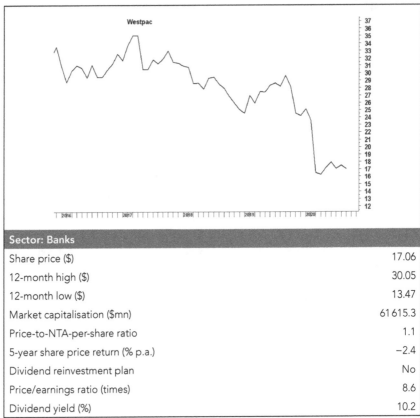

Sector: Banks	
Share price ($)	17.06
12-month high ($)	30.05
12-month low ($)	13.47
Market capitalisation ($mn)	61615.3
Price-to-NTA-per-share ratio	1.1
5-year share price return (% p.a.)	−2.4
Dividend reinvestment plan	No
Price/earnings ratio (times)	8.6
Dividend yield (%)	10.2

Sydney-based Westpac, which began trading in 1817 as the Bank of New South Wales, is one of Australia's big four banks, with interests in most areas of financial services. It is also one of New Zealand's leading banks and has some smaller businesses in the Pacific region. It owns St George Bank, BankSA and Bank of Melbourne. Its wealth management arm is BT. The bank also incorporates brands that include Asgard, Advance Asset Management, Capital Finance, XYLO Foreign Exchange and the RAMS home loans business.

Latest business results (March 2020, half year)

Profits crashed on both a statutory and cash basis as the bank's businesses were hit by the COVID-19 pandemic. In particular, it suffered from a $1.6 billion impairment charge related to expected credit losses from the pandemic. It also made a $900 million provision for a potential penalty relating to civil proceedings being brought against the bank by the government's Australian Transaction Reports and Analysis Centre. Westpac said that during the half it had put on hold 105 000 mortgage accounts worth $39 billion, together with 31 000 business loans worth $8.2 billion. Higher impairment charges drove profits down for all of the bank's key divisions, although the core Consumer division saw cash profits fall by a relatively modest 14 per cent from the 2019 first half, with an increase in deposits more than offsetting a decline in home loans and credit card lending. Business banking was hurt by a drop in loans and a reduction in the net interest margin.

Outlook

Westpac believes an economic recovery may start late in 2020, but it expects that caution will prevail well into 2021. It has a relatively high exposure to the mortgage market and will be strongly influenced by trends in domestic housing. It sees the economic downturn as feeding through to house prices, and it believes these could fall nationally by around 10 per cent during 2020, with no recovery likely until 2021. It is now working to streamline its operations in order to concentrate on its core Australia and New Zealand banking activities. It has already sold or closed parts of its wealth management business. It has created a new Specialist Businesses division for its remaining wealth management activities, along with its insurance and vehicle finance operations, and it plans to conduct a strategic review of these, with a view to possibly selling them. It is also applying a range of cost-cutting measures to boost productivity.

Year to 30 September	2018	2019
Operating income ($mn)	22 165.0	20 655.0
Net interest income ($mn)	17 187.0	16 953.0
Operating expenses ($mn)	9 698.0	10 031.0
Profit before tax ($mn)	11 655.0	9 830.0
Profit after tax ($mn)	8 065.0	6 849.0
Earnings per share (c)	236.23	198.18
Dividend (c)	188	174
Percentage franked	100	100
Non-interest income to total income (%)	22.5	17.9
Cost-to-income ratio (%)	43.7	48.6
Return on equity (%)	12.8	10.5
Return on assets (%)	0.9	0.8
Half year to 31 March	2019	2020
Operating income ($mn)	10 103.0	10 341.0
Profit before tax ($mn)	4 729.0	1 943.0
Profit after tax ($mn)	3 293.0	993.0
Earnings per share (c)	95.67	27.70
Dividend (c)	94	0
Percentage franked	100	~
Net tangible assets per share ($)	15.09	15.41

Woolworths Group Limited

ASX code: WOW   www.woolworthsgroup.com.au

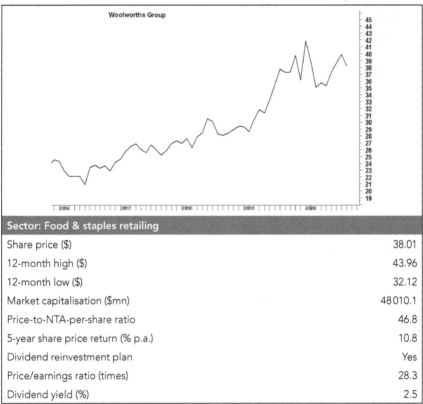

Sector: Food & staples retailing	
Share price ($)	38.01
12-month high ($)	43.96
12-month low ($)	32.12
Market capitalisation ($mn)	48010.1
Price-to-NTA-per-share ratio	46.8
5-year share price return (% p.a.)	10.8
Dividend reinvestment plan	Yes
Price/earnings ratio (times)	28.3
Dividend yield (%)	2.5

Woolworths, founded in Sydney in 1924, is one of Australia's retail giants. Its 3350 outlets across Australia and New Zealand include Woolworths, Metro, Countdown, SuperValue and FreshChoice supermarkets, Big W mixed goods stores and the majority-owned Endeavour Group, which incorporates Dan Murphy's, BWS, Cellarmasters and the company's clubs and hotels business. In August 2020 it announced the acquisition of a 65 per cent stake in the leading food distribution business PFD Food Services.

Latest business results (June 2020, full year)

Woolworths recorded higher sales. But a significant rise in costs resulting from the COVID-19 pandemic, including the closure of hotels for several months, led to a decline in full-year profits, despite a double-digit rise in earnings in the first half. Note that the June 2020 financial year contained 52 weeks, compared with 53 weeks for June 2019. The core Australian Food division reported a rise in sales and profits, although on a normalised basis profits actually edged down as the COVID-19 pandemic added $290 million to second-half costs. Online sales jumped 40 per cent to $2 billion. The New Zealand Food division reported excellent growth, including a double-digit rise in profits. For a period during the strict New Zealand lockdown, major supermarkets were among the only retail operations allowed to remain open. Big W sales rose by more than 10 per cent on a normalised basis, and this business moved back into the black, with a small profit. Endeavour Drinks enjoyed a solid rise in sales and profits, but the hotel business saw revenues and profits sharply down.

Outlook

Woolworths continues to benefit from changing spending patterns, as consumers spend more time in their homes and buy more from supermarkets, although this is partially offset by high pandemic-related costs. It expects online sales to continue their strong growth, and it is investing to expand its digital capacity. It continues to restructure the Big W operation, with four more stores to close during the June 2021 year. The $552 million planned acquisition of a 65 per cent holding in PFD Food Services would give Woolworths a strong position in the business-to-business wholesale food distribution sector. It has been opposed by other food distribution companies, with calls for the Australian Competition and Consumer Commission to block it. In February 2020 Woolworths merged its Endeavour Drinks business with its ALH hotels business, to create Endeavour Group, in which it holds an 85.4 per cent equity interest. It plans to demerge from Endeavour Group during 2021.

Year to 28 June*	2019	2020
Revenues ($mn)	59 984.0	63 675.0
Australian food (%)	66	66
Endeavour Drinks (%)	15	15
New Zealand food (%)	10	11
Big W (%)	6	6
Hotels (%)	3	2
EBIT ($mn)	2 702.0	2 629.0
EBIT margin (%)	4.5	4.1
Gross margin (%)	29.1	29.2
Profit before tax ($mn)	2 596.0	2 507.0
Profit after tax ($mn)	1 751.0	1 691.0
Earnings per share (c)	134.10	134.43
Cash flow per share (c)	227.69	329.84
Dividend (c)	102	94
Percentage franked	100	100
Net tangible assets per share ($)	1.83	0.81
Interest cover (times)	25.5	21.5
Return on equity (%)	17.0	17.9
Debt-to-equity ratio (%)	19.7	20.6
Current ratio	0.7	0.6

* 30 June 2019

PART II
THE TABLES

Table A
Market capitalisation

A company's market capitalisation is determined by multiplying the share price by the number of shares. To be included in this book, a company must be in the All Ordinaries Index, which comprises the 500 largest companies by market capitalisation.

	$mn
BHP	183 049.0
Rio Tinto	154 638.9
Commonwealth Bank	117 988.3
Westpac Banking	61 615.3
Fortescue Metals	53 943.5
Wesfarmers	52 995.7
ANZ Banking	49 632.2
Woolworths	48 010.1
Macquarie Group	44 722.9
Aristocrat Leisure	18 556.1
ASX	16 629.8
Brambles	16 359.7
REA	14 858.7
Ramsay Health Care	14 809.8
Cochlear	12 483.2
Magellan Financial	10 667.0
Northern Star Resources	9 733.0
Evolution Mining	9 408.4
Medibank Private	6 995.2
Orica	6 912.0
JB Hi-Fi	5 718.9
IDP Education	5 416.4
Harvey Norman	5 407.7
Mineral Resources	5 297.0
Ansell	4 683.5
Altium	4 459.4
Alumina	4 319.8
Breville	3 761.8
Beach Energy	3 238.7
Brickworks	2 653.9
Regis Resources	2 647.6
Pro Medicus	2 639.2
Technology One	2 448.6
Bapcor	2 379.3
Super Retail	2 359.6
ARB	2 103.5
NIB Holdings	2 014.6
IRESS	1 979.3
Platinum Asset Management	1 966.2
Codan	1 897.1
CSR	1 815.3
Pendal	1 775.4
Adbri	1 631.8
Perpetual	1 622.8

IPH	1 447.2
InvoCare	1 389.1
Dicker Data	1 314.2
Credit Corp	1 255.4
Collins Foods	1 186.7
AUB Group	1 177.4
Objective	1 104.1
SeaLink Travel	1 098.5
GUD	977.1
Lifestyle Communities	963.9
Data#3	948.5
Pinnacle Investment	908.9
Accent	859.4
Jumbo Interactive	853.3
Sandfire Resources	836.0
Integral Diagnostics	811.8
Service Stream	767.1
Hansen Technologies	763.2
Smartgroup	757.5
Nick Scali	683.6
GWA	683.6
Integrated Research	661.7
Infomedia	621.6
Adairs	581.3
Baby Bunting	540.9
Select Harvests	535.3
Australian Pharmaceutical	527.1
Australian Ethical Investment	518.1
PWR Holdings	491.4
SG Fleet	453.5
MNF Group	396.3
Money3	383.5
Clover	367.6
McPherson's	323.9
Pacific Smiles	284.0
OFX	279.4
Beacon Lighting	259.2
Servcorp	238.2
Class	228.7
Schaffer	221.5
Supply Network	187.9
Fiducian	180.5
Vita Group	178.5
1300SMILES	145.1
DWS	118.6
Mortgage Choice	95.6

Table B

Revenues

This list ranks the companies in the book according to their most recent full-year revenues figures (operating income for the banks). The figures include revenues from sales and services, but other revenues — such as interest receipts and investment income — are not generally included.

	$mn
Woolworths	63 675.0
BHP	62 218.8
Rio Tinto	61 664.0
Wesfarmers	30 846.0
Commonwealth Bank	23 761.0
Westpac Banking	20 655.0
ANZ Banking	19 029.0
Fortescue Metals	18 579.7
Macquarie Group	12 325.0
Ramsay Health Care	12 160.3
JB Hi-Fi	7 918.9
Brambles	6 860.3
Medibank Private	6 769.6
Orica	5 878.0
Aristocrat Leisure	4 397.4
Australian Pharmaceutical	4 010.7
Harvey Norman	3 545.8
Super Retail	2 825.2
NIB Holdings	2 473.1
Ansell	2 338.7
CSR	2 212.5
Mineral Resources	2 124.7
Northern Star Resources	1 971.7
Evolution Mining	1 941.9
Dicker Data	1 758.5
Beach Energy	1 728.2
Data#3	1 623.8
Adbri	1 517.0
Bapcor	1 462.7
Cochlear	1 352.3
Collins Foods	981.7
Breville	952.2
ASX	949.0
Service Stream	928.0
Brickworks	918.7
Accent	829.8
REA	820.3
Vita Group	773.1
Regis Resources	755.8
Magellan Financial	672.6
Sandfire Resources	656.8
SeaLink Travel	623.7
Alumina	604.9
IDP Education	587.1

IRESS	508.9
InvoCare	500.3
Pendal	491.3
Perpetual	483.9
ARB	465.4
SG Fleet	451.6
GUD	438.0
Baby Bunting	405.2
GWA	398.7
Adairs	388.9
IPH	369.6
Credit Corp	354.8
Servcorp	349.1
Codan	348.0
AUB Group	303.5
Hansen Technologies	301.4
Select Harvests	298.5
Technology One	285.0
Platinum Asset Management	285.0
Integral Diagnostics	275.6
Altium	274.1
Nick Scali	262.5
Beacon Lighting	251.6
Smartgroup	249.8
MNF Group	230.9
McPherson's	222.2
Mortgage Choice	172.8
DWS	167.9
Schaffer	155.1
OFX	137.2
Supply Network	136.8
Lifestyle Communities	126.9
Money3	124.0
Pacific Smiles	120.6
Integrated Research	110.9
Infomedia	94.6
Clover	76.7
Jumbo Interactive	71.2
Objective	70.0
PWR Holdings	65.7
Pinnacle Investment	60.4
Pro Medicus	56.8
Fiducian	54.7
Australian Ethical Investment	49.9
Class	43.9
1300SMILES	39.8

Table C
Year-on-year revenues growth

Companies generally strive for growth, though profit growth is usually of far more significance than a boost in revenues. In fact, it is possible for a company to increase its revenues by all kinds of means — including cutting profit margins or acquiring other companies — and year-on-year revenues growth is of little relevance if other ratios are not also improving. The figures used for this calculation are the latest full-year figures.

	%
SeaLink Travel	150.7
IPH	44.0
Northern Star Resources	40.7
Mineral Resources	40.5
Money3	35.3
Select Harvests	34.3
Fortescue Metals	34.2
Hansen Technologies	30.3
Evolution Mining	28.6
Codan	28.5
Breville	25.3
Aristocrat Leisure	25.3
Clover	21.8
Australian Ethical Investment	21.8
Magellan Financial	20.9
Integral Diagnostics	18.6
Dicker Data	18.0
Brickworks	17.0
Regis Resources	15.8
Data#3	14.8
Class	14.7
Altium	14.2
Rio Tinto	14.1
Pro Medicus	13.4
Credit Corp	13.0
Adairs	12.9
Objective	12.9
Bapcor	12.8
Technology One	12.7
Ansell	12.3
Infomedia	11.8
Fiducian	11.8
JB Hi-Fi	11.6
Pinnacle Investment	11.3
Sandfire Resources	10.9
Wesfarmers	10.5
Supply Network	10.4
Baby Bunting	10.1
Integrated Research	10.0
AUB Group	9.8
IRESS	9.5
Orica	9.4
Jumbo Interactive	9.1
Service Stream	9.0
Collins Foods	8.9
ASX	8.7
Beacon Lighting	7.7
Brambles	7.5
MNF Group	7.1
OFX	6.6
Woolworths	6.2
McPherson's	5.6
Ramsay Health Care	5.3
ARB	4.8
GWA	4.4
Servcorp	4.3
NIB Holdings	4.2
Super Retail	4.2
Accent	4.2
InvoCare	4.1
Harvey Norman	3.7
Smartgroup	3.1
DWS	2.7
Vita Group	2.6
Medibank Private	1.7
BHP	1.2
GUD	0.9
Commonwealth Bank	0.8
PWR Holdings	0.5
Australian Pharmaceutical	−0.4
Mortgage Choice	−0.9
1300SMILES	−1.3
Pacific Smiles	−1.3
ANZ Banking	−1.7
IDP Education	−1.8
Nick Scali	−2.1
Macquarie Group	−3.4
Platinum Asset Management	−3.5
CSR	−4.7
Perpetual	−4.9
Cochlear	−5.2
REA	−6.2
Westpac Banking	−6.8
Adbri	−7.0
SG Fleet	−11.1
Lifestyle Communities	−11.9
Pendal	−12.0
Beach Energy	−16.8
Schaffer	−23.6
Alumina	−34.7

Table D
EBIT margin

A company's earnings before interest and taxation (EBIT) is sometimes regarded as a better measure of its profitability than the straight pre-tax or post-tax profit figure. EBIT is derived by adding net interest payments (that is, interest payments minus interest receipts) to the pre-tax profit. Different companies choose different methods of financing their operations; by adding back interest payments to their profits we can help minimise these differences and make comparisons between companies more valid.

The EBIT margin is the EBIT figure as a percentage of annual sales. Clearly a high figure is to be desired, though of course this can be achieved artificially by inflating borrowings (and hence interest payments). And it is noteworthy that efficient companies, like some of the retailers, can operate most satisfactorily on low margins. Woolworths, for example, has one of the lowest EBIT margins of all the companies in this book.

The EBIT margin figure has little relevance for banks, and they have been excluded.

	%
Magellan Financial	84.8
Alumina	78.1
Platinum Asset Management	77.0
ASX	67.1
Pinnacle Investment	54.4
Fortescue Metals	53.9
Pro Medicus	52.5
Jumbo Interactive	52.3
Lifestyle Communities	48.9
REA	48.4
Money3	47.0
Pendal	40.8
Regis Resources	37.8
Beach Energy	37.8
BHP	37.2
Smartgroup	36.7
Rio Tinto	36.5
Credit Corp	35.1
Altium	34.1
Brickworks	33.6
Fiducian	31.1
Evolution Mining	30.6
IPH	30.1
PWR Holdings	28.0
Integrated Research	28.0
AUB Group	27.3
Infomedia	27.0
Mineral Resources	26.9
Select Harvests	26.8
Technology One	26.6
Schaffer	26.2
Australian Ethical Investment	26.0
1300SMILES	25.7
Nick Scali	25.6
Codan	25.5
Aristocrat Leisure	25.0
Perpetual	24.9
InvoCare	24.3
Class	23.0
Harvey Norman	20.2
Objective	19.5
OFX	19.4

IRESS	19.0
Clover	18.6
GUD	18.4
Northern Star Resources	18.4
IDP Education	18.4
GWA	18.0
Sandfire Resources	17.3
ARB	17.1
Brambles	16.2
Integral Diagnostics	15.8
Cochlear	15.3
Adairs	15.2
DWS	14.7
Ansell	13.4
Beacon Lighting	13.3
Hansen Technologies	13.1
SG Fleet	13.1
Adbri	12.3
Breville	11.9
Accent	11.4
Orica	11.3
McPherson's	11.3
Supply Network	11.2
MNF Group	10.4
Servcorp	10.4
Collins Foods	10.4
Pacific Smiles	10.3
Bapcor	9.8
Super Retail	9.7
Wesfarmers	9.5
CSR	9.5
Service Stream	9.4
SeaLink Travel	8.5
Baby Bunting	8.2
Ramsay Health Care	7.8
Mortgage Choice	7.6
Medibank Private	6.7
JB Hi-Fi	6.5
NIB Holdings	5.2
Vita Group	4.8
Dicker Data	4.6
Woolworths	4.1
Australian Pharmaceutical	2.3
Data#3	2.1

Table E

Year-on-year EBIT margin growth

The EBIT (earnings before interest and taxation) margin is one of the measures of a company's efficiency. So a rising margin is much to be desired, as it suggests that a company is achieving success in cutting its costs. This table does not include banks.

	%
Technology One	174.8
Select Harvests	120.2
InvoCare	51.0
Evolution Mining	39.9
Dicker Data	33.3
Schaffer	32.0
Mineral Resources	25.4
Beacon Lighting	24.3
Collins Foods	22.9
JB Hi-Fi	22.9
Australian Ethical Investment	20.9
Adairs	20.2
McPherson's	19.6
Servcorp	15.9
Northern Star Resources	15.8
Baby Bunting	15.6
Harvey Norman	15.3
Data#3	15.2
Super Retail	15.0
Nick Scali	14.4
IDP Education	13.0
Accent	12.9
Objective	12.7
Fortescue Metals	11.4
MNF Group	10.7
Codan	9.2
Rio Tinto	8.7
Supply Network	8.5
Clover	8.5
AUB Group	7.7
Australian Pharmaceutical	6.2
Regis Resources	6.1
Vita Group	4.4
Altium	3.6
Platinum Asset Management	3.6
Infomedia	3.0
Hansen Technologies	1.9
Pro Medicus	1.7
Aristocrat Leisure	1.0
Ansell	0.5
Integral Diagnostics	0.5
Brambles	0.5
Magellan Financial	0.2

Smartgroup	0.0
Orica	−1.7
Fiducian	−2.0
Credit Corp	−2.0
Pacific Smiles	−2.1
OFX	−2.3
ARB	−2.3
Integrated Research	−2.5
Pinnacle Investment	−2.8
1300SMILES	−2.9
IRESS	−3.2
ASX	−3.3
BHP	−3.4
REA	−4.1
PWR Holdings	−5.1
Service Stream	−5.1
Pendal	−5.5
Brickworks	−6.2
Jumbo Interactive	−7.2
DWS	−7.2
Breville	−7.3
Beach Energy	−7.4
Money3	−8.0
Woolworths	−8.3
Wesfarmers	−9.7
IPH	−10.5
GUD	−10.6
GWA	−11.9
Bapcor	−12.5
Lifestyle Communities	−13.0
Alumina	−14.8
CSR	−16.7
Ramsay Health Care	−18.3
Medibank Private	−22.2
Perpetual	−23.0
Adbri	−26.7
Class	−27.8
SG Fleet	−28.9
Mortgage Choice	−31.4
Sandfire Resources	−32.9
SeaLink Travel	−35.7
Cochlear	−41.0
NIB Holdings	−41.4

Table F
After-tax profit

This table ranks all the companies according to their most recent full-year after-tax profit.

	$mn
Rio Tinto	14 819.0
BHP	13 130.4
Commonwealth Bank	7 296.0
Fortescue Metals	6 862.3
Westpac Banking	6 849.0
ANZ Banking	6 470.0
Macquarie Group	2 731.0
Wesfarmers	2 083.0
Woolworths	1 691.0
Aristocrat Leisure	698.8
Brambles	691.6
ASX	498.6
Harvey Norman	480.5
Alumina	466.6
Beach Energy	461.0
Magellan Financial	438.3
Evolution Mining	405.4
Orica	372.0
Ramsay Health Care	336.9
Mineral Resources	334.0
JB Hi-Fi	332.7
Medibank Private	315.6
REA	268.9
Northern Star Resources	258.3
Brickworks	234.2
Ansell	229.0
Regis Resources	199.5
Pendal	163.5
Platinum Asset Management	155.6
Super Retail	154.1
Cochlear	153.8
CSR	134.8
Adbri	122.9
NIB Holdings	90.1
Bapcor	89.1
Perpetual	82.0
Credit Corp	79.6
IPH	77.7
Breville	75.0
Sandfire Resources	74.1
IDP Education	67.9
IRESS	65.1
InvoCare	63.9
Codan	63.8
Smartgroup	61.4

Service Stream	58.8
Technology One	58.5
ARB	57.3
Accent	55.7
Australian Pharmaceutical	55.1
Dicker Data	54.3
AUB Group	53.4
Select Harvests	53.0
GUD	50.9
Collins Foods	47.3
GWA	44.9
Altium	44.8
Lifestyle Communities	42.8
Nick Scali	42.1
SeaLink Travel	37.2
SG Fleet	36.7
Adairs	35.3
Pinnacle Investment	32.4
Servcorp	30.6
Money3	30.3
Jumbo Interactive	26.5
Hansen Technologies	26.2
Integrated Research	24.1
Data#3	23.6
Schaffer	23.6
Pro Medicus	23.1
Integral Diagnostics	23.0
Vita Group	22.4
OFX	21.4
Baby Bunting	19.3
Beacon Lighting	19.1
Infomedia	18.6
DWS	16.9
MNF Group	16.6
McPherson's	16.3
PWR Holdings	13.0
Fiducian	12.7
Objective	11.0
Clover	10.1
Supply Network	9.5
Mortgage Choice	9.4
Australian Ethical Investment	9.3
Pacific Smiles	8.1
1300SMILES	7.1
Class	6.8

Table G
Year-on-year earnings per share growth

The earnings per share (EPS) figure is a crucial one. It tells you — the shareholder — what your part is of the company's profits, for each of your shares. So investors invariably look for EPS growth in a stock. The year-on-year EPS growth figure is often one of the first ratios that investors look to when evaluating a stock. The figures used for this calculation are the latest full-year figures.

	%
Select Harvests	250.8
Technology One	168.3
Evolution Mining	85.2
Dicker Data	66.6
Mineral Resources	62.6
Fortescue Metals	55.7
Northern Star Resources	53.0
InvoCare	47.4
Australian Ethical Investment	41.3
Codan	39.0
JB Hi-Fi	33.2
Clover	33.1
Rio Tinto	33.1
Baby Bunting	32.9
Data#3	30.5
Aristocrat Leisure	28.9
Money3	22.4
Regis Resources	22.0
Hansen Technologies	21.3
Objective	21.2
Pro Medicus	20.3
Adairs	17.5
McPherson's	17.4
Magellan Financial	17.3
Beacon Lighting	15.6
IPH	15.1
Orica	14.2
Ansell	13.5
Harvey Norman	12.9
Brambles	12.8
Breville	10.5
Integrated Research	10.0
Supply Network	9.9
Infomedia	9.5
AUB Group	8.7
MNF Group	7.5
Wesfarmers	7.3
Fiducian	5.3
Collins Foods	5.0
Servcorp	4.8
OFX	4.5
Schaffer	3.8
Brickworks	3.6
Pinnacle Investment	3.5
Accent	2.9

BHP	2.3
Smartgroup	2.0
ANZ Banking	1.6
ASX	1.3
Super Retail	0.9
DWS	0.8
IRESS	0.7
Australian Pharmaceutical	0.7
Woolworths	0.2
ARB	−0.1
Nick Scali	−0.1
IDP Education	−0.5
Platinum Asset Management	−1.0
Jumbo Interactive	−3.2
Service Stream	−4.6
Credit Corp	−7.5
1300SMILES	−8.1
Integral Diagnostics	−8.1
PWR Holdings	−8.1
Vita Group	−8.9
REA	−9.0
Bapcor	−9.3
Pacific Smiles	−9.4
SeaLink Travel	−9.9
Macquarie Group	−11.0
Commonwealth Bank	−11.4
GWA	−11.6
Westpac Banking	−16.1
GUD	−16.6
Beach Energy	−17.8
Pendal	−20.1
Lifestyle Communities	−22.2
CSR	−24.4
Class	−25.0
Medibank Private	−27.9
Perpetual	−29.7
Mortgage Choice	−31.3
Adbri	−35.8
Sandfire Resources	−35.8
Altium	−39.3
SG Fleet	−39.6
NIB Holdings	−39.9
Ramsay Health Care	−44.0
Cochlear	−44.6
Alumina	−44.9

Table H
Return on equity

Shareholders' equity is the company's assets minus its liabilities. It is, in theory, the amount owned by the shareholders of the company. Return on equity is the after-tax profit expressed as a percentage of that equity. Thus, it is the amount of profit that the company managers made for you — the shareholder — from your assets. For many investors it is one of the most important gauges of how well a company is doing. It is one of the requirements for inclusion in this book that all companies have a return on equity of at least 10 per cent in their latest financial year.

	%
Technology One	63.4
Dicker Data	62.1
Nick Scali	52.4
Magellan Financial	49.2
Australian Ethical Investment	49.1
Platinum Asset Management	48.6
Data#3	47.6
Pro Medicus	42.2
Fortescue Metals	40.0
Aristocrat Leisure	36.1
Fiducian	34.9
Jumbo Interactive	33.9
Objective	33.7
Integrated Research	31.6
JB Hi-Fi	31.0
REA	30.4
OFX	29.4
Codan	27.8
Adairs	27.3
InvoCare	26.3
Regis Resources	25.7
IDP Education	24.9
Rio Tinto	24.6
PWR Holdings	24.3
DWS	24.3
Clover	24.3
Supply Network	23.7
Beacon Lighting	22.5
IPH	22.0
Smartgroup	21.6
Wesfarmers	21.6
Schaffer	21.3
Pacific Smiles	20.8
Baby Bunting	20.8
Breville	20.4
Class	19.4
BHP	19.2
Vita Group	19.0
Service Stream	18.7
Mineral Resources	18.4
GUD	18.4
Pendal	18.1
Woolworths	17.9
Beach Energy	17.8
Pinnacle Investment	17.7

1300SMILES	17.6
McPherson's	17.5
Super Retail	17.1
Infomedia	17.0
Altium	16.9
Medibank Private	16.8
Alumina	16.7
Evolution Mining	16.6
ARB	15.9
GWA	15.9
Northern Star Resources	15.9
Lifestyle Communities	15.7
IRESS	15.2
Credit Corp	15.0
MNF Group	15.0
NIB Holdings	15.0
Brambles	14.7
Harvey Norman	14.5
Cochlear	14.5
Macquarie Group	14.1
Accent	13.7
Select Harvests	13.5
Collins Foods	13.4
SG Fleet	13.3
Servcorp	13.3
ASX	13.1
Integral Diagnostics	13.0
Orica	12.7
AUB Group	12.6
Perpetual	12.5
Money3	12.4
CSR	12.0
Ansell	11.4
Brickworks	11.1
Sandfire Resources	11.0
ANZ Banking	10.8
Mortgage Choice	10.7
Australian Pharmaceutical	10.7
Ramsay Health Care	10.7
Westpac Banking	10.5
Bapcor	10.5
Hansen Technologies	10.5
Commonwealth Bank	10.3
Adbri	10.1
SeaLink Travel	10.0

Table I

Year-on-year return on equity growth

Company managers have a variety of strategies they can use to boost profits. It is much harder to lift the return on equity (ROE). Find a company with a high ROE figure, and one that is growing year by year, and it is possible that you have found a real growth stock. This figure is simply the percentage change in the ROE figure from the previous year to the latest year.

	%
Technology One	392.7
Select Harvests	235.2
Wesfarmers	81.9
Evolution Mining	79.1
InvoCare	49.9
Dicker Data	48.0
Baby Bunting	36.3
Fortescue Metals	27.7
Rio Tinto	25.6
JB Hi-Fi	23.4
Codan	21.7
Australian Ethical Investment	21.2
Data#3	20.3
Mineral Resources	19.0
McPherson's	18.9
Money3	17.6
Hansen Technologies	16.4
Orica	14.6
Clover	13.0
Servcorp	11.5
Ansell	10.8
Harvey Norman	9.8
Beacon Lighting	9.5
Adairs	7.8
Brambles	6.9
Regis Resources	6.7
Woolworths	5.5
Nick Scali	5.0
ASX	4.3
Australian Pharmaceutical	4.3
BHP	4.0
DWS	3.1
Aristocrat Leisure	2.3
Objective	2.1
Collins Foods	1.4
Platinum Asset Management	1.2
Accent	1.0
Supply Network	-0.4
Northern Star Resources	-0.8
Brickworks	-1.1
IRESS	-1.6
ANZ Banking	-1.8
Pacific Smiles	-3.4
IPH	-3.5
AUB Group	-3.8

OFX	-4.5
Fiducian	-4.5
REA	-5.1
Pro Medicus	-7.0
Integrated Research	-7.8
Magellan Financial	-8.4
Schaffer	-8.5
ARB	-9.4
Smartgroup	-9.5
Breville	-10.3
Super Retail	-11.1
1300SMILES	-11.5
Commonwealth Bank	-14.2
MNF Group	-14.4
PWR Holdings	-14.8
Service Stream	-16.7
GWA	-16.7
Westpac Banking	-17.8
GUD	-17.8
Vita Group	-18.9
Macquarie Group	-19.5
Credit Corp	-19.7
Jumbo Interactive	-20.2
Pinnacle Investment	-20.2
CSR	-20.4
Pendal	-24.1
Bapcor	-24.4
Medibank Private	-27.6
Perpetual	-28.9
Integral Diagnostics	-31.9
Mortgage Choice	-32.6
Beach Energy	-33.3
Adbri	-34.4
Lifestyle Communities	-34.6
Infomedia	-37.6
SeaLink Travel	-38.7
Class	-39.0
NIB Holdings	-41.4
SG Fleet	-41.5
Sandfire Resources	-41.8
Alumina	-41.8
Altium	-46.1
IDP Education	-52.5
Ramsay Health Care	-55.6
Cochlear	-65.1

Table J
Debt-to-equity ratio

A company's borrowings as a percentage of its shareholders' equity is one of the most common measures of corporate debt. Many investors will be wary of a company with a ratio that is too high. However, a company with a steady business and a regular income flow — such as an electric power company or a large supermarket chain — is generally considered relatively safe with a high level of debt, whereas a small company in a new business field might be thought at risk with even moderate debt levels. Much depends on surrounding circumstances, including the prevailing interest rates. Of course, it is often from borrowing that a company grows, and some investors are not happy buying shares in a company with little or no debt.

There are various ways to calculate the ratio, but for this book the net debt position is used. That is, a company's cash has been deducted from its borrowings. For inclusion in this book no company was allowed a debt-to-equity ratio of more than 70 per cent. Some of the companies had no net debt — their cash position was greater than the amount of their borrowings — and so have been assigned a zero figure in this table. The ratio has no relevance for banks, and they have been excluded.

	%				
Altium	0.0	OFX	0.0	InvoCare	12.1
ARB	0.0	Pendal	0.0	Schaffer	14.8
ASX	0.0	Platinum Asset Management	0.0	Australian Pharmaceutical	14.9
Australian Ethical Investment	0.0	Pro Medicus	0.0	Select Harvests	17.6
Baby Bunting	0.0	PWR Holdings	0.0	Rio Tinto	18.0
Beach Energy	0.0	Regis Resources	0.0	Pacific Smiles	18.2
Beacon Lighting	0.0	Sandfire Resources	0.0	IPH	18.8
Breville	0.0	Servcorp	0.0	Supply Network	18.8
Class	0.0	Service Stream	0.0	1300SMILES	20.2
Cochlear	0.0	Super Retail	0.0	Woolworths	20.6
Codan	0.0	Technology One	0.0	Brickworks	21.0
Credit Corp	0.0	Vita Group	0.0	BHP	26.1
CSR	0.0	Wesfarmers	0.0	AUB Group	30.0
Data#3	0.0	Adairs	0.7	SeaLink Travel	31.7
Fiducian	0.0	Fortescue Metals	1.9	Clover	32.0
Harvey Norman	0.0	Smartgroup	4.8	Adbri	34.6
IDP Education	0.0	Alumina	4.8	DWS	35.8
Infomedia	0.0	SG Fleet	5.2	Brambles	39.0
Integrated Research	0.0	NIB Holdings	5.8	Lifestyle Communities	44.1
JB Hi-Fi	0.0	Northern Star Resources	6.2	Hansen Technologies	45.1
Jumbo Interactive	0.0	Pinnacle Investment	7.4	Dicker Data	45.8
Magellan Financial	0.0	Accent	7.6	Money3	50.1
Medibank Private	0.0	Evolution Mining	7.7	Orica	50.9
Mineral Resources	0.0	Ansell	7.9	GWA	51.1
MNF Group	0.0	IRESS	8.7	GUD	51.7
Mortgage Choice	0.0	McPherson's	10.2	Integral Diagnostics	54.2
Nick Scali	0.0	Bapcor	10.5	Collins Foods	56.2
Objective	0.0	Perpetual	11.0	Aristocrat Leisure	64.1
		REA	12.1	Ramsay Health Care	64.3

Table K
Current ratio

The current ratio is simply the company's current assets divided by its current liabilities. Current assets are cash or assets that can, in theory, be converted quickly into cash. Current liabilities are normally those payable within a year. The current ratio helps measure the ability of a company to repay in a hurry its short-term debt, should the need arise. Banks are not included.

Company	Ratio
Alumina	34.2
Money3	10.8
Magellan Financial	9.8
Platinum Asset Management	8.7
Infomedia	5.8
Sandfire Resources	5.4
Credit Corp	5.0
Clover	4.9
Pro Medicus	4.8
Adbri	4.3
Pinnacle Investment	3.8
PWR Holdings	3.4
Jumbo Interactive	3.2
ARB	3.1
IPH	3.0
Regis Resources	2.7
GUD	2.7
IDP Education	2.5
Brickworks	2.5
Australian Ethical Investment	2.5
Breville	2.4
Schaffer	2.4
Supply Network	2.4
Fiducian	2.4
Ansell	2.4
CSR	2.3
Fortescue Metals	2.3
Codan	2.2
MNF Group	2.2
Class	2.2
Select Harvests	2.1
Mineral Resources	2.0
Evolution Mining	2.0
Bapcor	2.0
InvoCare	2.0
Altium	2.0
Aristocrat Leisure	1.9
Integrated Research	1.8
Cochlear	1.8
Lifestyle Communities	1.8
Pendal	1.8
Medibank Private	1.8
GWA	1.7

Company	Ratio
Northern Star Resources	1.7
NIB Holdings	1.7
IRESS	1.7
Harvey Norman	1.7
Rio Tinto	1.6
Hansen Technologies	1.6
Beacon Lighting	1.6
Smartgroup	1.5
McPherson's	1.5
BHP	1.4
Service Stream	1.4
Orica	1.4
Mortgage Choice	1.3
Perpetual	1.3
Australian Pharmaceutical	1.3
Objective	1.2
Dicker Data	1.2
REA	1.2
AUB Group	1.2
Brambles	1.1
Beach Energy	1.1
Wesfarmers	1.1
ASX	1.1
Integral Diagnostics	1.1
1300SMILES	1.1
Super Retail	1.1
Ramsay Health Care	1.1
DWS	1.1
Nick Scali	1.1
Data#3	1.1
Baby Bunting	1.0
Accent	1.0
Collins Foods	1.0
JB Hi-Fi	0.9
Technology One	0.9
Vita Group	0.8
Adairs	0.8
Servcorp	0.8
Pacific Smiles	0.8
SeaLink Travel	0.7
Woolworths	0.6
OFX	0.0
SG Fleet	0.0

Table L
Price/earnings ratio

The price/earnings ratio (PER) — the current share price divided by the earnings per share figure — is one of the best known of all sharemarket ratios. Essentially it expresses the amount of money investors are ready to pay for each cent or dollar of a company's profits, and it allows you to compare the share prices of different companies of varying sizes and with widely different profits. A high PER suggests the market has a high regard for the company and its growth prospects; a low one may mean that investors are disdainful of the stock. The figures in this table are based on share prices as of 4 September 2020.

Company	PER	Company	PER
DWS	7.0	Supply Network	19.7
Beach Energy	7.0	McPherson's	19.8
Servcorp	7.8	1300SMILES	20.3
ANZ Banking	7.8	Ansell	20.7
Fortescue Metals	7.9	Dicker Data	21.8
Vita Group	8.0	AUB Group	22.0
Westpac Banking	8.6	Medibank Private	22.2
Alumina	9.3	NIB Holdings	22.3
Schaffer	9.4	SeaLink Travel	22.4
Pendal	9.6	Lifestyle Communities	22.5
Australian Pharmaceutical	9.6	MNF Group	22.7
Select Harvests	10.0	Bapcor	23.1
Mortgage Choice	10.2	Evolution Mining	23.2
Rio Tinto	10.5	Magellan Financial	24.2
Sandfire Resources	10.9	Brambles	24.3
Harvey Norman	11.1	Collins Foods	25.3
Brickworks	11.3	Wesfarmers	25.4
Smartgroup	12.1	Aristocrat Leisure	26.5
SG Fleet	12.3	IRESS	27.0
Money3	12.5	Integrated Research	27.5
Platinum Asset Management	12.7	Pinnacle Investment	27.7
Service Stream	13.0	Baby Bunting	28.0
OFX	13.0	Woolworths	28.3
Regis Resources	13.3	Hansen Technologies	29.1
Beacon Lighting	13.4	Infomedia	29.2
CSR	13.7	Codan	29.7
Super Retail	13.8	Jumbo Interactive	32.2
BHP	13.9	Class	32.5
Adbri	14.0	ASX	33.4
Fiducian	14.2	Integral Diagnostics	33.5
Credit Corp	14.2	Pacific Smiles	34.8
GWA	15.2	Northern Star Resources	35.3
Macquarie Group	15.4	ARB	36.7
Accent	15.4	PWR Holdings	37.6
Mineral Resources	15.9	Clover	37.8
Commonwealth Bank	16.2	Ramsay Health Care	40.0
Nick Scali	16.2	Data#3	40.1
Adairs	16.5	Technology One	41.1
Perpetual	16.8	Breville	48.2
JB Hi-Fi	17.2	Australian Ethical Investment	54.5
Orica	17.4	REA	55.3
InvoCare	17.4	Cochlear	71.3
IPH	18.4	IDP Education	74.5
GUD	19.2	Altium	99.6
		Objective	99.9
		Pro Medicus	114.3

Table M
Price-to-NTA-per-share ratio

The NTA-per-share figure expresses the worth of a company's net tangible assets — that is, its assets minus its liabilities and intangible assets — for each share of the company. Intangible assets, such as goodwill or the value of newspaper mastheads, are excluded because it is deemed difficult to place a value on them (though this proposition is debatable), and also because they might not have much worth if separated from the company. The price-to-NTA-per-share ratio relates this figure to the share price.

A ratio of one means that the company is valued exactly according to the value of its assets. A ratio below one suggests that the shares are a bargain, though usually there is a good reason for this. Profits are more important than assets.

In some respects, this is an 'old economy' ratio. For many high-tech companies in the 'new economy' the most important assets are human ones whose worth does not appear on the balance sheet.

Companies with a negative NTA-per-share figure, as a result of having intangible assets valued at more than their net assets, have been omitted from this table.

Company	Ratio
ANZ Banking	0.9
Westpac Banking	1.1
Sandfire Resources	1.1
Servcorp	1.1
Beach Energy	1.2
Mortgage Choice	1.2
Brickworks	1.3
Harvey Norman	1.6
Select Harvests	1.7
Money3	1.7
Commonwealth Bank	1.8
CSR	1.8
Alumina	1.9
Adbri	1.9
Schaffer	1.9
Credit Corp	2.1
Australian Pharmaceutical	2.3
Mineral Resources	2.4
Macquarie Group	2.5
BHP	2.7
Fortescue Metals	2.8
Rio Tinto	2.9
Regis Resources	3.2
Lifestyle Communities	3.3
Beacon Lighting	3.5
InvoCare	3.6
Orica	3.7
Evolution Mining	3.8
Supply Network	4.4
Brambles	4.5
Northern Star Resources	4.6
OFX	4.6
Pinnacle Investment	4.8
Medibank Private	4.9
Pendal	5.3
Platinum Asset Management	6.2
ARB	6.2
Perpetual	6.6
Infomedia	7.2
Clover	7.8
NIB Holdings	8.0
MNF Group	8.7
Nick Scali	9.4
Wesfarmers	9.6
Dicker Data	9.8
Ansell	9.9
Fiducian	10.5
Bapcor	10.7
Pacific Smiles	10.8
Vita Group	11.3
Magellan Financial	11.5
Codan	11.8
Baby Bunting	12.2
Integrated Research	12.4
PWR Holdings	12.5
Cochlear	12.6
McPherson's	12.7
ASX	13.6
Breville	14.1
Jumbo Interactive	15.8
Accent	17.0
Super Retail	20.2
IDP Education	20.5
1300SMILES	21.3
Altium	22.9
Australian Ethical Investment	24.9
Data#3	25.6
AUB Group	26.3
Class	35.0
Woolworths	46.8
Objective	61.8
Pro Medicus	63.8
REA	69.5
JB Hi-Fi	77.0
Service Stream	89.0
Technology One	172.8

Table N
Dividend yield

Many investors buy shares for income, rather than for capital growth. They look for companies that offer a high dividend yield (the dividend expressed as a percentage of the share price). Table N ranks the companies in this book according to their historic dividend yields. Note that the franking credits available from most companies in this book can make the dividend yield substantially higher. The dividend yield changes with the share price. The figures in this table are based on share prices as of 4 September 2020.

	%
Westpac Banking	10.2
Fortescue Metals	10.0
ANZ Banking	9.0
Mortgage Choice	8.4
Pendal	8.2
Servcorp	8.1
Alumina	7.6
Smartgroup	7.5
Australian Pharmaceutical	7.2
Platinum Asset Management	7.1
DWS	6.7
Rio Tinto	6.0
Accent	5.8
SG Fleet	5.8
Select Harvests	5.7
Nick Scali	5.6
Perpetual	5.2
Schaffer	4.9
BHP	4.8
Service Stream	4.8
Medibank Private	4.7
IRESS	4.5
Commonwealth Bank	4.5
GWA	4.4
Beacon Lighting	4.3
IPH	4.2
InvoCare	4.2
1300SMILES	4.2
Harvey Norman	4.1
OFX	4.1
Sandfire Resources	4.1
Fiducian	4.0
Money3	3.9
Dicker Data	3.8
JB Hi-Fi	3.8
Magellan Financial	3.7
McPherson's	3.6
Mineral Resources	3.5
Macquarie Group	3.4
Supply Network	3.4
GUD	3.3
Wesfarmers	3.3
Orica	3.2
Brickworks	3.2
Adairs	3.2
NIB Holdings	3.2
AUB Group	3.1
Regis Resources	3.1
Pinnacle Investment	2.9
Evolution Mining	2.9
ASX	2.8
Class	2.7
CSR	2.7
Brambles	2.7
Jumbo Interactive	2.6
Infomedia	2.6
Bapcor	2.5
Baby Bunting	2.5
Woolworths	2.5
Integral Diagnostics	2.3
Data#3	2.3
Vita Group	2.2
SeaLink Travel	2.2
Hansen Technologies	2.1
Ansell	2.0
Collins Foods	1.9
Credit Corp	1.9
Aristocrat Leisure	1.9
Adbri	1.9
Integrated Research	1.9
Super Retail	1.8
Codan	1.8
Technology One	1.6
ARB	1.5
Breville	1.5
Beach Energy	1.4
MNF Group	1.3
Pacific Smiles	1.3
Northern Star Resources	1.3
PWR Holdings	1.2
Altium	1.1
Australian Ethical Investment	1.1
Clover	1.0
REA	1.0
Ramsay Health Care	1.0
IDP Education	0.8
Cochlear	0.8
Lifestyle Communities	0.6
Objective	0.6
Pro Medicus	0.5

Table O
Year-on-year dividend growth

Most investors hope for a rising dividend, and this table tells how much each company raised or lowered its dividend in its latest financial year.

	%		
Fortescue Metals	309.3	Brambles	0.0
Select Harvests	166.7	Class	0.0
Mineral Resources	127.3	Integrated Research	0.0
Codan	105.6	IRESS	0.0
Evolution Mining	68.4	Lifestyle Communities	0.0
Pro Medicus	50.0	MNF Group	0.0
Objective	40.0	Pinnacle Investment	0.0
Dicker Data	38.6	Regis Resources	0.0
Clover	35.7	Service Stream	0.0
Rio Tinto	34.9	Jumbo Interactive	−2.7
Hansen Technologies	33.3	Integral Diagnostics	−5.0
JB Hi-Fi	33.1	REA	−6.8
Technology One	32.3	Westpac Banking	−7.4
Data#3	29.9	Woolworths	−7.8
Northern Star Resources	25.9	Medibank Private	−8.4
Baby Bunting	25.0	Platinum Asset Management	−11.1
Aristocrat Leisure	21.7	Servcorp	−13.0
Magellan Financial	16.0	Pendal	−13.5
Altium	14.7	Wesfarmers	−14.6
Schaffer	14.3	IDP Education	−15.4
IPH	14.0	Sandfire Resources	−17.4
Accent	12.1	BHP	−18.7
Ansell	11.6	Money3	−20.0
Breville	10.8	OFX	−20.6
InvoCare	10.8	Adairs	−24.1
Infomedia	10.3	DWS	−25.0
McPherson's	10.0	Macquarie Group	−25.2
Beacon Lighting	9.9	SeaLink Travel	−26.7
AUB Group	8.7	PWR Holdings	−30.6
Mortgage Choice	8.3	Commonwealth Bank	−30.9
Supply Network	6.9	GUD	−33.9
Orica	6.8	GWA	−37.8
Brickworks	5.6	Perpetual	−38.0
Nick Scali	5.6	NIB Holdings	−39.1
ASX	4.5	SG Fleet	−43.5
Smartgroup	3.6	Harvey Norman	−45.5
Australian Pharmaceutical	3.3	Credit Corp	−50.0
Fiducian	3.1	Cochlear	−51.5
1300SMILES	3.0	Pacific Smiles	−58.6
Bapcor	2.9	Ramsay Health Care	−58.7
Collins Foods	2.6	Super Retail	−61.0
ARB	0.0	CSR	−61.5
ANZ Banking	0.0	Alumina	−64.8
Australian Ethical Investment	0.0	Vita Group	−73.9
Beach Energy	0.0	Adbri	−75.0

Table P
Five-year share price return

This table ranks the annual average return to investors from a five-year investment in each of the companies in the book, as of September 2020. It is an accumulated return, based on share price appreciation (or depreciation) plus dividend payments.

	% p.a.
Jumbo Interactive	75.5
Clover	71.6
Codan	64.1
Pro Medicus	63.6
Fortescue Metals	62.9
Australian Ethical Investment	53.3
Altium	52.7
Mineral Resources	49.4
Objective	49.0
Northern Star Resources	47.8
Data#3	45.5
Service Stream	44.7
IDP Education	42.5
Pinnacle Investment	42.5
McPherson's	40.5
Evolution Mining	39.4
Breville	36.3
Dicker Data	35.8
Regis Resources	32.0
Schaffer	31.1
Aristocrat Leisure	30.9
Magellan Financial	29.6
Lifestyle Communities	29.5
Collins Foods	29.2
Fiducian	28.6
JB Hi-Fi	25.8
Nick Scali	24.3
REA	23.2
ASX	21.7
Supply Network	20.9
Integral Diagnostics	20.6
Beach Energy	20.3
Cochlear	19.4
Rio Tinto	19.0
SeaLink Travel	18.6
Smartgroup	18.6
Money3	18.1
Technology One	17.8
Baby Bunting	17.7
AUB Group	17.4
Bapcor	16.9
ARB	16.6
Infomedia	16.6
Macquarie Group	15.6

Integrated Research	14.9
Credit Corp	14.8
Wesfarmers	14.7
Alumina	13.8
Ansell	12.8
PWR Holdings	12.6
BHP	12.4
NIB Holdings	11.9
Accent	10.8
Woolworths	10.8
CSR	10.2
GUD	9.7
MNF Group	9.7
Hansen Technologies	9.3
Adairs	9.2
Super Retail	8.6
Harvey Norman	8.4
Class	8.3
DWS	7.8
Medibank Private	7.3
IPH	6.7
IRESS	6.6
Brickworks	6.3
Orica	5.8
GWA	5.6
Brambles	5.3
Commonwealth Bank	3.8
Ramsay Health Care	3.2
Perpetual	1.2
1300SMILES	0.8
InvoCare	0.8
Sandfire Resources	0.7
ANZ Banking	−0.4
Pacific Smiles	−0.6
Vita Group	−1.1
Adbri	−1.8
Australian Pharmaceutical	−2.3
Westpac Banking	−2.4
SG Fleet	−2.8
Pendal	−3.4
Platinum Asset Management	−3.6
Beacon Lighting	−4.1
Mortgage Choice	−5.5
Select Harvests	−8.5
OFX	−9.7
Servcorp	−11.4

Table Q
Non-interest income to total income

The final three tables rank the banks only. Many of the banks are working to diversify away from their traditional lending and deposit-taking businesses into other operations where they see potential for faster growth and higher profits (although these ventures are not always successful — recently we have been seeing some of the banks divest themselves of money management subsidiaries that did not live up to expectations). This table ranks them according to their success, showing how much of their income derives from non-interest sources.

	%
Macquarie Group	84.9
ANZ Banking	24.6
Commonwealth Bank	21.7
Westpac Banking	17.9

Table R
Cost-to-income ratio

All the banks are working to reduce their high costs. The cost-to-income ratio — expressing costs as a percentage of operating income — is one of the measures commonly used by analysts to ascertain their success.

	%
Commonwealth Bank	45.9
ANZ Banking	48.3
Westpac Banking	48.6
Macquarie Group	72.0

Table S
Return on assets

Banks have large assets, and the return on assets ratio — after-tax profit as a percentage of average total assets — is another popular measure of their efficiency.

	%
Macquarie Group	1.2
Westpac Banking	0.8
Commonwealth Bank	0.7
ANZ Banking	0.7

Best-selling author Alan Hull presents the complete sharemarket solution for novices to experts. Whether you're managing your portfolio, trading tactically on the sharemarket or investing in blue chip shares, Alan Hull explains the ins and outs of investing and trading in easy-to-understand and engaging language.

Available in print and e-book formats